D1237261

X-EFFICIENCY: THEORY, EVIDENCE AND APPLICATIONS

Second Edition

Topics in Regulatory Economics and Policy Series

Michael A. Crew, Editor
Graduate School of Management, Rutgers University
Newark, New Jersey, U.S.A.

Previously published books in the series:
Rowley, C., R. Tollison, and G. Tullock:
Political Economy of Rent-Seeking
Frantz, R.:
X-Efficiency: Theory, Evidence and Applications
Crew, M.:
Deregulation and Diversification of Utilities
Shogren, J.:
The Political Economy of Government Regulation
Hillman, J., and R. Braeutigam:
Price Level Regulation for Diversified Public Utilities
Einhorn, M.:
Price Caps and Incentive Regulation in Telecommunications
Crew, M.:
Competition and the Regulation of Utilities
Crew, M., and P. Kleindorfer:
Competition and Innovation in Postal Services
Thompson, H.:
Regulatory Finance: Financial Foundations of Rate of Return Regulation
Crew, M.:
Economic Innovations in Public Utility Regulation
Crew, M., and P. Kleindorfer:
Regulation and the Nature of Postal and Delivery Services
Oren, S., and S. Steven:
Service Opportunities for Electric Utilities: Creating Differentiated Products
Kolbe, A.L., W.B. Tye, and S.C. Myers:
Regulatory Risk: Economic Principles and Applications to Natrual Gas Pipelines
Pechman, C.:
Regulating Power: The Economics of Electricity in the Information Age
Gordon, R.K.:
Regulation and Economic Analysis: A Critique over Two Centuries
Blackmon, G.:
Incentive Regulation and the Regulation of Incentives
Crew, M.:
Incentive Regulation for Public Utilities
Crew, M., and P. Kleindorfer:
Commercialization of Postal and Delivery Services
Abbott, T.:
Health Care Policy and Regulation
Goff, B.:
Regulation and Macroeconomic Performance
Coate, M.B., and A.N. Kleit:
The Economics of the Antitrust Process
Crew, M.:
Pricing and Regulatory Innovations Under Increasing Competition
Crew, M., and P. Kleindorfer:
Managing Change in the Postal and Delivery Industries

X-EFFICIENCY: THEORY, EVIDENCE AND APPLICATIONS

Second Edition

Roger S. Frantz
San Diego State University
San Diego, California, U.S.A.

Kluwer Academic Publishers
Boston/Dordrecht/London

Distributors for North America:
Kluwer Academic Publishers
101 Philip Drive
Assinippi Park
Norwell, Massachusetts 02061 USA

Distributors for all other countries:
Kluwer Academic Publishers Group
Distribution Centre
Post Office Box 322
3300 AH Dordrecht, THE NETHERLANDS

Library of Congress Cataloging-in-Publication Data
Frantz, Roger S.
  X-efficiency : theory, evidence and applications / by Roger
Frantz. -- 2nd ed.
     p. cm. -- (Topics in regulatory economics and policy ; 23)
  Includes bibliographical references and index.
  ISBN 0-7923-9768-1
  1. Industrial efficiency. 2. Industrial productivity.
  3. Industrial policy. I. Title. II. Series
  HD56.F725 1997
  338'.06--dc20   96-28940
                                                      CIP

Printed on acid-free paper.

Printed in the United States of America

Harvey Leibenstein — 1922–1994.

This book is dedicated to Harvey Leibenstein,
founder of X-Efficiency Theory, and my mentor,
who I miss very much.

CONTENTS

List of Figures and Tables

PREFACE

My interest in X-Efficiency (XE) dates back to 1978. At the time, I was writing the dissertation for my Ph.D. at Washington State University. My dissertation was concerned with the role of attitudes in the school-to-work transition among young men. I was advised by Professor Millard Hastay (a member of my committee) to look at Leibenstein's "new" book, *Beyond Economic Man*. One of the things that caught my attention was his behavioral description of (selective) rationality. It seemed that Leibenstein's behavioral description of a (selectively) rational individual was very similar to what psychologists such as Abraham Maslow were reporting as being the product of a particular motivational system. In other words, I was impressed with the idea that what Leibenstein was referring to as X-inefficiency was being discussed by psychologists as "the way it (often) is." So from the beginning I always considered the concept of X-(in)efficiency to be a valuable one for understanding human behavior. I have since come to believe that this is particularly true when considering behavior in non-market environments, i.e., within the firm.

Work on this book, however, can most realistically said to have started with work which I began in 1982 while I was a Visiting Scholar at Harvard University. Professor Leibenstein suggested that I consider how some empirical evidence which was being cited as evidence for the role of property rights might also be consistent with XE theory. (The consistency, in both directions, is considerable.) This led to an investigation of empirical research that cited XE as a possible explanation for the reported results. This literature seemed large, but not as large as theoretical work citing XE. Taken together, I was organizing a very large literature and one of which many of my colleagues and others with whom I spoke were not generally aware. My impression is that this body of literature on XE theory continues to be unknown by many in the economics profession.

My greatest indebtedness for this book is to Harvey Leibenstein, who has been generous with both his time and his encouragement for this and other projects. I have known him to be one who is not afraid to think outside the orthodox framework, and whose insights have firmly impressed me as being keen, educational, and wonderfully refreshing. While Professor Leibenstein and I might disagree on certain points, I believe it fair to exclaim at the outset of this book that, "I am an X-ist."

Many others have read portions of this book or otherwise given of their time and expertise for the benefit of this project. In particular I wish to acknowledge Michael Crew (Rutgers University) who is the editor for the series of which this is part; Joan Anderson (University of San Diego) with whom I have worked on several projects; and Richard Hattwick (Western Illinois University), the editor of the *Journal of Socio-Economics* who has been particularly supportive of my ideas. Others who have helped me considerably have been Don Lecraw (Western Ontario), Walter Primeaux (University of Illinois), and T. Y. Shen (University of California, Davis).

Several of my colleagues of San Diego State have also given generously of their time and expertise. Harinder Singh has read almost all of the manuscript and has provided me with very valuable comments and ways of organizing the material. Michael Naughton has tutored me on the economics of regulation. My deficiencies in this area are my own. Other colleagues whom I wish to acknowledge are George Babilot, Ray Boddy, Fred Galloway, Lou Green, Ibrahim Poroy, Fred Seebold, Robert Seidman, and Yiannis Venieris.

I also wish to thank my friend Aurliano Cruz for his help in making possible my research on XE in Mexico. Without Aurliano the work in Mexico could not have been done. Finally Judi Bakke and Mark Crooks have provided their considerable artistic talents.

The Center for Public Economics at San Diego State University has provided me with financial support for this project and published my working paper in 1984 which has been expanded into this book. I wish to thank its director, George Babilot, for the immense assistance he has provided toward the development of this project. Chapter 9 of this book, "X-Efficiency, Its Critics and a Reply," was first published in the *Quarterly Review of Economics and Business.* I thank the editor of that journal, Paul Uselding, for allowing me to borrow so freely from that work.

ROGER S. FRANTZ

Forward to the First Edition

Most teachers of basic economics come across students who disbelieve some of the theory they are taught. "That's not the way it's done in real firms," or "That's not the way it's done in my father's firm," the student will argue. In attempting to answer such challenges and rationalize standard theory to their students, economics teachers frequently develop handy responses such as: "One needs a simplified model to understand such a complex phenomenon as the operation of an economy," "All science simplifies," "What may appear to be deviant behavior is not if we understand it more thoroughly," "We cannot start with all the complexities right off the bat."

Is it possible that in some sense the use of such justifications is wrong and the objections of the students are right? Granted that simplification is necessary, can we economists argue that we have hit on just the right set of simplifying postulates to achieve the valid and useful kind of economics we wish to build? This is a problem that has concerned me for several decades. In this foreword I want to indulge in a number of speculations about this general question, as well as some related issues.

My work on X-efficiency was basically the outcome of an accident- having underutilized research assistants, who were willing to search out the details of technical reports on visits enterprises in less developed countries (LDCs), mostly from the ILO and the United Nations, that were buried in the University of California library. Their work revealed a number of clear-cut, empirical examples of firms that appeared to be operating non-optimally and in other ways that contradict standard micro theory. I was forced by the data to reconsider my previously held positions. The original 1966 article on X-efficiency was the result of these concerns. I did not predict the large number of citations that the article would receive, the stimulation it would serve to other people's work, or some of the controversies that it would generate.

The size of the reaction to X-efficiency theory raises questions about the current nature of microeconomics. Is microeconomics a cumulative science? Does it build on previous triumphs exclusively in a gradual manner? Is its current state the consequence of just small accretions to our knowledge? Does it involve step-by-step progress? In general, there have been two major "revolutions" in microeconomics: the Smithian revolution of 1776, and the marginalist revolution in the 1870s (which includes the works of Walras). The first revolution occurred over 200 years ago, and the second over a century ago. Since the 1870s, work seems to have proceeded in terms of small changes involving mostly refinements and elaborations of the mathematical interpretation of the theory.

The general view among economists is that this process of refinement has led to gains in understanding, and especially in rigor. However, side by side with the gains there have been losses. Part of the process of refinement has been to rid the theory of what seemed like unnecessary intellectual baggage. Frequently this loss went unnoticed since the focus was on the refined theory and its implications rather than on the ideas and elements that were left aside. This clearly seems to have been the fate of the central notion of efficiency. Somehow, efficiency became transformed into allocative efficiency and nothing else. In fact, one of the great triumphs of economics was believed to have been the 1930s volume by Lionel Robbins in which economics was defined as the logic of the allocation of scarce resources to alternative uses. Markets were then studied from the viewpoint that they allocated society's economic resources efficiently to alternative uses.

What got lost in this progression of economics was the businessman's idea and the engineer's idea of efficiency, which signify how well or poorly people and machines are working. Once allocative efficiency is combined with the maximization-of-utility or -profits postulate there is no longer any room for the businessman's and the engineer's concepts of efficiency. Thus, the idea disappeared that suboptimal operations by the firm and inside the firm are possible. I believe that my 1966 article contributed to the revival of the idea that various forms of suboptimal behavior are possible. This is one reason why it engendered controversy. Businessmen, engineers, and psychologists are aware of suboptimal behavior, but standard economic theory somehow does not easily or readily lend itself to the possibility of suboptimal operations. X-efficiency theory raised the possibility that standard theory is incomplete in a fundamentally important way. It is this idea, that standard theory might be incomplete, that has caused strong reactions.

The X-efficiency ideas have raised the basic theoretical question, What are the premises that restrict standard theory to incompleteness? If sub-optimal behavior does exist, how can we reformulate the basic theory, especially the theory of the firm, to readily and directly account for it?

X-efficiency theory has raised empirical questions as well. The first empirical question is whether X-inefficiency is factually important. A second empirical question is whether the implications of a reformulated theory of the firm fit known facts or empirical studies not yet undertaken. The three chapters by Frantz on empirical studies suggest rather forcefully that both empirical questions can be answered affirmatively. X-inefficiency is obviously factually important, and the implications, to the extent that studies check them out, seem to be upheld.

Another source of controversy arises from the basic conservatism inherent in every profession. The X-efficiency approach requires substituting for the maximization postulate another postulate, which we may specify as the Max/Nonmax postulate, that allows for nonmaximizing behavior but certainly does not preclude maximizing behavior. It is important to note that in all scientific fields as well as in mathematics, it is normal to change basic postulates in order to obtain alternative implications and results. An example of this occurred between 1840 and 1870 in the field of geometry when the non-Euclidean geometries were invented. Clearly this is also true of the relativity and quantum theory revolutions in physics. Examples in other fields can readily be found. Such changes are usually accompanied by controversy, so it is not surprising that controversy should result when it is attempted in economics.

In my view, alternative theories or models should be stated in such a way that empirical results can decide between alternative approaches. The three empirical chapters in Frantz's book speak very much to this issue. In general it seems to me that the authors of the empirical studies usually tried to give a fair interpretation of the alternative approaches being considered.

On one issue I have definitely changed my mind from what I stated in earlier writings. I no longer believe that inert areas depend necessarily or even usually on a balanced accounting of the benefits and costs of moving. Many people within their inert areas may not think of the costs or benefits of change. They may not be making any calculations at all. This follows from the fact that a variety of decisions, such as those based on habit or conventions, are usually of a noncalculating type. Rather my view now is that inert areas depend on basic psychological and physiological aspects of human nature. In other words, life would be almost impossible if we had to react to every external stimuli no matter how small. In fact, the opposite side of the coin of our ability to focus attention is the ability to ignore a variety of other stimuli that impinge on us simultaneously. This can also be understood in terms of the theory of arousal. We often have to be aroused beyond some threshold level for us to even consider taking action of any kind.

It is important to emphasize that this is very much Roger Frantz's book. It presents an approach to the questions raised by X-efficiency theory that, while obviously sympathetic, nevertheless represents an independent judgment. Of course, I would not look at every aspect in the same way that Frantz does. It is precisely because Frantz's book represents an independent interpretation of both the theory and the facts, as well as the attempt to carefully connect the two, that makes this book of special value.

HARVEY LEIBENSTEIN
Harvard University

Forward to the Second Edition

Recently the *Economic Journal* has published an interpretive essay, "Harvey Leibenstein as a Pioneer in Our Time." One point was that early in Leibenstein's career he did several, unusually innovative things: Work in (1) what is now called Experimental Economics, and (2) again in what is now called Demographic Economics. But it is his work in (3) X-efficiency Economics for what he is best remembered. How few of us are remembered at all, and how many fewer for what we are "best" recalled! Leibenstein was a rare, creative genius.

Real leadership or pioneering is a matter of the relationship between an individual and a crowd (perhaps a group of followers is a more felicific term). If the 'leader' is too far ahead, his leadership is simply a matter for the books. If he is not far enough ahead, can one say that there is real leadership? Leibenstein's leadership with regard to experimental economics and demographic economics can be demonstrated, but I chose to concentrate on what he did in creating a branch of micro micro economics, namely X-efficiency economics. This idea originally surfaced in print in   1966. His active scholarly life ended in 1987. In the 21 intervening years he published four major books, 13 articles, as well as about nine scholarly 'comments' on the subject. Between 1971 and 1975 reference in the Social Science Index listings averaged 64 per year, rising to 102 per year for 1976-1980, and peaking at 112 per year for 1981-85. The average from 1896-90 was 91, and 1991-57 was 57. These numbers attest both to his own creativity and to the fact of his leadership.Others and I have written much about Leibenstein's many specific contributions. What they actually were is initially a library job. In the case of X-efficiency economics one does not have to go to the 'stacks' to find out the dimensions. They can be found in this book. In his Foreword Professor Leibenstein gives a pithy review, and Professor Frantz does much of the remaining task by utilizing both the method of straight exposition and the method of analyzing the views of X-efficiency's critics. I think this book a polished gem — if Leibenstein's contribution is seen as the principal gen, — Frantz's is the highly-skilled polish.

May I add something new? It is a partial attempt to put Leibenstein's X-efficiency economics into a larger context.

Virtually all who have read about X-efficiency economics have realized that it was built on foundations quite different from the current, popularly-called neo-classical, set. Leibenstein himself stressed this point, asserting several times that his work was not predicated on a simple rational system. Indeed, he scoffed at the naivete of those who thought that any economics could get very far in terms of its explanatory powers if it insisted upon a professionally tight linkage of syllogisms.

My point is not to repeat the point about the simpleness of simple rationality — as many like Leibenstein have done. I want go on to an often-neglected aspect of Leibenstein's point, namely that it is not in the *processing* of information *(analyzing* is the usual word of art) about the non-maximizing behavior, wherein lies the rub (although difficulty resides there too). Rather it is in the adequacy of the basic *gathering* of that information. There are many reasons for the inadequacy of information gathering and hence for the absence of maximizing decisions, but I mention only three.

- No small part of the problem is identifying just what one is looking for. Sometimes that information is so obvious that even though it 'lies on one's eyeballs' it cannot be seen; more usually, however, it like rare truth (which as Churchill put it, has to be protected by a legion of falsehoods) the information is shielded by layers of irrelevancies.
- In our times the idea that economics has such pervasive epistemic roots that it cannot be part of the known scientific (ontological) disciplines goes back to the Maynard Keynes of *The Treatise On Probability*. And what is epistemic can defy logic, but it is truth notwithstanding.
- G.L.S. Shackle, a man and theorist much admired by Leibenstein (as did Shackle admire him), approached this matter of hidden truth in a different way. He used the phrase *unknowledge* — that is, information which cannot be known at the time a decision has to be made — to round-out the idea.

So there we have it — X-efficiency draws often on hard-to-find real facts; it draws on the subjective, that is opinions which serve functionally as facts, and in practice it draws on guesses (ranging from primitive estimates to tested intuition) which are employed in the case of unknowledge. X-efficiency is a system which explains how one can understand factory operations as we see them. Handled well it is an explanatory, not a predictive, theory. Handled sophisticatedly it suggests the limited areas where rational maximization is used. Most of all, it is a system which attracts those employing cognition insofar as it gives them reasons

It is likely that Leibenstein's derived his contributions in this area empirically rather than through reading or excogitation. Yet, irrespective of their origins, I think that Leibenstein deserves the credit for their modern application: it was his call for a new "micro-micro" theory which dates the message.

One of my brilliant colleagues, Alvin Roth, has commented perspicaciously that it is the last, not the first, discoverer of something who gets the credit — after *him*, what is new stays discovered. Leibenstein, enough of a innovational scholar so as not to need boastfully to attribute to himself complete originality, regularly mentioned that the idea of X-efficiency analysis did not spring either from his or perhaps some earlier brow; indeed, he would modestly report that it was simply his interest in the juxtaposition of economics and individual psychology which led him to the literature and then to his independent cognition, which explained his formulation of the topic. Leibenstein and his X-efficiency analysis is like a ratchet — whoever may be said by others to be the 'real' originator of micro micro analysis, it will be Leibenstein's contribution which keeps the idea from disappearing again.

It is a wise leader who knows his followers, and it is also a wise follower who understands his leader. My pleasure is to note at the beginning of this second edition of Professor Frantz's important book that that is what we have here.

MARK PERLMAN
University Professor of Economics (Emeritus)
The University of Pittsburgh

1

INTRODUCTION

1.1. Introduction

In 1983 at a conference on behavioral economics held at Princeton University, I delivered, for the first time, a very short review of the empirical literature that I had gathered on XE theory. The audience, probably responding to the brevity of my remarks, was polite. An individual approached me afterwards offering a two-part comment. First, he found the literature to be interesting but admitted to not being aware of the extent to which it existed. Second, he had an alternative, non X-efficiency explanation for the results reported in this body of literature. His explanation, which he briefly began to explain in the moment or two that we could muster, was, as he was quick to point out, completely consistent with neoclassical theory.

The fact is that microeconomics theory employs a language that "explains" any event or empirical results. For me, these explanations prove one thing: the speakers are well versed in the current orthodoxy. The orthodox response often seems the result of some perceived challenge to a sacred belief. On the other hand, make no mistake about it: X-efficiency theory, property rights theory, rent-seeking, the theory of transactions costs, and other such theories attempt to explain the same phenomena. Some of the literature and empirical evidence ascribed to each can be and often are consistent with the others. Clinching the case for any one of these theories exclusive of the others has not been accomplished. The authors of the 55 studies presented in chapters 6 through 8 choose an X-efficiency approach, and I present their studies as such.

Still, my preference is for X-efficiency theory because of its interdisciplinary nature, and because it takes problems seriously rather than as puzzles to be solved or phenomena to be "explained." I also prefer X-efficiency because of my repeated observance of seemingly non rational behavior on the part of people in all parts of my life, including economists. Finally, working on X-efficiency theory has allowed me work closely with Professor Leibenstein, a preeminent scholar and a very humane individual.

1.2. X and Allocative Efficiency and the Welfare Losses from Monopoly Power

Is there a need within (micro)economics for a concept such as X-efficiency? The X in X-(in)efficiency stands for a nonallocative (in)efficiency whose source was (and still is relatively) unknown. In 1954 Harberger estimated that the welfare loss to the U.S. economy due to monopoly power was approximately 0.01% of the GNP. Later estimates place this figure in the ballpark of 0.5% to 1% of GNP. Still, is the misallocation of resources so insignificant for economic welfare? Leibenstein believed the answer to be otherwise. First, he pointed out that these estimates take into account only the (net) output and price distortions caused by monopoly and/or tariffs. While some outputs and prices may be very distorted, on net, the distortions are not likely to be large. According to the estimates of Harberger and others, they are not.

Second, Leibenstein pointed out that these estimates assumed that firms are cost minimizers, that is, they purchase and utilize all inputs "efficiently." X-efficiency (XE) theory was motivated to show that protection from competitive pressure produces not only allocative inefficiency but also another type of inefficiency that is manifest as excess unit costs of production among firms sheltered from competitive pressure. Being of an unknown nature, Leibenstein referred to it as X-inefficiency. He believed then, as evidence as shown since, that the costs of X-inefficiency exceed those of allocative inefficiency.[1]

1.3. X-Efficiency and the Neoclassical Production and Cost Functions

X-efficiency was unknown because the orthodoxy of the day (and largely of today) assumes that firms are producing on both their production and cost function. That is, firms are assumed to be maximizing output from given inputs, including technology. Firms are assumed to be cost minimizers. So long as firms are producing on their production and cost function, then the firm is merely a technological relation, and orthodox theory is correct in ignoring X-efficiency.

If, however, production and cost processes are not primarily a technological relation, then the orthodox textbook presentation needs to be modified. XE theory is one such modifica-tion: XE theory assumes that neoclassical theory is accurate when firms are producing on their production and cost functions. For this reason XE theory considers neoclassical theory to be a "limiting case." Once again, it considers neoclassical theory most applicable when firms are producing on their production and cost functions.

------

[1]   Estimates of the relative magnitude of X and allocative efficiency can be found in Greer (1991) and Scherer and Ross (1990).

In chapter 2 of this book I focus on the technological or mechanistic nature of textbook microeconomic theory in order to show that this theory <u>assumes away</u> the possibility of X-(in)efficiency. Neoclassical arguments against XE theory become redundant: there is simply no place in neoclassical microeconomics theory for X-(in)efficiency.

1.4. The Development of XE Theory

The development of XE theory in the early 1960s was not the only attempt by economists to explain the behavior of firms which the profit-maximizing, cost-minimizing models seem incapable of doing. Baumol (1959) was developing a model of the firm based on the goal of sales maximization. Baumol notes that at least part of the impetus for this model was based on his own experiences as a consultant to business. In addition, Marris (1963, 1964) was developing a model in which the firm's goal is growth, while the managers in Williamson's (1964) firm were interested in perquisites. Simon (1957, 1961) was developing his theory of satisficing, which helped earn him a Nobel Prize. Simon's colleagues Cyert and March (1963) were developing a behavioral theory of the firm, and Gordon Tullock (1967) was developing the concept of rent-seeking. Others were working along the same path.

As I have already alluded to, Leibenstein's development of the X-efficiency concept was primarily driven by (various types of) data. One type was the observation that his graduate research assistant at Berkeley was underutilized! This lead him to wonder whether the underutilization of inputs was a more generalized phenomena than simply this isolated example.

Another observation was a difference between formal models of economic development on the one hand, and his own experiences and the experiences of several colleagues working in less developed countries on the other. Finally, data were available that seemed inconsistent with neo- classical theory: some data showed that firms were able to increase their output by making relatively simple changes in the internal organization of the plant; other data showed that firms were not operating according to the principles of marginal analysis; and macrodata indicated that something other than physical labor and physical capital was playing an important role in the growth rates of several industrialized nations.

All three types of "data" seemed to warrant an investigation into alternative theories of the firm, which might fill a lacuna in economic theory that relied exclusively on the concept of allocative-market-inefficiency. How could these three types of data be explained? Leibenstein developed XE theory as a response to these data. In chapter 3, the data seemingly inconsistent with neoclassical theory as well as the initial statement of XE theory are presented. In addition, several other (non-profit-maximizing) theories of the firm are also presented so that the reader can be given a sense of the environment in which XE theory was being formulated.

1.5. XE Theory and Generalized Neoclassical Theory

The nature of XE theory, and the fact that it differs in some fundamental ways from the currently dominant theory, neoclassical theory, means that a contrast between the two is inevitable. In the first few pages of this book, I have already mentioned this point several times. However, I will refer to two versions of neoclassical theory: first, the version that assumes profit maximization and cost minimization, and second, the generalized version which assumes utility maximization and cost minimization. In this generalized version, costs are minimized subject to the manner in which the employees choose to maximize their utility. Thus, for example, if employees are assumed to be utility maximizers which includes "on-the-job leisure", then the firm will be minimizing their unit costs subject to this goal of the employees, which is not to work with high amounts of either mental or physical effort.

Some of the assumptions of XE theory are consistent with the generalized version of neoclassical theory. That is, the latter makes use of concepts that can explain the third type of data discussed above, or the central postulates of XE theory, as well as the empirical findings consistent with the implications of XE theory. For example, X-inefficiency may result from the fact that labor contracts are "open" thereby providing workers with effort discretion, or from the the assumption of "inert areas," that is, that individuals discover a comfortable level of effort and tend to maintain this effort level, sometimes appearing oblivious to the demands of the environment. Given the existence of an appropriate level of transactions and monitoring costs, these assumptions central to XE theory can be argued to be consistent with the generalized version of neoclassical theory. In chapter 9, I will discuss how generalized neoclassical theory "explains" some of the empirical work on XE theory.

1.6. XE as a Research Design

XE theory is not consistent with generalized neoclassical theory in one very important way. XE theory assumes that individuals may be both maximizers and nonmaximizers. More specifically, not all environments will result in an individual exhibiting maximizing, that is, calculating behavior. Maximization, in other words, is to be observed, not assumed. To assume maximizing behavior is to assume away X-(in)efficiency. This is one reason why assumptions are important!

Table 1 illustrates this point.[2] There are two hypotheses about individual behavior: individuals are (always) maximizers and individuals are not (always) maximizers. There are also two actual types of behavior that individuals engage in: they may maximize or they may not. Thus there are two types of errors that can be

---

2   This way of presenting XE theory and neoclassical theory was suggested by my colleague
     Harindar Singh. It is also discussed in Rozen (1985).

actual / hyp.	max.	non max.
max.	OK	type 2 error
non max.	type 1 error	OK

Table 1. Methodological consequences of implicit type 1 and type 2 errors

made: type 1 and type 2. A type 1 error in this context means that an individual is hypothesized not to maximize when, in fact, he does maximize. A type 2 error means that the individual is hypothesized to maximize when, in fact, he does not maximize. Neoclassical theory, by ignoring the possibility of nonmaximizing behavior, sets type 1 errors to be zero (by assumption). Accordingly, the neoclassical framework makes the probability of a type 2 error very high. And, in fact, within this context neoclassical theory represents a vigorous pursuit of type 2 errors. That is, a conscious effort is made to show that what may appear at first glance to be non-maximizing behavior is, in fact, maximizing behavior if all relevant factors are taken into account. As I shall point out in chapters 1 and 8, these factors are usually asserted to be the "missing link." At this juncture, I will simply name some of these factors: utility, rent-seeking, risk aversion, and property rights.

In contrast to the neoclassical framework, XE theory acknowledges the possibility of both maximizing and nonmaximizing behavior and thus acknowledges the possibility of both type 1 and type 2 errors. As a research design, XE theory is better able to recognize the trade-off between these errors and to attempt to keep both within manageable limits so that empirical tests can be accomplished. This is also shown in table 1 by the diagonal elements, in which an individual is hypothesized to maximize when he does, and is hypothesized not to maximize when he doesn't. Thus, neoclassical theory, by assuming that all behavior is maximizing behavior, limits itself to type 2 errors (quadrant 4). However, neoclassical analysis in this regard attempts to show why all behavior (maximizing and "seemingly" nonmaximizing) actually falls into quadrant 1: individuals are always maximizers.

On the other hand, XE theory represents a more comprehensive research design because it allows behavior to be consistent with any of the four quadrants. By acknowledging this possibility, XE theory exhausts all eventualities. Chapters 4 and 5 of this book are devoted to presenting the theory. Chapter 4 focuses on the psychology of the individual worker, while chapter 5 also considers the individual as a member of a group. As we proceed through these chapters, I ask the reader to consider table 1 and how the research design implied by XE theory differs from that of neoclassical theory, and what, if any, contribution it makes.

1.7. Empirical Research on XE Theory

Chapters 6 to 8 summarize 55 empirical studies consistent with the implications of XE theory. Chapter 6 presents empirical evidence on regulated firms, most notably, public utilities. Chapter 7 presents evidence on market structure, including ownership form, firm size, and market concentration, while chapter 8 presents evidence on input ratios and international trade. However, some of the research reported in these chapters may seem not to fit because some of the research covers more than one topic area, and some of the research was placed where it appears because it is most complementary to other research presented there.

1.8. Critics of XE Theory

In Chapter 9, I take up arguments against XE theory and some of the empirical work consistent with its implications. Four schools of criticism are discussed: those emphasizing rent-seeking, those emphasizing on-the-job leisure as output, those emphasizing competition among utility maximizing managers, and those emphasizing property-rights. Despite the fact that these schools overlap each other in certain ways, this taxonomy has proved useful. As I will argue, these criticisms of XE theory rely heavily on terms that are used extensively, but not exclusively, in a tautological fashion. Considering XE theory and neoclassical theory throughout the book, I conclude with what I believe are their individual strengths and weaknesses and some suggestions for future research on XE theory.

2
PRODUCTION, COST, AND WELFARE: A REVIEW

2.1. Introduction

The efficient use of resources is the major focus of economics. For historical and other reasons, this means primarily the allocation of resources by prices and markets. The term *allocative efficiency* means the efficiency with which markets allocate resources among their competing uses. Allocative efficiency exists when perfectly competitive firms price their output at marginal cost, and hence when the industry produces the socially optimum rate of output (SORQ).

Market power adversely affects allocative efficiency. Power gives a firm the ability to raise price above marginal cost and to restrict output in such a way that the industry's output rate is below SORQ. The market is inefficient because the optimum amount of resources has not been allocated to the production of the commodity. The industry's output rate being below SORQ, an underallocation of resources exists.

However, the firm with market power is efficient so long as it sets its output rate correctly, where $MR = MC$; sets its price correctly, where $P = MB$, and; minimizes its costs of production for a given rate of output. Since these three conditions are assumed, the firm is efficient even when the market is inefficient. Stated in different terms, the firm is *always* assumed to be efficient.

Since firms are assumed efficient, efficiency means allocative-market-efficiency. Whether these assumptions are realistic, and whether realism of assumptions is important is not the issue here. What is important is that these assumptions have allowed economic theory to focus on the efficiency of markets while placing much less attention on the internal efficiency of firms.

The purpose of this book is to show that (in)efficiency also applies to firms. This type of (internal) efficiency is called X-efficiency, so named by Harvard economist Harvey Leibenstein. This book will also show that X-(in)efficiency may be more important than allocative-market-efficiency.

In order to understand X-efficiency, it is necessary to understand the theory that assumes that firms are efficient, as well as the concept of allocative-market-efficiency. The purpose of this chapter is to present the essential aspects of this theory of efficient firms and the concept of allocative-market-efficiency as it appears in most intermediate-level microeconomics textbooks. I am assuming that these textbooks are faithful representations of the current state of the art.

This chapter thus serves as background material for the remainder of the book. If you are not already familiar with this material, you may find this chapter somewhat confusing. On the other hand, if you are familiar with this material, you will probably find both my emphasis and my insistence on making implicit assumptions explicit to be worth the time necessary to read through the chapter.

In the next two sections of this chapter, I will present the theory of the firm in the short run and in the long run, respectively. The efficiency and welfare effects of market power will follow.

2.2. The Firm in the Short Run

2.2.1. Short-Run Production Function

In the short run the relationship between inputs and outputs is written as $Q = f(K, L)$, where Q is output, K is a fixed amount of capital, and L is labor. This relationship is the short-run production function. The important point to keep in mind is that this function indicates the *maximum* (assumed to be the actual) output attainable from any given amount of labor, holding the capital stock constant. This is shown in figure 1. Here we see that one unit of labor combined with 1 unit of capital can yield maximum of 10 units of output. Figure 1 also shows that two units of labor combined with one unit of capital can yield a maximum of 30 units of output, etc.

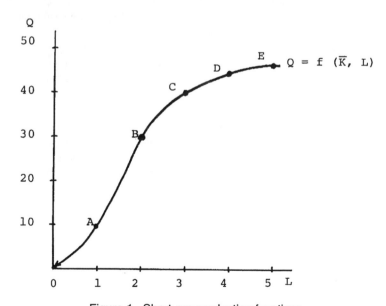

Figure 1. Short-run production functions.

Because the production function indicates the maximum output rate attainable from any given amount of labor, it also indicates the minimum amount of labor necessary to produce a given output rate. Thus in figure 1 we also see that 10 units of output can be produced with a minimum of one worker, while 30 units can be produced with a minimum of two workers, etc.

Of course, a firm cannot produce more than maximum from a given set of inputs: that is, a firm cannot produce above its production function. On the other hand, we assume that it does not use more inputs than necessary. That is, we assume that X-inefficiency is zero so that the firm does not actually fall below its production function. The firm, therefore, always produces *on* its production function, by assumption.

2.2.2. Short-Run Cost Function

Obviously, the firm's expenses emanate from the process of production. Therefore the production and cost functions of the firm will be related. Consider again the production function showing the following labor-output combinations: $L = 1$, $Q = 10$; $L = 2$, $Q = 30$, etc. In figure 1, these are shown as points A and B, respectively. Since the firm is assumed to minimize its use of inputs for any level of output, then given the prices of inputs, the resulting total costs—TC = (PlL + PkK)—are the firm's *minimum* attainable costs for each output rate. This yields the firm's ATC curve, shown in figure 2.

Of course, the firm cannot incur costs less than the minimum costs. That is, the firm cannot incur costs represented by a point below its cost function. On the other hand, by assuming that X-inefficiency does not exist economic theory does not

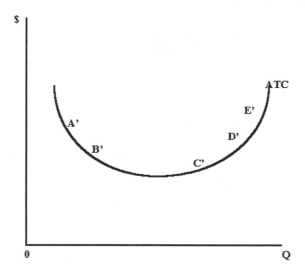

Figure 2. Short-run average total cost curve.

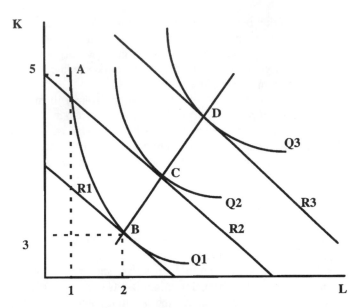

Figure 3. Long-run production function and the firm's expansion path.

allow for a firm to produce above its cost function. The firm, therefore, always produces *on* its cost function, by assumption.

2.3. The Firm in the Long Run

2.3.1. The Long-Run Production Function

In the long run, any output rate can be produced with any one of potentially numerous capital:labor combinations. The combinations that we are interested in are those which minimize the number of inputs for any rate of output. In figure 3, the minimum input combinations capable of producing output rate Q1 is the line denoted Q1, which is an isoquant line.

In figure 3, the isoquant Q1 indicates that Q1 can be produced for example, with 5K and 1L (point A) or with 3K and 2L (point B). That the rate of substitution is 1L for 2K is not important in this context. Figure 3 also shows isoquant Q2, where Q1 < Q2.

The important point about the isoquant is that it conforms to the interests of economy theory and therefore indicates the minimum amount of inputs necessary to produce a given output rate. For example, in figure 3, if five units of capital are used to produce Q1, then the minimum amount of labor necessary is one unit. If one unit of labor is used, then the minimum amount of capital required is five units.

Because the isoquant indicates the minimum necessary inputs required to produce a given output rate, it also indicates the maximum output rate attainable from given inputs. Figure 3, therefore, also shows that Q1 is the maximum output rate attainable from any of the capital—labor combinations represented by the isoquant Q1. Minimum inputs for a given output rate and maximum output for given inputs are two sides of the same coin.

2.3.2. Optimal-Cost Minimizing-Input Combinations

What input combinations can the firm use in order to minimize its costs of production for any given output rate? Potentially, any input combination represented by a point on the isoquant could minimize the firm's costs. However, each set of input prices will, in fact, allow only one input combination to result in minimum costs for the firm.

In order to determine this cost-minimizing input ratio, the firm needs to know several things. First, the firm needs to know how many inputs it can purchase for any given rate of expenditures (R). The ability to purchase inputs depends upon R, the price of labor (Pl), and the price of capital (Pk). Hence R =(PlL) + (PkK). All maximum amounts of capital and labor that can be purchased for a given R are called an isocost curve. One such isocost curve is R1 in figure 3. In figure 3, R1 represents lower costs than does R2 while R3 represents even higher costs.

To make a long story short, the firm minimizes its costs (R) for output rate Q1 by using the input combination such that the isoquant is just tangent to the lowest isocost curve. In figure 3 this is point B. For Q2 and Q3, the points are C and D, respectively. Because firms are assumed to be X-efficient, the theory focuses only on the cost-minimization points, as if noncost minimization is not important. In fact, since it is assumed not to exist, it is not important.

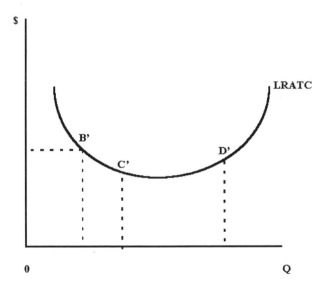

Figure 4. Long-run average total cost curve.

2.3.3. Expansion Path and Long Run Cost Function

Points B, C and D map out the firm's expansion path, its minimum long run total costs for each level of output. Therefore, for Q1, its minimum long run total costs are (3Pk + 2Pl). Dividing by Q gives us the long-run average total cost curve. In figure 4, this is shown as point B'. Similarly, points C' and D' represent the minimum long-run average total costs for Q2 and Q3, respectively.

Of course, the firm cannot incur costs less than the minimum costs. That is, the firm cannot incur costs represented by a point below its cost function. On the other hand, by assuming that X-inefficiency does not exist economic theory does not allow for a firm to produce above its cost function. The firm, therefore, always produces *on* its cost function, by assumption.

2.3.4. The Emphasis is on Minimum Cost

The emphasis in economic theory is on minimum cost and maximum output points:points: on the production and cost functions and the expansion path. Unfortunately this emphasis tends to make us forget that other possibilities exist. By default, points on the production function have become both maximum and actual levels of output. Points on the cost function (curve) have become both minimum and actual costs. Nonoutput maximization and noncost minimization are thus not perceived as either existing or important. In some cases, they are said not to be part of economics. As presented, X-inefficiency *cannot* exist within microeconomic theory. These beliefs, however, are more a statement about the interests of economists than one about the (real) world.

2.4. Firms, Markets, and Efficiency

2.4.1. Introduction

The production and cost functions presented here assume that the firm is maximizing its output for any level of inputs (production function) and minimizing its costs for any level of output (cost function). Under these conditions, the firm may be considered as a "black box": nothing more than a technological relation that converts (given) inputs into (maximum) outputs at technologically minimum necessary costs. What occurs inside the firm becomes irrelevant if we assume that the firm is operating on its production and cost functions. Activities within the firm are especially irrelevant if we assume that all activities taking place within the firm is done efficiently. The firm so modeled *cannot* be inefficient in any meaningful sense, and hence only allocative market (in)efficiency is an issue. It is as if the "theory of the firm" does not contain a firm.

2.4.1. Allocative Efficiency

Having assumed the internal efficiency of the firm, the economist's concern about efficiency focuses on the market. That is, does the market allocate resources efficiently? To understand the answer to this question, we will utilize figures 5 and 6. Figure 5 shows market equilibrium as Pe and Qe. The demand curve reflects the

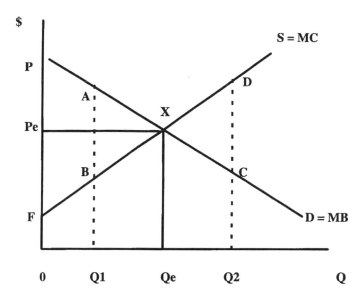

Figure 5. Market equilibrium and allocative-market-efficiency.

marginal benefits (MB) of consumption, while the supply curve reflects the marginal costs (MC). Market equilibrium is thus a price:output combination for which MB = MC and thus for which total benefits minus total cost is at its maximum value; market equilibrium maximizes net economic welfare.

At any output rate less than Qe, MB exceeds MC, and hence mutually beneficial voluntary exchange is possible. Increases in both consumer and producer surplus, or economic welfare are also possible. Consumer surplus is the difference between the maximum that consumers are willing to pay for what they receive and what they actually pay for it (actual expenditures). Consumer surplus is thus the difference between total benefits and total expenditures. Since the demand curve reflects marginal benefits, it follows that total benefits are measured as the area under the demand curve.

The producer surplus is the difference between the revenues that a firm receives and the minimum price that it is willing to accept for supplying any given rate of output. Each point on a supply curve shows the minimum price for any output rate.

For Q1, buyers are willing to pay AQ1 while sellers are willing to accept BQ1. Clearly, a price between AQ1 and BQ1 will generate both consumer and producer surplus. Therefore, any output rate less than Qe generates both consumer and producer surplus, and hence is worthwhile. Any output rate below Qe is thus an underallocation of resources and represents allocative-market-inefficiency.

On the other hand, any output rate greater than Qe, for example, Q2 is one for which MB (=CQ2) is less than MC (=DQ2), and hence net economic welfare would

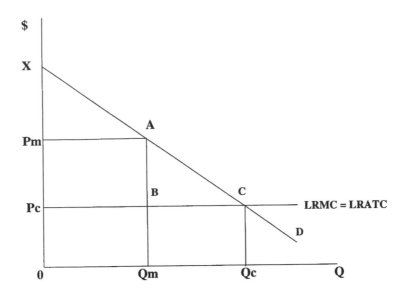

Figure 6. The firm and allocative-market-efficiency.

decrease were it produced. Any output rate above equilibrium is thus an overallocation of resources and also represents allocative-market-inefficiency.

Thus welfare is maximized at competitive market equilibrium. Competitive market equilibrium is this allocative-market-efficiency, the socially optimum rate of output. The important point is that since X-inefficiency is assumed to be nonexistent, efficiency means that which occurs at a competitive market equilibrium; efficiency means allocative-market-efficiency.

Allocative efficiency is also shown in figure 6. Whereas figure 5 showed allocative inefficiency from the point of view of the market as a whole, figure 6 shows it for a firm. In figure 6, the competitive firm is shown to produce output Qc at price Pc while the monopolist produces a lower output, Qm, at a higher price, Pm. The firm, regardless of market structure, is assumed to be part of a constant cost industry. Hence, long-run average total cost (LRATC) is constant and equal to long-run marginal cost.

To discuss allocative efficiency as part of the welfare costs of market power, we begin by estimating the amount of consumer surplus existing under perfect competition and market power. Under perfect competition, the surplus of consumers is their total benefits (0XCQc) minus their total expenditures (0PcCQc). In Figure 6, this is the area XCPc. Under monopoly, total benefits to consumers equal 0XAQm while consumer expenditures equal OPmAQm. Under monopoly, the consumer surplus is thus XAPm. Market power thus reduces the consumer surplus by an amount equal to PmACPc.

This lost consumer surplus—PmACPc—is divided into two segments: ABC and PmABPc. The area PmABPc is monopoly profits. This is the monopoly price (Pm) minus its average cost (Pc) times its output rate (Qm). Profits, however, are treated as a transfer of income from buyer to seller rather than a welfare loss.

The area ABC is allocative-market-inefficiency. The perfectly competitive industry produces the socially optimum rate of output which maximizes consumer and producer surplus. The monopolist produces less and charges a higher price such that consumer and producer surpluses are still increasing. Qm thus represents an underallocation of resources, or market-allocative-inefficiency. Allocative inefficiency—Qm—is a deadweight welfare loss because both the consumers and the producers are sacrificing welfare for which nothing else is gained.

The costs of monopoly power are thus economic profits, and allocative inefficiency. Implicit in this analysis is the assumption is that X-inefficiency is zero and hence that both the perfectly competitive firm and the monopolist produce with the same—minimum—average and marginal costs. To the extent that a monopolist produces with higher costs

than perfectly competitive firms, these higher costs represent X-inefficiency. This is yet another effect of monopoly power. The implications of this, the crux of the book and of X-efficiency theory, will be discussed in later chapters. However, the next section will introduce these ideas.

2.4.3. Minimum Costs and Allocative (In)Efficiency

In figure 6, the assumption is that competitive firms and monopolists have the same cost curves. That is, costs are assumed to be determined by technical factors such as input prices, output rates, and technology. Assuming minimum costs allows us to focus on the market. This assumption has lead us to assume that the only inefficiency created by monopoly is allocative inefficiency. In other words, X-inefficiency *cannot* exist. These beliefs, however, are more a statement about the way in which microeconomic theory is presented than it is about the (real) world.

2.5. Implications

In the theory of the firm presented in this chapter, the firm is assumed to have a single goal that it carries out in a coherent fashion. This goal is assumed to be profit maximization. Second, in maximizing profits, the firm is assumed to make smooth and quick adjustments to changes in its environment. For example, a relative increase in the price of labor is predicted to result in a decrease in the labor:capital ratio. Another example is that an increase in the marginal productivity of labor is predicted to increase the labor:capital ratio per unit of output. As a final example, an increase in the firm's available funds for expenditures is predicted, ceteris paribus, to increase output. Third, the firm is assumed to perform as if it were a textbook case. That is, the firm maximizes its profits and minimizes its costs; it maximizes output for given inputs and minimizes costs for a given output rate. Fourth, the firm's behavior is assumed to be independent of its size, or form of ownership. The firm is treated as if it were a single individual. In the next chapter, and throughout the book, this framework for viewing firms will be questioned as we present an alternative—XE theory—framework.

3

X-EFFICIENCY:
THE INTELLECTUAL SETTING AND
AN INTRODUCTION TO THE THEORY

3.1. Introduction

In the previous chapter, we reviewed microeconomic theory with respect to production, cost, and the welfare costs of monopoly power. We know that microeconomics assumes that the firm is a cost minimizer and that efficiency means allocative efficiency. That is, the firm produces maximum output for given inputs, incurs minimum its cost for a given output, and only markets can be inefficient. Leibenstein questioned these assumptions in postulating a nonallocative type of (in)efficiency. In 1966 he called it X-efficiency. Data from both industrialized and less developed countries, showing that firms were neither always internally efficient nor always maximizing their profits, led him to postulate the existence of an X-(in)efficiency.

Leibenstein was not the only one at this time who was questioning the assumptions of microeconomics. Scitovsky, Baumol, Williamson, Marris, Simon, Tullock, and Monsen and Downs, among others were questioning the profit-maximization assumption. For each of these writers, the firm is assumed to maximize something other than profits: the firm has a "complex objective function." Tullock was questioning the cost-minimization assumption, but in a different way and with his eyes on a different "prize" than Leibenstein. Simon was questioning the rationality postulate of economic theory, and along with his colleagues at Cyert and March was delving into the internal workings of the firm. Leibenstein's work, while similar to theirs, was also different in important aspects.

In this chapter I shall discuss the way in which Leibenstein's work differed from that of these other authors, the data that motivated Leibenstein and his original statement of XE theory, and Leibenstein's original formulation of XE theory.

3.2. Complex Objective Functions

3.2.1. Introduction

Nonprofit objectives of individuals and groups within firms are certainly neither a startling nor novel idea in economics. Alfred Marshall in his *Industry and Trade*

(1932); Berle and Means in their often quoted book, *The Modern Corporation and Private Property* (1932); and Keynes in his *Essays in Persuasion* (1935) spoke about nonprofit objectives of decision makers in modern firms. Hicks (1935) argued that a "quiet life" was perhaps the best form of monopoly profits. More contemporary writers discussing this issue have included Cole (1959), Gordon (1961), and Barnard (1962). These writers have argued that, rather than profits, one or more of the following are apt to be the primary objective of managers: power, prestige, professional competence, salary, security, and status.

In this section I will discuss the response of four other economists to the apparent non-profit maximizing behavior of firms. In order of discussion they are Tibor Scitovsky (1943), William Baumol (1959), Robbin Marris (1963,1964), Oliver Williamson (1964), and R. Joseph Monsen, Jr. and Anthony Downs (1965).

3.2.2. Scitovsky

Scitovsky's paper, although appearing over 20 years before Leibenstein's original treatment of XE theory, was original in its approach and served as a paradigm for the others. Scitovsky's attention focused on the question of whether an entrepreneur (or a manager) with a utility function containing income and leisure could maximize both his utility and the firm's profits simultaneously.

Scitovsky's conclusion is that the simultaneous maximization of both utility and profits is possible only if the entrepreneur's marginal utility for profits and work effort is infinite and his or her marginal utility for leisure is zero. Are entrepreneurs possessed of such a psychology?

Scitovsky believes that entrepreneurs may possess such a psychology. However, this "need not apply to every businessman, and may conceivably be untrue even about the representative entrepreneur" (p. 358). Profit maximization may thus not be descriptive, but, according to Scitovsky, it "makes economic analysis so much simpler" (p. 352).

3.2.3. Baumol

William Baumol's thesis—that the "typical" oligopoly attempts to maximize sales (total revenue) subject to the firm earning some "minimum" level of profits—was the outgrowth of his work with a business consulting firm. Baumol does not consider this objective to be inconsistent with rational behavior, saying, "People's objectives are whatever they are. Irrationality surely must be defined to consist in decision patterns that make it more difficult to attain one's own ends, and not in choosing ends that, for some reason, are considered to be wrong" (p. 46). The desire to maximize sales is due in part to the positive correlation between sales and the salaries of executives. Second, maximum sales are desired because of the disadvantages of declining sales—a loss of customers, a loss of receptivity from the capital markets, a loss of distributors, and more onerous industrial relations. Baumol reports that when profits and sales conflict with each other, business people almost always prefer to maintain or increase sales. While unprofitable lines are eventually discontinued, this occurs only after "much heart searching and delay" (p. 47).

Sales maximization requires a concern for future sales and hence funds to finance the necessary expansion. Baumol thus defines the minimum profit constraint as a level of profits necessary to finance this expansion. Some "intermediate level of profits" is thus likely to be "optimal" for achieving long-run sales maximization. Once this minimum profit level is achieved, sales maximization becomes the primary objective of the firm. Baumol reports that, in his experience, only once had the president of a major corporation been quoted in the press as stating that he wanted to make his company the most profitable, not the largest firm in the industry. He comments, "It is interesting that this man had once been an academic economist" (p. 52). As to whether long-run sales maximization is consistent with long-run profits, Baumol adds that in large firms goals are not always discussed and explicitly formulated, thus making the concept of long-run goals difficult to understand.

3.2.4. Marris

For Robin Marris, the modern corporation is characterized by the separation of ownership from finance. In Marris's model, managers maximize utility that is a function of the growth of the firm and their own security. Growth is measured as the growth in assets and reflects the satisfactions received from association with a large and growing firm, e.g., salary, power, and prestige. Security is measured by the firm's valuation ratio, that is, the ratio of the firm's market value to the book value of its assets. As the valuation ratio falls, the firm becomes a more likely target for a takeover which threatens management's position. With respect to this utility function, Marris states that management maximizes growth subject to a security constraint. That is, management's first goal is to minimize the chance for a takeover, and having succeeded at that, management then sets out to maximize the growth of the firm's net assets.

More security (profits) and more growth, however, are not necessarily compatible. First, higher growth by reducing the rate-of-return to capital "lowers" profits. Second, growth is not necessarily compatible with efficiency. In contrast to more traditional neoclassical models that assume all workers and teams to be homogenous, Marris assumes that new organization members, however qualified, are not fully efficient at nonroutine decisions until they become familiar with the culture of the organization. He thus postulates that management's average decision-making efficiency is a function of two elements: the average efficiency of new members compared with the average efficiency of old members and the total number of new members as a percentage of the organization's total membership. Because the firm's growth increases the ratio of new to total members, growth reduces average tenure and hence long-run average efficiency.

Marris seems to have been one of the first economists to hypothesize that management is constrained by the threat of a takeover. However, while neoclassical theory assumes that non-profit maximization always leads to a takeover—the assumption being that the capital markets are perfect—Marris assumes that the capital market is not perfect. This provides management with some discretion away from profit maximization. The explanation rests in part on the scarcity of capable "raiders." The neoclassical assumption of a completely known production function and homogeneous workers leads to the theory that any management team should generate the same profits. Marris rejects this theory in favor of the assumption that these elements affect productivity and profits.

Marris assumes that most capitalists are not capable managers, while most management specialists are not capitalists. With an imperfect capital market, managers have some allowable discretionary behavior. This leads Marris to conclude that the most efficient firms grow the fastest, less efficient firms grow more slowly, and the least efficienct are taken over.

3.2.5. Williamson

Oliver Williamson incorporated nonmonetary values into his model of motivation and behavior with an "expense-preference function." Williamson assumes that managers operate the firm so as to maximize their own utility which is a function of staff, emoluments, and discretionary profits. Managers attempt to maximize this utility function subject to the constraint that after-tax profits be greater than or equal to some minimum level. The conventional wisdom during the time of Williamson's writing included the assumption that managers are indifferent towards all types of costs or expenses: a dollar is a dollar. In his model of expense-preference, managers' attitudes towards costs are asymmetric, that is, some types of expenses are preferred over others. In the category of preferred expenses are those that yield utility to the manager but that cannot be assumed to have a positive impact on his productivity.

Managers' expense preferences include staff expenses—general administration and selling expenses—and emoluments or perks. Can managers simultaneously maximize both their utility and corporate profits? They can if and only if the marginal utility (MU) for staff and emoluments is zero, which means that both are valued only because of their contribution to profits. Since Williamson considers this situation unlikely, he concludes that profits and utility maximization are incompatible.

Williamson recognizes that the modern organization is a coalition, an organization rather than a "representative firm." However, he adds that it is a coalition of equals only during times of crises, when there is a threat to jobs and income. During "normal" times, management becomes the chief member of the coalition. This gives management access to information that others do not have, which, in turn, gives management the power to make decisions. While the threat of takeover serves to influence management's behavior, it is only a partial check. The potential power of investors has thus "largely gone unexercised" (1964, p. 22), leaving the capital markets as an imperfect mechanism through which investors control their managers. Therefore, Williamson concludes that the motives and behaviors of managers are important.

3.2.6. Monsen and Downs

Monsen and Downs begin by stating that traditional price theory treats the firm as if it were a single person with known and ordered preferences and the ability to carry out these preferences. By contrast, Monsen and Downs show that large managerial firms (those firms with at least 1000 employees whose management does not have controlling interest in the firm) are not managed with the prime objective of maximizing profits. Rather, Monsen and Downs assume that in these firms owners want steady dividend income and gradually increasing stock prices, while managers attempt to maximize their lifetime income.

As in the Marris and Williamson models, Monsen and Downs assume that capital markets are not perfect, thus reducing the ability of owners to control managers toward profit maximiza-tion. This imperfection arises because owners are relatively unaware of all the alternatives open to the firm ex ante. They learn about the firm's performance ex-post from managers who screen the information that is "leaked." Stockholders, therefore, cannot really determine whether profits are being maximized. Furthermore, owners cannot "accurately judge small differences in the quality of performance"(p. 225). Thus, so long as stock prices meet the criterion of "satisfactory growth" and dividends do not fall, managers will have reason to feel secure about their jobs.

As for the managers, their income includes both monetary compensation and nonmonetary compensations such as leisure, prestige, and power. It is from these two categories that they attempt to maximize their lifetime income. Given the lack of information flowing to the stockholders, managers will be especially vigorous only when their lifetime incomes are affected. Managers will thus direct the firm so that it pays steadily rising dividends and experiences steadily increasing stock prices. In addition, managers will be risk averse will avoid variability in corporate earnings, and will reduce corporate growth. In other words, large firms, especially large managerial firms, will be less efficient then smaller, owner-managed firms. Therefore, similar to both Williamson's and Scitovsky's models, utility (lifetime income) maximization and profit maximization are not compatible with each other.

3.3. Rent-Seeking Behavior

XE theory would consider deviations from cost minimization as evidence of X-inefficiency. On the other hand, the theory of rent-seeking would explain these apparent deviations from cost minimization as being the product of rational behavior. As in the case of market equilibrium, the assertion of rent-seeking behavior tends to assume away X-inefficiency.

Rent is that part of a payment to any resource in excess of its opportunity cost. That is, rent is another name for profits. In traditional economic theory the pursuit of economic profits within an ordered—competitive—market structure is a motivator of private behavior and a servant of the public interest. Profit seeking within an ordered market structure thus results in allocative efficiency.

However, when the allocation of resources is made via a political process rather than through the market process, then the outcome is different. The motivations of the participants are assumed to be the same in the political process as they are in the market profit-seeking process, e.g., the pursuit of individual gain. The result, however, is the creation of social waste rather than social surplus. This follows from the assumption that the political process grants someone or some group a monopoly position and hence monopoly profits. Those granted this monopoly status and those who covet it both understand that political decisions are not etched in stone. Hence both of these groups are motivated to allocate resources in an attempt to either maintain or receive the government's favor. The political process thus generates rent-seeking behavior. However, the resources allocated in this fashion do not produce goods or services with market value. Rather, they are used to create a favorable (from the spender's point of view) distribution of wealth. Therefore, rent-seeking behavior, while rational from the individual's point of view, creates social waste. Because rent-seeking is assumed to be rational behavior, it follows that rent-seeking, and in particular the higher costs incurred by the firm because of rent-seeking, does not imply any inefficiency on the part of the firm. Thus, once rent-seeking behavior is assumed to be the cause of higher costs among, for example, regulated firms, then X-inefficiency as a result of government regulation has been assumed away.

3.3.1. Tullock on the Welfare Costs of Monopoly

Tullock's 1967 paper on the welfare costs of monopoly is an interesting statement not only in its own right but also because of the differences between this orthodox approach to regulation and the X-efficiency approach. Tullock begins his article by quoting Robert Mundell's (1962) lament about how the small estimates of the welfare losses of monopoly power can lead some to conclude that economics is not very important. Mundell's answer was to reexamine the "tools upon which these estimates are founded" (p. 622). Tullock then cites Leibenstein's original 1966 paper on X-inefficiency, which discussed why small allocative losses (measured by the welfare triangle) may not be the only or necessarily the largest welfare losses created by monopoly power. Tullock's response to Leibenstein is to reject the possibility that these other losses represent nonallocative losses. Instead, he takes the route suggested by Mundell, i.e., that the tools used should be reevaluated while maintaining the exclusive concern with allocative (in)efficiency. It seems useful to recognize this point at the outset.

Our presentation of the research on rent-seeking by Tullock and others is illustrated in figure 7, which shoes several examples of the welfare costs of government. First, we examine the case of an excise tax. We might imagine that in the absence of this tax and with a constant cost Co, a domestic price of Pc results in quantity Qc. However, the imposition of an excise tax raises the price to Pm and reduces quantity to Qm. The welfare cost is the area ABC, while the area PmABPc is a transfer from the buyers of this commodity to the recipients of the public funds. But suppose, says Tullock, that the revenues raised are completely wasted by, for

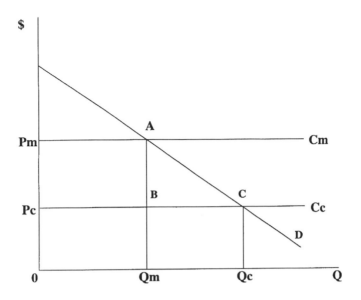

Figure 7. Welfare costs of taxes, tariffs, and rent seeking.

example, producing tunnels that go nowhere. Under these conditions, the total welfare cost of the government's tax program is the entire area PmACPc. That is, under these conditions, there is not only an allocative inefficiency ABC but also an expenditure of PMABPc for which nothing is received. There is no transfer involved here—only a waste of scarce resources.

Second, we examine the case of a tariff. Let us assume constant costs. Without a tariff, Qc units will be bought at a price Pc. The imposition of a tariff results in Qm units bought at a price Pm.

The welfare cost of the tariff includes the triangle ABC. However, if the domestic producers are less efficient than foreign producers then their costs are Cm, while the cost that of foreign goods is Cc. The imposition of a prohibitive tariff raises the price to Pm, reduces the demand to Qm, and allows the less efficient domestic producers to control the entire market. In this case, not only is there allocative inefficiency, ABC, but also a reallocation of resources to inefficient domestic producers. This waste is measured by the area PmACPc. And in both cases—excise taxes and tariffs—the total welfare cost of government policies exceeds the traditional measure of welfare losses due to monopoly power (area ABC).

Rent-seeking expenditures are a function of the size of the expected or potential return from incurring the favor of the government. Assuming rational behavior, these expenditures are a rational investment from the point of view of the interest group making these expenditures. Thus X-inefficiency has already been assumed away. Consequently, government regulation cannot, by definition, create X-inefficiency. What it does do is to create an incentive for the employees to make privately rational investments that are socially wasteful.

3.4. Simon and the Carnegie School

3.4.1. Introduction

In the Introduction to their 1963 book, *A Behavioral Theory of the Firm*, Cyert and March state,

> This book is about the business firm and the way it makes economic decisions. We propose to make detailed observations of the procedures by which firms make decisions... We believe that, in order to understand contemporary economic decision making, we need to supplement the study of market forces with an examination of the internal operation of the firm.

Clearly, Cyert and March's "Carnegie School" approach has similarities with the ideas Leibenstein published in his 1960 book, *Economic Theory and Organiztional Analysis*, and which he was further developing through XE theory. It is possible not only to summarize some of these similarities but also to point out some of the differences.

3.4.2. Bounded Rationality and Satisficing

Simon's work on organizations, including his 1961 book, *Administrative Behavior*, makes it clear that he considers decision making central to the problem of how organizations perform. One important determinant of the quality of decision making and hence performance is the motivational system operating inside the firm. Unlike orthodox economic theory, which implicitly assumes that both the motivational system and performance are optimal, Simon assumes neither. Rather, he maintains that factors such as peer pressure can influence individuals to the extent that identical workers operating in close physical proximity can have noticeably different output rates.

Peer pressure is only one among many factors that determine the degree of rationality. The salient feature of rationality is that it is the outcome of a process that workers follow. This process is necessarily limited, and hence an individual's rationality is "bounded rationality." In his 1957 book, *Models of Man*, Simon points out that the boundaries on human rationality come not from instinct or intent but from the limits to human neurological functioning. Simon's concern is thus the *process* by which decisions are made. Leibenstein was squarely in Simon's camp here.

Humans may thus intend to be rational, but we are bound by our brains in how much we can attain. Humans are thus satisficers rather than maximizers. That is, we choose to attain an acceptable level of achievement rather than to maximize our achievement.

3.4.3. The Carnegie School

The Carnegie School developed and used several concepts that were similar to concepts used by Leibenstein in discussing the nonallocative effects of monopoly power. These include standard operating procedures, resistance to change except under duress, organizational slack, and multiplicity of goals. Leibenstein made use of the concept of inertia (resistance to change), habitual decision making (standard operating procedures), and principal-agent problems (multiple goals expressed as an *aspiration* level) to explain how X-inefficiencies are created. His claim that firms did not always minimize cost takes the form of organizational slack, or payments in excess of those necessary to keep the organization functioning. Finally, both approaches offer alternatives to the maximization postulate.

Hence the similarities between Leibenstein's work and that of the Carnegie School are clear. There are also differences however. First, satisficing is similar to maximizing in that both are goal-oriented, directed behavior. On the other hand, X-inefficient behavior stems not from aspiring rather than maximizing, but from sloppiness, laziness, and the like. Second, and a related point, organizational slack is treated as having the positive effect of helping to stabilize the organization during times of crises by providing it with a cushion. This cushion helps the firm to cut into its excess costs without equal cutbacks in resource usage. Leibenstein's general approach was to call organizational slack a form of inefficiency. Third, the Carnegie School takes more of an operations research and organizational behavior approach, while XE theory orients itself within an economic theory framework. In fact, Leibenstein insisted that he was a neoclassical economist, but one who did not believe that human behavior was always maximizing.

3.5. XE Theory: An Introduction

3.5.1. Introduction
In this section, I present some of the data that motivated the development of XE theory, as well as a summary of Leibenstein's 1966 paper. Two types of data motivated XE theory: first, data apparently showing that firms are not internally efficient, and second, data showing that firms were not maximizing their profits because they were not following the behavioral rules of marginal analysis.

3.5.2. Internal Efficiency
Internal efficiency: micro data. In 1962, Peter Kilby reported the results of International Labor Organization Productivity Demonstration Missions in various industries in several less developed countries. The results of this work showed that "simple alterations in the physical organization of a plant's productive process" can lead to relatively large increases in labor productivity and hence relatively large decreases in unit labor and capital costs. These "simple alterations" included changes in plant layout, changes in the utilization of machines, the handling of materials, work flows throughout the plant, waste control, method of payment to employees and worker training and supervision. The results for all nine countries listed in this study showed an average increase in labor productivity of 75% and an average decrease in both unit labor and unit capital costs of approximately 35%.

Kilby also reported data for five rubber factories in Nigeria. In this case, all the plants were located in the same region, and they all sold their product to the same market, hired labor from the same market, and used identical capital in plants with similar physical layouts. Despite this, unit labor requirements varied by as much as 134%, while unit capital requirements varied by as much as 270%. The most efficient firms—those with the lowest unit input requirements—were owned and operated by Greeks. The most inefficient firms were privately owned Nigerian firms. Clearly, Kilby's data suggest that production and costs are not technologically determined, and that the organization of the firm is an important determinant of both output and cost.

L. Rostas's 1962 study of relative labor productivity in 31 U.S. and U.K. manufacturing industries showed U.S. labor productivity to be, on average, 120% higher. Such differences are not necessarily surprising. However he notes that "... in a number of industries (or firms) where the equipment is very largely identical in the U.S. and U.K...., there are still substantial differences in output per worker in the U.K. and U.S."(p. 64). These other factors included plant layout; work flow; lighting, heating, and other internal factory conditions; number of hours worked; method of wage payments; labor turnover; and motivation. He says, "It is of importance to know more about these 'other' factors and the extent to which they influence output per worker. These factors, which are independent of mechanization or the technique of production, are partly 'organizational' factors, partly factors affecting the willingness and ability of the worker" (p. 64).

Rostas did not provide any quantitative estimates of these other factors. C.F. Pratten (1976), however, did provide such estimates in his study of productivity differentials among plants of multinational corporations. Pratten reports estimates for the effects of economic and "behavioral" factors on productivity differentials between U.K. and German plants, U.K. and French plants, and U.K. and North American plants of multinational corporations. On the average, labor productivity among plants in the U.K. was lower than for plants in Germany (27%), France (15%), or North America (50%). Economic factors include output rates, length of production runs, capital, product mix, and capacity utilization. Behavioral factors include strikes and work norms, including the effects of industrial relations that affect productivity. Among plants in the U.K. and Germany, economic factors "explain" 13 percentage points, while behavioral factors explain 12 percentage points. For U.K.—German differences, economic and behavioral causes explain 9 and 5.5 percentage points, respectively. For U.K.—North America differences, economic and behavioral factors explain 35 and 11 percentage points, respectively.

Frederick Harbison (1956) also looked at the contribution of "organization," in his case to the process of economic development. Harbison defines the organization as more than the sum of the individuals who manage, plan, coordinate, administer, and supervise. However, the factor called "organization" reflects and is the "integrated aggregation" of these functions. Harbison adds that "...the organization that employs labor is probably the principal factor—the dominant force—in determining labor productivity with constant technology" (p. 372).

The factor "organization" is thus an important determinant of variations in labor productivity that is "frequently" observed within a firm. For example, Harbison reports on two petroleum refineries located less than one-half mile from each other in Egypt. The productivity of labor in one was double that in the other for years. "But recently, under completely new management, the inefficient refinery was beginning to make quite spectacular improvements in efficiency with the same labor force" (p. 373). These reports can be interpreted to mean that these firms were not producing on either their production or cost functions.

Productivity and growth: macro data. In 1957, Robert Solow (1957) published his study of the aggregate production function for the private nonfarm sector of the U.S. economy, a study that would eventually lead him to a Nobel Prize. His data covered the period 1909 to 1949. His results may be summarized as follows: a 1% increase in the capital stock increases output by 0.35%, a 1% increase in labor increases output by 0.65%, and "technological change" increases output by an average of 1.5% per year. Solow defined technological change as any kind of shift in the production function, that is, any change in our ability to produce with given inputs of capital and labor. Factors included as technological change include "...all sorts of things...," including "organization" (p. 312).

In 1959, Solow published another study of the private nonfarm sector of the U.S. economy for the period 1919-1953. Here he reported that 1% increases in capital and labor results in 0.30% and 0.70% increases in output, respectively. Technological change, however, increases output by an average of 2.5% per year.

Odd Aukrust (1959) published a similar study for the entire Norwegian economy for the period 1900—1955. His data showed that, a 1% increase in capital increases output by 0.20%, a 1% increase in labor increases output by 0.76%, and the annual increase in output due to better "organization" is 1.8%. Aukrust defines "organization" in the same fashion as Solow defines technological change. In particular, he mentions the knowledge of management and other employees, the motivation to work, the social climate at work, and the international environment.

Olavi Niitamo (1958) published yet another similar study for the manufacturing sector of the Finnish economy for the period 1925—1952. His data showed that, a 1% increase in capital increases output by 0.26%, a 1% increase in labor increases output by 0.74%, and the annual increase in output from better organization is 1.2%. Taken together, these studies point to a nontraditional factor that exerts a significant influence on production. These findings are not proof by any means of X-(in)efficiency. They are included here because Leibenstein knew of and considered them while formulating XE theory.

3.5.3. Profit Maximization

Beginning in the late 1930s, a number of studies began to show that neither a firm's conduct or performance was profit maximizing. One of the first of these studies was by R. Hall and C. Hitch (1939). Hall and Hitch were part of a group of economists from Cambridge, England, who studied the practices of business firms as part of their study of business cycles. The Hall and Hitch study was based on the responses of 38 entrepreneurs, 33 of who were in manufacturing.

In contrast to the assumption of economic theory that firms produce until marginal revenue (MR) is equal to marginal cost (MC) and set their price according to demand, the most "striking feature" of the responses given by the 38 entrepreneurs is that firms do not equate MR with MC. In addition, they do not set prices by demand. Rather, they practice "full cost pricing." That is, they try to estimate their average total cost and then charge a price that reflects these costs plus a mark-up for profits. In other words, "... in pricing they try to apply a rule of thumb which we shall call 'full cost,' and that maximum profits, if they result at all from the application of this rule, do so as an accidental (or possibly evolutionary) by-product" (pp. 18-19). The majority of the firms claimed to adhere to full-cost pricing. Hall and Hitch also report that the full-cost pricing policy is used because entrepreneurs do not know either the demand curve for the product or the price elasticity of demand! Without this, maximization is not possible.

A second study of this nature is that of Richard Lester (1946). Lester sent questionnaires to 430 firms in the southern U.S. who were paying substantially lower wages in their southern plants as compared to their nonsouthern plants. His data are based on 68 completed questionnaires. In asking about what determines employment, 28 firms replied that only product market demand was relevant. Of the 28 firms that listed two or more factors, 65% listed product market demand, 9.7% listed changes in technology, 9.5% listed non-labor costs, 5.1% listed profits, and only 7.6% listed wages and changes in wages. These results are surprising not only because of the emphasis put on the labor demand curve in economic theory but also because for these 28 firms, labor costs represented approximately 30% of total costs. At the time of the study, labor costs were approximately 20% of all costs for all U.S. manufacturing firms. Hence one would suppose that firms would be very sensitive to wages and wage changes when making employment decisions. The firms in Lester's study were not.

Lester also asked these entrepreneurs how they would react to a relative increase in the wages of their southern workers vis-a-vis their northern workers. Of the 43 firms replying, the largest percentage (29.6%) said they would improve internal efficiency by improving management, the work or product flow throughout the plant, the plant layout, and experimenting with incentives. Only 4% gave the "correct" response: reduce output. Lester also reports that the entrepreneurs from his sample do not generally think about marginal cost and that in general they consider it very difficult to estimate either marginal cost or marginal product.

Here again, one is faced with behavior that seemingly contradicts economic theory. If firms do not operate in the way economic theory describes, then how do they operate? What modus operandi do they use, and what is the effect on their performance and on the use of scarce resources? Furthermore, the performance of the firms described in the Kilby, Rostas, Pratten, and Harbison studies appears to be inefficient but not in the sense of allocative inefficiency. That is, these firms can not be described as inefficient because they are producing less and charging a higher price then would a perfectly competitive firm. Rather, they might be described as internally inefficient: producing less than possible at a higher cost then necessary.

3.6. X-Efficiency

To explain these data, Leibenstein developed XE theory. What theoretical conditions support the existence of these nonallocative inefficiencies? That is, why are given inputs not transformed into predetermined outputs? Leibenstein discussed four factors. First, labor contracts are incomplete. Specifically, while the payment portion of the labor contract is clearly specified, the performance aspect is not. Management can state in no uncertain terms that an employee will receive $X an hour, $X per week, or $X per year. On the other hand, management would find it much more difficult to specify and monitor the sequence and the details of each and every activity that the employee should perform.

Thus, workers have effort discretion that makes their performance dependent upon motivation. Leibenstein adds, "A good deal is left to custom, authority, and whatever motivational techniques are available to management as well as to individual discretion and judgment" (p. 407). In contrast to this treatment of labor contracts, neoclassical economics implicitly treats labor contracts in the same fashion as other contracts and assumes that work effort is fixed.

Second, the production function is not completely specified or known. The process of production always contains an experimental element to it such that the firm does not always know in advance the quantity of output that will be received from given inputs and input ratios. Thus, given inputs are associated with a variety of output rates. In figure 8, we have thus drawn the production function as a thick band rather than as a thin line. Given one unit of capital and two workers, output may vary between Q1 and Q2. In chapter 2, we showed a production function as a

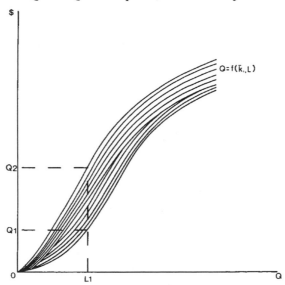

Figure 8. Discretionary behavior and the short-run
production function as a "band".

thin line, implying that given inputs convert into predetermined and maximum outputs.

Third, not all inputs are marketed and/or equally accessible to all buyers. For example, management knowledge is neither well defined nor traded in a well-organized market. The motivations of management, at the same time, may be the decisive factor in a firm "finding" other inputs at the right price, i.e., finances. The role of knowledge and motivation are significant in determining X-efficiency. While standard microeconomic theory assumes maximization and hence that all available knowledge is fully utilized, XE theory assumes that motivation will influence the use of knowledge. Leibenstein says,

> ... knowledge may not be used to capacity just as capital and labor may be underutilized. More important, a good deal of our knowledge is vague. A man may have nothing more than a sense of its existence, and yet this may be the critical element. Given a sufficient inducement, he can then search out its nature in detail and get it to a stage where he can use it. People normally operate within the bounds of a great deal of intellectual slack. Unlike underutilized capital, this is an element that is very difficult to observe (p. 405).

Fourth, firms may imitate each other rather than compete. Under this circumstance, there is no reason to believe that the firm will necessarily produce on its production and cost functions. Leibenstein adds, "The simple fact is that neither individuals nor firms work as hard, nor do they search for information as effectively, as they could. The importance of motivation and its association with degree of effort and search arises because the relation between inputs and outputs is not a determinant one" (p. 407).

If output and costs are not completely predetermined, then what factors do determine these variables? Certainly, technology is important. However, XE theory introduces a variable called "pressure." Pressure is a condition whereby the individual feels relatively driven to realize some potential. In XE theory, pressure is said to be created by competition and adversity. In this original formulation of the theory, costs were shown to be determined by pressure. This is, of course, different from the standard formulation that shows costs as a function of output for a given technology. While costs in this standard formulation are always assumed to be technologically minimum costs, in XE theory costs are not assumed to be *always* minimized: sometimes, but not always.

In figure 9, we show the effect of pressure on costs. To do this, Leibenstein assumed that the unit costs of any firm will be influenced by the average level of costs for the industry as a whole. This means that each firm reacts to industrywide costs in a way that influences its own costs. In particular, when industrywide unit costs rise, then any one firm can allow its costs to rise while remaining competitive. On the other hand, when industry wide unit costs fall each firm will attempt to lower their own unit costs in order to stay competitive. In figure 10, we are assuming that industrywide costs in the previous period (t-1) will serve to formulate the firm's expectation of the current period (t) industrywide costs, and hence to influence the

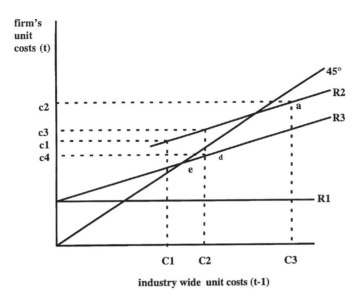

Figure 9. Pressure, technological change, and costs.

firm's unit costs in the current period. The 45 degree line is the locus of all points for which industrywide unit costs in period t-1 are equal to the firm's unit costs in period t. In other words, the firm makes a proportional adjustment to industrywide costs such that both are equal to each other.

R1 shows the reaction curve for a cost minimizer. This firm's costs do not react to industry pressure as defined above. On the other hand, reaction curve R2 is for a firm whose costs do react to pressure. For example, if the firm expects industry-wide unit costs to be C1, then its costs will be c1. If the expectation is that industrywide unit costs will be C2, then its costs will be c2. The precise shape of the reaction curve can certainly be different than what we are showing here. The important point is that the firm's costs are influenced by the performance of other firms.

Reductions in cost by increases in X-efficiency and increases in knowledge are shown with the addition of reaction curve R3. Assume that we begin at point a, with industrywide costs C2 and firm costs c2. If industry costs falls to C3, then the firm's costs would fall to c3 by moving along R2 to point b. If knowledge increases, it would be felt by a downward shift in the entire curve to R3. The firm's costs would then fall to c4 as the firm moves from point b to point d. Again, if industry costs fell further, then the firm's costs would again be lowered and shown by a movement along R3 to another point such as e. Regardless of the actual process, the firm's costs are not assumed to be predetermined, but influenced by motivations for cost reduction and, of course, knowledge (technology). We will thus draw the cost curve not as a thin line but as a thick band. This is shown in figure 10.

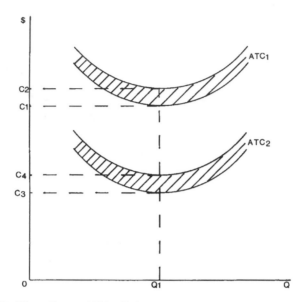

Figure 10. The effects of X-inefficiency and technological change on costs.

The meaning of ATC1 in figure 10 is that any level of output can give rise to a level of costs that varies according to pressure and motivations. For example, Q1 will be produced in the range C1C2, the exact unit cost being determined by pressure or motivation for cost reduction. This range is similar to the movement from point a to point b in figure 9, which results from changing pressure. On the other hand, an increase in knowledge will shift the entire ATC curve downward to ATC2. Output Q1 can now be produced with unit costs C3 but will be produced in the range C3C4, depending upon pressures for cost reduction. This downward shift in the ATC curve is similar to the downward shift in the reaction curve in figure 9 from R2 to R3 and the subsequent movement from point d to point e. Leibenstein summarizes these points by stating,

> ...for a variety of reasons people and organizations normally work neither as hard nor as effectively as they could. In situations where competitive pressure is light, many people will trade the disutility of greater effort, of search, and the control of other peoples' activities for the utility of feeling less pressure and of better interpersonal relations. But in situations where competitive pressures are high, and hence the costs of such trades are also high, they will exchange less of the disutility of effort for the utility of freedom from pressure, etc" (p. 413).

As we proceed we will see that this idea of utility maximizing effort decisions is given no more probability than that of non-maximizing behavior.

3.7. Conclusions

Nonprofit maximizing theories of the firm did not begin with Leibenstein. In this chapter, I have reviewed a class of nonprofit-maximization theories known as "complex objective functions," including that of Scitovsky, and those who are Leibenstein's contemporaries:- Baumol, Marris, Williamson, and Monsen and Downs. I have also discussed the relationship between Leibenstein's and Tullock's work on rent-seeking. Each of these theories assumes that firm members apply fully rational behavior in the pursuit of maximizing profits plus some other variable. In the case of Simon (and his colleagues at Carnegie Mellon), the possibility was raised that individuals are satisficers, but not maximizers. This work is closest to Leibenstein's own attempt to incorporate nonmaximizing behavior into economic theory. In the next two chapters, I will present in XE theory in greater detail.

4
X-EFFICIENCY THEORY: 1

4.1. Introduction

In the last chapter, we examined data (seemingly) inconsistent with orthodox neoclassical theory, as well as Leibenstein's initial attempt to provide a explanation for these data. In the next two chapters we will analyze this explanation—XE theory—in more detail.

The X in X-efficiency represents an unknown factor responsible for a nonallocative type of inefficiency. That is, the data presented in the last chapter revealed unexploited, low-cost opportunities for increasing intrafirm productivity and hence for reducing the firm's costs. These (X) unexploited opportunities are due to factors such as lack of motivation, human inertia, and biases in human decision making that lead to non-maximizing behavior, suboptimal performance, and waste. These unexploited opportunities are a form of inefficiency, but not allocative inefficiency. These inefficiencies are not related to prices and markets per se. They are related to intrafirm activities and to both type-1 and type-2 errors made by individuals, which affect the firm's performance.

One of the tasks of the next two chapters is thus to explain how the individual's "internal" environment (personality) and "external" environment can produce both these types of behaviors. XE theory will be discussed in the following sequence. First, we will discuss the psychology and behavior of the individual. Second, we will discuss the individual as a group member. Third, we will present the implications of the theory. Fourth, we will provide an application of the theory to the determination of productivity.

4.2. The Individual in XE Theory

XE theory is largely a reaction to two things: orthodox economic theory which presents production as technologically determined, and formal and anecdotal evidence seemingly inconsistent with this theory. If production is not the outcome of merely technological forces, then what does determine input:output relations? In part, XE theory explains both these issues by exploring the component parts, or meanings, of some commonly used words and terms, including decision making, effort (physical and/or mental), pressure, maximization, and rationality. In each case, the reader will see a tendency to think of these as being defined by a range of possibilities; for example, decision making can be either "tight" or "loose," and effort and pressure can vary from a little to a great deal. The reader will also recognize a tendency for XE theory to inquire about the behavioral or procedural aspects of these words. For example, what are the component parts of effort, and under what conditions is a high effort level more likely to be forthcoming? Similar to Herbert Simon, rationality is used in a procedural sense. That is, what procedures are necessary for a rational decision to be made?[1]

4.2.1. The Dual Personality

The concept that an individual can contribute to X-(in)efficiency arises from the dual nature of the human personality. On the one hand, we want to adhere to standards, to strive for the maximum, and to strive by being calculating and attentive to details. In other words, this aspect of the personality is our rational self, the part of us that uses "tight," focused, or rational decision-making procedures. Leibenstein refers to this aspect of our personality as the "superego function." (Although this term was used by Freud, it would be incorrect to assess its use here as implying that Leibenstein is attempting to incorporate Freudian psychology into economic theory.) The other tendency is for each of us to "kick back," to use "loose" decision-making procedures, to follow our "animal spirits." Leibenstein refers to as the "id function." It is the id function that leads us to be "unconstrained," that is, unwilling but not necessarily unable to be calculating, attentive, rational.

XE theory assumes that, on the average, each individual is influenced by both functions in a way that leads to a compromise between the two. That is, each of us forges a compromise between the way we feel we must behave and the way we would like to behave were it not for a sense of obligation to duty or to a set of standards. In other words, each individual strikes a compromise that provides them with a sense of (psychological) "comfort."

The words "constrained" and "unconstrained" have been used in the context of an individual's ability and willingness to be attentive to details, to calculate, to be rational. "Constrained" and "unconstrained" are now going to be considered as the two end points of a personality trait that could be measured on a continuous scale. That is, the personality could exhibit complete constraint concern, at one end of the spectrum, and a complete lack of concern for constraints at the other end. Thus, an individual could employ the full power of his or her attention to details and to calculating costs and benefits. Such an individual would be completely or fully rational. On the other hand it is possible to imagine an individual placing less than 100% of this power on the details and calculations necessary to make a fully informed decision. Such an individual is referred to as "selectively rational." Rationality is thus a continuous variable with an "economic person" exhibiting

---

1   See Simon (1957, 1959, 1978) for a discussion of procedural vs. substantive rationality. Some similarities and differences between Simon's concepts and that of X-efficiency are discussed in Leibenstein (1976, 1979, 1985).

complete constrain concern. The economic person is thus a limiting case: a characteristic of the decision-making procedures used by some people at some times but not necessarily characteristic of all people at all times.

4.2.2. Selective Rationality

An extended look at the behavioral or procedural elements consistent with full and selective rationality will now be undertaken. The purpose of this element of the theory is to develop a list of decision-making procedures that are as consistent as possible with full, and hence selective, rationality. Such a list gives the concept of rationality a behavioral meaning and, therefore, denies that rationality can simply be assumed.

Six elements of rational decision making[2] will be explored. These are: realism in assessing the environment, nonreflexive assessments of the environment, independence of judgment, magnitude sensitivity, nondeferral of decisions and actions, and learning from experience. Some of these elements may overlap each other; for example, a nonreflexive (nonknee-jerk) assessment may imply a more realistic one. Be that as it may, our major concern here is in creating a framework or research agenda in which rationality can be studied, and in order to do this the concept of rationality has to be made operational. The above list is one possible approach.

Each of the elements in this list is believed to be a continuous variable. For example, a decision can be based either on a completely realistic assessment of the environment or on completely wishful thinking. Another possibility is that a decision will be made on the basis of a realistic assessment of some parts of the environment and wishful thinking towards other parts. The assessment of the riskiness of a project should make the importance of realism apparent.

A reflexive assessment of the environment is a knee-jerk reaction or decision. It is a noninformed decision based on the first impulse experienced by the decision maker. On the other hand, a nonreflexive assessment is characterized by a cool appreciation of the relevant facts. The term "knee-jerk" is not synonymous with "spontaneous"; "spontaneous" implies an almost instantaneous decision made by an expert nonreflexively but "unconsciously."

Independence of judgment may also vary from completely independent to completely dependent. Dependence would include at least the following decision making procedures: accepting advice from those with less information than that possessed by oneself; behaving simply to please others or gain their approval; and noncritical emulation. (In)dependence, as is true of the other elements of rationality, is often a matter of degree, rather than an all-or-nothing event.

Complete constraint concern—complete rationality—is seen as the outcome of a decision that is sensitive to changes in the environment. Only those who are (highly) magnitude sensitive are able to take advantage of (small) changes in

---

2   See Frantz (1980) for a discussion of similarities between Leibenstein's concept of (selective) rationality and that of the psychologist Abraham Maslow.

relevant environmental data - prices, income, demand, etc.—which warrant an appropriate response in terms of a change in their behavior.

Never put off until tomorrow what you can do today, but especially when you are betting that tomorrow will never come. (It always does!) Time deferral refers to this behavior or pattern, and to the practice of implementing "loose" decision making procedures today in the hope that you will gain the ability and/or willingness to be highly rational tomorrow. Time deferral is clearly distinguished from delaying a decision until the information search and analysis are completed.

The result of a decision depends upon its informational content. Some decisions are based upon all relevant past experiences, regardless of whether they were successful or un- successful. At other times we may remember only the successful experiences and base our current decisions accordingly. Ceteris paribus, the outcome of a decision will be different depending on this degree of selective learning, or how we learn from past experiences. In all people, the components of rationality are believed to be continuous, not binary (all-or-nothing) variables, and the degree of rationality exhibited by any one individual at any time is the outcome of the dual influences of both the superego and id functions on the individual's behavior. Furthermore, complete rationality is seen as the outcome of a decision-making procedure characterized by the optimal use of realism, nonreflexivity, independence, a high degree of magnitude sensitivity, nontime deferral, and a willingness and ability to learn from all (relevant) past experiences.

4.2.3. Deductive Thinking

The fact is, we are not prone to logical or deductive thinking. Although we make good decisions—even optimal ones—despite our lack of logical reasoning ability I want to make this point: our formal logical decision-making abilities are limited. Deductive reasoning is neither our usual practice nor is it natural. Much of the time we reason nondeductively, that is, inductively. Deductive thinking is believed to be product of our first 12 to 15 years of life, a skill that needs to be developed rather than an inherited part of adult reasoning. As a result, logical thinking is not a *given*.

In addition we suffer from many biases that distort our decision making abilities. Although these biases may be the product of human evolution, they reduce our ability for optimal decision-making, and they are correctable. Before we can minimize our biases, we must recognize them. Seventeen biases are listed and discussed briefly below.

4.2.4. Common Biases in Human Decision Making[3]

Bias # 1: Acquiescence to Majority Opinion. Studies have shown that even when asked to judge the length of a line, individuals knowingly answer incorrectly in order to agree with the (overwhelming) majority. Individuals also violate their own

---

3   Biases in human decision making are discussed in Mullen and Roth (1991) and Frank (1991).

personal judgments when faced with a presumed representative of community standards.

Bias # 2: Reactions to Excessive Stress. Excessive stress is anathema to deliberative or reflective decision-making. The decision-making affects of excessive stress include distorting facts, denial of one's true values or goals, maintenance of the status quo, procrastination, knee-jerk decision-making in order to reduce the stressful situation, "passing the buck," and hypervigilance to immediate and trivial details at the expense of the total costs and benefits of various alternatives.

Bias # 2a: Approach-Avoidance Conflict. Some situations or things both attract and repel us at the same time: the possibility of profits but the risk of losses, the possibility of publishing an article but the fear of rejection by the publisher, the pure joy and pure horror of chocolate chip cookies. The danger inherent in an approach-avoidance conflict is a source of stress, leading to vacillation rather than to a rational decision.

Bias # 2b: Approach-Approach Conflict. At times we must choose between two equally desirable alternatives: for example, choosing which school to attend, which neighborhood to live in, which woman to date (the "so many women, so little time" syndrome). The desire to avoid regret is a source of stress, leading us to decide in an arbitrary way as much as in a rational way.

Bias # 2c: Avoidance-Avoidance Conflict. At times we must choose the lesser of two evils. The undesirable outcome that awaits us is a source of stress, leading us to become preoccupied with trivial details as a way of denying or withdrawing from the stress.

Bias # 3: Need for a Consistent and Coherent View of Ourselves and Our Relationship With the World. Consider the fact that on the one hand I hold to the belief that I am a hardworking tenured full professor, but on the other hand my student evaluations are below par and I haven't published anything since Haley's Comet appeared over the night sky. These inconsistent facts are disturbing or troublesome and are called cognitive dissonance. The reaction to cognitive dissonance is often to accept the most psychologically comfortable alternative. In my case, this may be the rationalization that students are in no position to evaluate me, and the referees of the journals to which I have submitted articles are simply jealous! The important issues of my commitment to teaching and (scholarly) research will never be resolved if I take this approach of eliminating the dissonance without eliminating the conflict that gave rise to it in the first place.

Bias # 4: Confirmation Bias. Once I've decided that the students cannot realistically evaluate me, then I listen only to those colleagues who agree with me and even overestimate their ability for clarity in these matters.

Bias # 5: Halo Effect. We tend to experience clusters of properties and evaluate something or someone on the basis of the cluster as a whole. The quiet CPA with a wife and three children who attends church regularly with his entire family could never be a child molester. The Halo Effect distorts our ability to correctly evaluate information and hence to make appropriate decisions.

Bias # 6: Ignoring the Odds. We ignore the odds even when they suggest that we are incorrect. This bias is also known as the representative heuristic. (A heuristic is a shortcut device for making decisions.) For example, is Michele a librarian or a salesperson? She is shy and withdrawn, a meek soul, always helpful, has a need for order, and a passion for detail. You probably believe that Michele is a librarian because her personality more adequately fits the description of a librarian. Odds are, you're wrong. Don't worry: approximately 67% of 1000 business executives surveyed made the same error. They, and perhaps you as well forgot to figure the odds: there are approximately 200,000 librarians in the U.S. but 75 times as many salespersons - approximately 14 million. Despite certain personality traits, Michele is more likely to be selling something than she is to be stacking books at the local library.

Bias # 7: The Self-Serving Bias. We tend to attribute desirable outcomes in our life to our own intelligence, effort, or diligence. On the other hand, we blame the external environment for undesirable outcomes. We also overestimate the chance of positive things happening to us (winning the lottery) but underestimate undesirable outcomes happening to us (being in a car accident). Distorting our abilities and the reasons for success and failure cannot help but reduce our decision-making abilities.

Bias # 8: Sour Grapes. We tend to devalue a goal simply because of our fear that it is unattainable. Although this can be a healthy response to the truly unattainable goal, it is costly if we have a tendency for underestimating our abilities and then convincing ourselves that we do not want to attain that goal in the first place.

Bias # 9: Discounting the Future. Especially during times of duress and stress, we tend to place more importance on the present and to overly discount the future. On the other hand, economic success requires us to postpone immediate gratification and sacrifice for the future.

Bias # 10: Overconfidence. We allow overconfidence to lead us to believe that what we do know is accurate and complete - especially when the information at hand is incomplete - and that what we don't know isn't worth knowing. (College professors suffer a great deal from this mistake.) An example of this mistake is buying a product about which, in fact, you have very limited information and relying only on the information given to you by the seller.

Bias # 11: Data are Good. We rely on (inadequate or irrelevant) data just because they are data. Psychologists Amos Kahneman and Daniel Tversky (1974) refer to this as an anchoring heuristic. For example, in a study of anchoring, a group of real estate agents were shown a house, were given a talk about the neighborhood and home values, and were told that the asking price was $65,900. The agents' evaluation of the house placed its value at $66,755, on average. Another group of agents shown the same house and given the same talk was told that the asking price was $83,900. They evaluated the same house at $73,000, on average, or approximately 10% above the average figure given by the other group of agents. We tend to use any data given to us and to "anchor" our judgments with them.

Bias # 12: Overestimating Memorable Events. We tend to overestimate the frequency of events that we more easily remember, as well as dramatic and memorable events. This bias is referred to as the availability heuristic. For example, do words beginning with the letter R occur more often than words whose third letter is the letter R? The answer is "no." However, most persons surveyed give the incorrect answer, perhaps because it is easier to think of words beginning with R than words whose third letter is R. Buying the stock of a company that announces a hot new product is another example of how dramatic events affect our inferences. We infer that a hot new product will increase company profits, while ignoring all other - less dramatic - information about the company, the industry, and the economy in general. Persons who have just seen an automobile accident are more likely to overestimate the frequency of such accidents. Approximately 70% of persons surveyed believe that murder is more common than suicide in the U.S. However, although we hear more about murders than suicides, suicides out numbered murders 3 to 2 in 1987.

Bias # 13: We See Patterns Where They Don't Exist. We underestimate the role of chance in everyday events. We "see" patterns that which, in fact, are random or chance events. Professor Werner De Bondt of the University of Wisconsin estimates that by chance alone - not related to superior management - approximately 15% of mutual funds that invest in stocks will outperform the average equity fund for three consecutive years. Or, in flipping a coin 20 times, there is an 80% chance that you will draw either three heads or three tails in a row. Drawing three consecutive heads (tails) is not a pattern; the statistical odds of drawing a head is .50; the odds of two consecutive heads is (.50) x (.50), or .25; the odds of three in a row is (.50) x (.50) x (.50), or .125.

Bias # 14: Principle of Proportionality. We don't always treat a dollar as a dollar. Research has shown that three out of four people will go ten blocks to save $25 on a clock radio, paying $25 rather than $50. This is a saving of 100%. However, only one in five will go ten blocks to save $25 on a $1500 stereo system. This same $25 is a saving of approximately 1.5%. The fact that you will not walk ten blocks to save 1.5% is not rational; it is a mistake created by a common bias in human decision making. And the bias is costly because the people who sell expensive items tend to know this.

Bias # 15: Mental Accounts. We mentally "pigeonhole" money and create mental accounts that may not make sense. For example, people who win $1,000 gambling in Las Vegas are more likely to bet even more the next day than people who discover an additional $1000 in their savings account: $1000 is obviously not just $1000. Some people are more likely to purchase something by charging it to their credit card - paying in the range of 18% interest - than to purchase it with money in their bank, which is earning an interest rate of 5% to 8%. It is also the case that the people who overwithhold on their income taxes in order to guarantee that they won't owe any taxes at year's end, and won't have to draw on their savings are often the same people who build up large indebtedness on their credit cards and who, in effect, draw on their savings.

Bias # 16: Sunk Costs. We often throw good money after bad money. Once we pay for something, we have a tendency to become irrationally committed to it. The money paid is a sunk cost. Yet, decisions should be made regardless of sunk costs—regardless of the past. Individuals have been known to react to a drastic fall in the price of their stock by investing more as a way of trying to recoup their (paper) losses. Throwing good money after bad simply as a way of avoiding acknowledgment of a bad decision and a loss is not rational.

Bias # 17: Opportunity Costs. We think too much about obvious out-of-pocket expenses and not enough about less obvious lost opportunities (opportunity costs). Professor Richard Thaler (1980) finds this a curious phenomenon. When asked hypothetically, people who have won a ticket to the Super Bowl will sell it only at a very high price. However, they would spend only approximately half as much had they not owned a ticket but wanted to attend the game. Thaler's explanation is that we are more aware of how much money we would have to take out of our pocket to buy the ticket, but less aware of how much we could put into our pockets by selling the ticket\(lost opportunity). Theoretically, the two prices should be approximately equal to each other.

Given the range of these seventeen biases there would seem to be no lack of opportunities for X-inefficient decision making.

4.2.5. Selective Rationality and Heuristics

Some of the 17 biases above are referred to as heuristics or shortcut methods for making decisions. A heuristic is a method of reducing complexity without loss of accuracy. Purchasing the same brand names and/or quality of goods as your neighbors is an often used heuristic: those subscribing to it believe it reduces their need to search while giving the appearance of correctness and good taste. Screening potential employees by their educational attainment is a commonly used heuristic. However, while useful, heuristics can also lead to serious errors in judgment and to X-inefficiency.

4.2.6. Some Psychological Studies on Human Cognition

A tradition within psychology, studies of human cognition date back to the work of E.H. Weber (Geldard, 1972) and G.T. Fechner (1860) of the mid-nineteenth century (in 1860, Fechner coined the term psychophysics to refer to the study of human cognition), to Tanner and Swets' 1954 seminal paper on signal-detection theory (Tanner and Swets, 1954), and to Estes' (1980) work on decision making. These and other related papers have led to the conclusion that the human nervous system makes errors in judgment, and that both human and animal decisions are based not only upon costs and benefits but also upon motivations and our (not totally reliable) nervous system. In this regard, two characteristics of the human sensory system are discussed: the difference threshold, and adaptation. All sensory systems have difference thresholds. That is, if changes in the environment are to be perceived, then the change must be greater than some minimum amount. Some environmental changes, therefore, are not noticed. The difference limen is then defined as this minimum amount of environmental change necessary for it to be noticed. Sensory systems are also characterized by adaptation, that is, the sensory effects of a constant amount of energy varies. Thus, if you immerse your hand in hot water, the sensation of hot gradually is replaced by thermal neutrality. These "imperfections" in our sensory system which increase the likelihood of habitual behavior and reduce magnitude sensitivity. Habits, of course, need not be inefficient. But by reducing our awareness of the environment, they increase the likelihood of our being out of step with our environment.

Individuals may have preferences, but not necessarily the ability or the willingness to make clearcut distinctions about changes in their environment. That is, we do not always know when a choice about two different states can be made. Secondly, while we do make choices based on our preferences, at times our habits mitigate both our choices and our preferences. In other words, we may be selectively rational, but not necessarily completely rational. The question of effort levels illustrates these ideas.

Some effort levels are certainly preferred to others. For example, most of us prefer not to be bored or excessively overworked. However, between boredom and exhaustion there are many effort levels. Some of these are more likely to be indistinguishable from each other because of our cognitive limits, discussed above. Hence it would not be accurate to state that we have preferences among indistinguishable effort levels. In addition, we also want to admit the possibility that apart from these cognitive limits, we simply do not always think in terms of the maximizing type of behavior assumed essential to economic man. Hence it would not be accurate to state that we have preferences among "indistinguishable" effort levels. In other words, whether motivated by cognitive limits or a simple lack of concern, we often "don't care one way or the other." While such inertia can occur at any satisfaction (or effort) level, let us assume, for the purposes of illustration only, that it occurs at relatively high levels of satisfaction.

4.3. Conclusions

In this chapter, we have discussed the psychology of the individual with no regard for his or her external environment. In the next chapter, we will discuss some aspects of the external environment. The first aspect to be discussed is the individual's relations with others. This will allow us to investigate group behavior, particularly group-determined effort levels. We will then ask how these effort levels are affected by the market structure within which the firm operates; the second aspect of the external environment that we will consider. The internal and external environments will then be shown to simultaneously affect the degree of X-(in)efficiency. An application of XE theory to the determination of productivity and to government regulation will conclude the next chapter.

X-EFFICIENCY THEORY: 2

5.1. Introduction

In the last chapter, we focused on some elements of individual decision making that lead to X-inefficiency. In this chapter, we will investigate the individual's effort decision, the individual as a group member, group behavior, and some elements that compose the external environment and that influence the firm's degree of X-efficiency. We will begin with the individual's effort decision.

5.2 Individual Effort and the Inert Area

Firms do not automatically convert inputs into the technologically maximum output rate for several reasons, including the fact that firms buy labor time, while production requires labor effort, or what Leibenstein refers to as "directed effort, at or beyond some level of skill." That is, the essential element of human inputs—directed effort—is not directly purchased, and this is one of many distinctions between human and nonhuman inputs. Effort is thus viewed as the outcome of an individual's response to motivations provided by his or her own psyche or and/or by the external environment.

The term effort is used here to include both its physical and mental aspects. That is, physical effort refers to the exertion of the physical body in the form of walking, lifting objects, or speaking. Mental effort refers to exerting the mind. Both physical and mental effort can be exhibited to varying degrees; hence, both are variables. In addition to the biological reasons that account for this variability, the work environment provides its own stimuli.

A major element of this work environment is that employment contracts are "incomplete." Being incomplete, the employment contract is different from a nonemployment contract, for example, a "contract" with a restaurant. Ordering a bagel and cream cheese from a delicatessen represents a "complete" contract. That is, you order a bagel and cream cheese and you agree to pay a certain sum of money. You know exactly what you ordered (bought), and the firm knows exactly what it will receive as a result of the sale. In the case of an employment contract, however, the firm purchases time but produces with the directed effort of the employees. This arrangement or contract is incomplete because there is no fixed tradeoff between the time purchased and the effort used. The delicatessen agrees and does in fact place a bagel and cream cheese in front of you, and you agree and do in fact pay an agreed-upon sum of money. In the employment contract, however, the agreeing and the doing are not necessarily the same. In other words, most workers on most jobs have a certain amount of discretion. The elements of effort, and hence the way in which their discretion is manifest, will now be discussed.

Effort is said to have four elements: the activities (A) that constitute the job, the pace (P) at which work is performed, the quality (Q) of output, and the time pattern (T) of work. Other elements are possible, and perhaps some of these overlap each other. These elements constitute one, perhaps not the most exhaustive, list. In order to make the concept of effort operational, however, a list is necessary. What activities constitute a particular job? What activities would increase the likelihood that the job is done well? Most individuals begin a job with some information. However, it is very unlikely that they receive an exact, detailed account of the tasks that compose the job. The individual may thus make a calculated (fully rational) decision about how to perform the job, or he may simply begin and proceed in some fashion, or may emulate others, or, may use any one of many other possible decision- making techniques. For the sake of brevity, but with some hesitation, I will refer to the use of any of these decision-making techniques as the outcome of a choice. Thus, the individual must in some way choose or interpret the job. In this case, he or she must choose, with regard to at least some aspects of the job, what he or she is to do. The individual must also choose, with respect to at least some of these tasks, the pace at which to perform the activities. Some discretion about quality may also be possible, and here, the choice about quality relates to the attentiveness with which the individual works. Finally, he or she may be able to choose the time pattern or rhythm, including the hours of the day or the "stop-go" pattern.

Once chosen, these four decisions constitute the worker's "APQT bundle." To the extent that an individual chooses this effort level, he chooses his APQT bundle. Otherwise, the APQT bundle is preset by the firm. Thus far we have argued that, at least partially, free-choice APQT bundles exist. How common are free-choice APQT bundles likely to be? We will argue that they have many desirable properties and hence are likely to be common. What is the effect of a freely chosen APQT bundle on effort and the firm's X-efficiency? The important point is that effort becomes a variable that may or may not produce rational behavior, i.e., cost minimization and hence perfect X-efficiency.

Preset APQT bundles pose several problems for a firm. First, to preset an APQT bundle for all nonmanagerial employees requires an enormous amount of knowledge and hence an enormous amount of searching. Therefore, the search costs of preset APQT bundles are likely to be very high. Second, if management presets the APQT bundles, then presumably management will want to make sure that the nonmanagerial employees work according to these bundles. Hence, the monitoring costs of preset APQT bundles are also likely to be very high. Third, there are likely to be psychic costs of working for a firm that, in essence, doesn't trust you to make decisions about how best to perform your job. This will likely lead to absenteeism and low morale. Fourth, a preset APQT bundle doesn't allow the firm to take advantage of the knowledge   accumulated by the nonmanagerial employees through experience. This robs the firm of a significant source of human capital. Fifth, "working to rule" is often said to be the best way to sabotage an organization, since it significantly reduces the flexibility that a firm needs in a changing environment.

Sixth, and often overlooked, is that if nonmanagerial APQT bundles are preset, then those of managerial employees must also be preset. If the choices of nonmanagerial employees are to be completely controlled, then so must the choices of the monitors. Their APQT bundle must be preset so as to insure that the APQT bundles of the nonmanagerial employees are preset and adhered to. And who, one might ask, presets the APQT bundle of the managers? In addition to search and monitoring costs, preset APQT bundles are not likely to be commonly used because they imply an organizational structure that is uncomfortable to all employees.

We are left with the conclusion that effort is the outcome of an individual's response to both internal and external motivations, influenced by both his superego and id functions, and affected by the force of habit. Research on habitual or routinized behavior reveals several of its characteristics. First, similar environmental stimuli lead to similar—routinized or habituated—responses, without an explicit consideration of alternative responses. Second, habitual behavior reduces awareness of and responsiveness to the environment; the individual focuses on a narrower range of environmental cues. One implication is that the individual is more likely not to be aware when changes in the environment have taken place, that is, he or she becomes less magnitude sensitive. Third, decisions are made after a shorter time interval, that is, decisions become more reflexive.

5.2.1 The Inert Area in XE Theory

Figure 11 illustrates these ideas. The curve SE shows the relationship between effort levels and levels of satisfaction. Recall that each effort level corresponds to at least one APQT bundle, or effort point. This curve may be seen as having three parts. The first is area 1, or effort levels less than or equal to e1. Over this range, satisfaction is increasing at an increasing rate; individuals prefer more to less effort up to effort level e1. The second part is area 3, or effort levels greater than e2. Over this range, satisfaction is decreasing at an increasing rate; individuals prefer less effort to more effort for effort levels exceeding e2. The third is area 2, which is the range bounded by effort levels e1 and e2. Over this range, effort neither increases nor decreases as rapidly as in areas 1 and 2, respectively. In fact, area 2 is shown to have a relatively flat top.

The flat top means that there is a range of effort-satisfaction points such that, within this range, each point is indistinguishable from every other point. This may be due to the cognitive factors discussed above, due to the fact that the individual is not a maximizer, or because of transactions costs. This range of indistinguishability is referred to as an "inert area." In figure 11, the inert area is arbitrarily drawn as the area bounded by effort levels e1e2 and satisfaction levels s1s2.

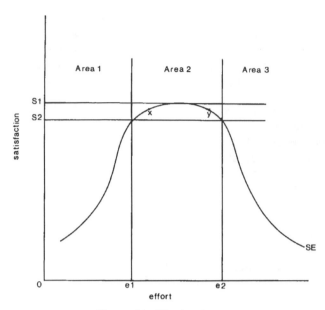

Figure 11. The inert area.

This inert area has several characteristics and implications. The first is that the individual is not always completely rational. That is, the individual is not always directing his or her abilities toward calculating and analyzing costs and benefits of various effort and satisfaction levels. Second, assuming that the individual is calculating, every effort level within the inert area is preferred to any effort level out of the inert area. Thus, the individual prefers effort level e1 to any lesser effort level and also prefers effort level e2 to any greater level of effort. Third, every effort level within the inert area is indistinguishable from every other point in the inert area. Thus, effort points x and y are indistinguishable from each other. Fourth, while satisfaction level s1 is preferred to any lower level, every level of satisfaction in s1s2 is indistinguishable from every other level.

The individual thus prefers any effort level within the inert area to any effort level out of the inert area. Effort levels out of the inert area, therefore, are not "equilibrium" effort levels. That is, an individual working with an effort level less than e1 will attempt to increase effort but working at an effort level greater than e2 will result in a (desired) movement toward less effort. On the other hand, any effort level within the inert area e1e2 can be an equilibrium effort level. The concept of an equilibrium effort level has two implications.

First, once the individual is working within the inert area he or she will be resistant to changing the effort level. Although any particular inert area need not be long lasting, the individual still must be exposed to a shock or surprise of sufficient magnitude before effort will transcend the boundaries of the inert area. On the other hand, since every effort level within the inert area can be an equilibrium position, then within this range the individual will be flexible. Therefore, individual inertia can produce resistance to change.

The assumption being made here is that, except in rare cases, the upper bound of the inert area—effort level e2—is below that which represents the optimal level of rationality for a given job. At the same time, however, inertia implies a (limited) willingness toward flexibility. Thus, within the inert area, an individual can be counted on to dovetail his or her activities with those of others, to change effort levels without detailed supervision, and to cope well with change. Thus, if management accepts the inert area of the nonmanagerial employees, then knowing their boundary points will allow management to "maximize" the workers' effort without creating undue friction. These friction could include grievances, strikes, or slow-downs. Of course, managers are also subject to inert areas.

5.3. Intrafirm Determinants of Individual and Group Effort

An individual's degree of rationality can be the outcome of his or her own independent choices, or it can be influenced by others. These "significant others" may be one's peers or supervisors. These relations Leibenstein refers to as horizontal and vertical relations, respectively. The third possibility is that one is affected by what has gone on in the past, which constitutes the traditions and history of the firm. Whether formalized or not, tradition can be, and often is, a very effective influence on behavior. Its effect often takes the form of the following question and answer:(Q): "Why do you perform this job as you do?" (A): "I don't know, but we have always done it this way." Perhaps "this way" is the very best way. However, there is no reason a priori why this should be so.

5.3.1. Tradition, Supervisors, and Peers

The effect of these other influences are shown in fiure 12. Figure 12 shows an individual's satisfaction:effort relation as SE and his inert area as e1e3. Recall that the inert area represents an absence of fully rational decision making. The inert area thus represents a situation whereby behavior is characterized by habit, nonattentiveness, and a relative absence of awareness of environmental changes. Recall also that the inert area may occur at any level of effort and satisfaction. However, for purposes of illustration, we are assuming that it occurs at relatively high levels of satisfaction.

Beginning with satisfaction:effort relation SE and inert area e1e3, we will now adjust this relationship to take into account the effect of vertical relations on the SE relation. In doing so, we will make two assumptions for the purposes of illustration. First, we assume that vertical relations create pressure for more effort and that the individual receives satisfaction from avoiding such pressure. Second, we will assume that the individual also receives satisfaction from receiving the approval of his supervisors. In other words, most of us find some satisfaction in avoiding "unnecessary hassles" and in receiving recognition for a job well done.

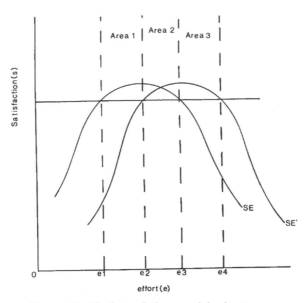

Figure 12. Vertical relations and the inert area.

If the individual receives some satisfaction from avoiding the pressure that comes from supervisors when he works at low effort levels, then at low effort levels the adjusted satisfaction:effort curve, SE', will lie below the unadjusted satisfaction:effort curve, SE. If he also receives some satisfaction from receiving approval for high effort then, SE' will lie above SE. Thus, for relatively low effort levels, SE' is below SE because pressure from supervisors reduces satisfaction. At the same time, SE' is above SE for relatively high effort levels because their approval increases satisfaction. Pressure from supervisors thus motivates the individual to be more willing to work with directed effort, i.e., to be more rational.

The adjusted relation, SE', produces its own inert area e2e4. As expected, both the lower (e2) and upper (e4) bounds of the adjusted inert area lie at higher effort levels than for the unadjusted inert area, e1 and e3, respectively. The individual's inert area within this supervisor:supervisee relation is thus e2e4. Clearly, area 1 in figure 12—the effort range e1e2—would no longer be part of the inert area. An individual who knows that he or she is working within area 1 would find it uncomfortable enough to force a movement into area 2. Area 2 is certainly in the new inert area, because it is common to both SE and SE'. Area 3 is also expected to be in the individual's new inert area because of the satisfaction of approval. Leibenstein (1976) has worked out many other senarios based on the needs and psychology of the individual.

5.3.2. Multiperson Effort and Inert Areas

The concept of a multiperson inert area follows from the concept of the individual's unadjusted and adjusted inert area. A multiperson inert area comprises

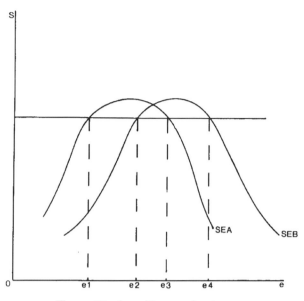

Figure 13. A multiperson inert area.

all effort points within the common inert areas of each group member. In figure 13 we assume the group to consist of two individuals. Individual A's adjusted SE relation is shown as SEa. Individual A's inert area is e1e3. Individual B's adjusted SE relation and inert are SEb and e2e4, respectively. The group inert area is thus e2e3. That is, within e2e4, neither individual has a tendency to exert pressure to change either his or her own or the other's effort point. For individual A, any effort level exhibited by individual B that is above e3 would be unwelcome and would bring a response to reduce B's effort. At the same time, any effort level exhibited by individual A that is less than e2 would bring a response by B to increase A's effort. However, so long as A works with at least effort level e2, and so long as B works with a maximum effort level of e3, then neither will be motivated to change either their own or the other's effort. This does not imply that either A or B will be at the most preferred effort level: they might not be happy about it, but neither will they attempt to change it.

As the size of the group becomes larger, group effort takes on the characteristics of a public good. We might expect that, ceteris paribus, an increase in the number of group members will reduce the size of the group's inert area. That is, an increase in the number of group members reduces the number of effort points that will be acceptable to everyone. On the other hand, it is not difficult to imagine that an increase in the number of group members will result in a more formalized group work ethic such as either a lower bound or an upper bound or both. In this case, each member agrees to "live and let live" so long as none of the other individuals violate the rule. The result is that the size of the inert area increases. In figure 13, this would be shown as the SE relation for each group member becoming more "satisfaction elastic." A precise result about group size and the inert area will not be attempted here. Suffice it to say that group relations affect effort.

The concept of the multiperson inert area also means that relatively low as well as relatively high effort levels will not be part of the group inert area. Thus, the effort level exhibited by the group will approach the average level of productivity of each group member. We may thus think of group effort as a "convention," an agreement. The implication of this for the determination of productivity will now be explored.

5.4. Productivity, Effort Conventions, and the Prisoner's Dilemma

The concepts of individual effort discretion and multiperson inert areas imply that no single person within a firm controls all the relevant variables determining effort. In this case, effort (or productivity) may be thought of as the outcome of a game. Leibenstein (1976, 1982a) makes use of the prisoner's dilemma (P.D.) game to illustrate the determina-tion of productivity. Briefly, the prisoner's dilemma is a situation in which each individual acts according to his own self-interest and the outcome is not optimal for any individual. Stated in another way, a prisoner's dilemma exists when the opportunities for adversarial behavior reduces cooperative (superior) behavior.

Productivity as a (P.D.) game is shown in table 2. Table 2 shows that both management (the firm) and the employees have three options with respect to the other side. Each can practice a strategy referred to as the golden rule (G.R.), peer group standards (P.G.S.),or individual maximization (I.M.). For the firm, the golden rule means to operate the firm almost entirely for the benefit of the employees. The golden rule strategy is one of cooperation. The other extreme is individual maximization, or cost minimization. Here the firm attempts to minimize the working conditions (including wages) provided to the employees, while at the same time attempting to get the most they can from the employees. This strategy is an adversarial one. The third option, or middle course, is to provide working conditions consistent with the philosophy "a fair day's work for a fair day's pay." As we will see, this is also a strategy of cooperation.

For the employees, the golden rule strategy is to work as if they owned the firm. That is, they work according to the best interests of the firm and in a manner consistent with how they wish the firm to treat them. The golden rule strategy for the employees is also one of cooperation. The other extreme is to supply as little effort as possible while remaining on the payroll. This strategy is an adversarial one. Individually, this may be thought of as the "free-rider" option. That is, the individual reasons that so long as he is the only shirker, the firm will not suffer and hence his shirking will go unnoticed. The free-rider strategy for any one individual is a rational one, since it minimizes work effort with no cost in benefits (working conditions). The middle course is the philosophy of "a fair day's work for a fair day's pay." Again, this will be shown to be a strategy of cooperation.

		FIRMS		
		G.R.	P.G.S.	I.M.
E M P L O Y E E S	G. R.	30 / 30	34 / 12	40 / 3
	P. G. S.	12 / 34	20 / 20	24 / 8
	I. M.	3 / 40	8 / 24	10 / 10

Table 2. Productivity as a prisoner's dilemma.

The P.D. aspect of this game is that if each side follows their own maximization strategy, both sides lose. For the firm, cost minimization requires that, regardless of which of the three strategies is used by the employees, the firm should give as little as possible, that is, the firm should always adopt an adversarial strategy of individual maximization. Cost minimization (profit maximization) requires that, for a given effort level of the employees, the firm should spend as little as possible on those employees. At the same time, the rational strategy for the employees is to give as little effort as possible for any given strategy adopted by the firm. In both cases, maximizing one's (benefit/cost) ratio requires an adversarial strategy of individual maximization. The result, of course, is the prisoner's dilemma: a firm characterized by low productivity and poor working conditions.

Fortunately, most of us aren't rational! In table 2, the numbers represent the value of satisfaction to each side from each joint choice. Thus, if both sides choose the golden rule strategy, then the satisfaction to both the firm (satisfaction of a certain level of profits) and to the employees (satisfaction from a given set of working conditions) is equal to 30. On the other hand, the value of the P.D. solution to each is only 10. The best joint choice for the firm is in the upper right-hand box. That is, the best choice for the firm is when it minimizes payments to the employees while the employees work according to the golden rule. In other words, the firm's best position is to act as an adversary while the workers cooperate. (The workers either have very little bargaining power or else they are a bunch of "saps.") This choice is worth a satisfaction level of 40 to the firm but only 3 to the employees.

On the other hand, the best joint choice for the employees is in the lower left-hand box. That is, the best choice for the employees is when they are treated royally but return it by being free-riders. In other words, the best joint choice for the employees is when they behave in an adversarial fashion but the firm adopts a strategy of cooperation. Ceteris paribus, the profits to the firm of this joint choice are going to be very low (high costs plus low productivity). This choice yields a level of satisfaction of 40 to the employees and only 3 to the firm. (Although the payoffs in table 2 are symmetrical, such symmetry among the joint choices is not necessary.) The other off-diagonal elements also represent the payoff to other adversarial strategies.

A cooperative joint choice of interest is the peer-group standard. The satisfaction of this joint choice to either party is 20. Leibenstein views the peer-group standard solution as an alternative to the P.D. solution. As seen in the payoff matrix of table 2, the peer-group standard is superior to the P.D. solution, although not as good as the golden rule solution. As already discussed, the peer-group standard represents an effort convention, or norm. Two questions arise about an effort convention: the rationale for its existence and how it affects behavior. The rationale for conventions has been developed by David Lewis (1968) and Edna Ullman-Margalit (1977). One basic rationale is that a convention solves a coordination problem.

Of particular interest for an effort convention is that more than one convention can solve the firm's coordination problem. In this case, any convention, whether optimal or nonoptimal, can be superior to not having any convention. One illustration of the benefits of any convention (cited by Leibenstein) is the decision as to what side of the road all cars are driven on.

Once an effort convention has been established, most people abide by it. New members observe the APQT bundles of more experienced members as a way of learning "how things are done." Clearly, if the effort convention is uncomfortable, the individual either adjusts his or her own standards or seeks employment elsewhere. But once accepted, individuals react to the convention in a type of "stimulus-response" pattern. That is, the convention is not reappraised each time its use is called for. The convention exists to be used. Will it ever be reappraised and changed? Of course, but only when a sufficient surprise shocks individuals out of their inert areas.

Returning to table 2, it is clear that the strategy of cooperation via the effort convention of the peer-group standard is superior to the adversarial strategy leading to the P.D. solution but inferior to the cooperative strategy of the golden rule. The effort convention is thus not an optimal solution. Why then would individuals and/or groups agree to abide by such a nonoptimal convention? One reason is that well-enforced sanctions would be applied against anyone violating the convention. The effort exhibited by any individual in a group is thus more likely to resemble an average effort level than one closer to his or her best. Another characteristic of the peer-group standard solution is that, except for the golden rule solution, it is both efficient and equitable. Clearly, the P.D. solution is not efficient. On the other hand, the off-diagonal elements would not be viewed as fair by at least one of the parties. For example, the employees would not perceive as equitable a situation in which they behave according to the golden rule while the firm behaves as an individual maximizer. At the same time, the firm would not perceive as equitable a situation in which it behaves according to the golden rule while the employees behave as individual maximizers. The other off-diagonal elements also represent a situation where one of the parties is giving more than the others. On the other hand, the peer-group standard solution in one whereby both give and receive the "same" amount.

5.4.1. Ford Motor Co., Louisville: A Digression[1]

The business literature contains many examples of firm turnarounds. This case of a Ford plant in Louisville illustrates how a P.D. solution is replaced with a more mutually advantageous solution. For at least several years prior to 1979, Ford's Louisville assembly plant was known as a "war zone," characterized as filthy, with openly hostile labor-management relations, autocratic managers, intransigent union leaders, mutual distrust, and little concern for (X) efficiency. Then, in 1979, the demand for the plant's cars declined sharply, and the night shift was laid off. Rumors circulated that the plant would close.

At the same time both, the plant's union chairman and plant manager jobs changed hands: both the new men believed that self-destructive behavior was not necessary. It also became evident that the plant had to turn things around in six months or it would be closed. Small but important employee requests were honored, such as lunch tables appearing on the plant floor. The company undertook a Quality-of-Work Life program and serious ongoing discussions with the employees, which resulted in many small changes that added up. One large change was to replace the tradition of having the designers send their designs to the manufacturers, who are then supposed to build the product. This process often involves a great deal of unnecessarily spent effort as manufacturers attempt to follow plans that are (unnecessarily) difficult. The Ford Louisville plant broke tradition by displaying those plans on the plant floor and inviting comments before the manufacturing phase began. By early 1980, the plant was turning out high-quality products, and by the end of 1980 Ford decided to invest $700 million in the production of the Ford Ranger. Whereas in pre-1979 days as many as 700 "concerns" per 100 cars would be recorded by quality inspectors, by 1982 the figure had dropped to 198, the lowest in Ford's U.S. history. Again, it was the "shock" caused by the apparent loss of jobs that changed a P.D. solution into something more mutually advantageous. (Were the workers and managers maximizing their utility through the behaviors exhibited both prior to and after 1979? While this is one possible

---

1   This example is discussed in Main (1983b).

explanation for their behavior, and one that would be consistent with neoclassical theory, I believe that it is far-fetched. This and similar issues will be discussed in chapter 9.

5.5. Market Structure, Pressure, and Effort

5.5.1. Introduction

The firm in XE theory purchases human time but uses directed effort. Workers have effort discretion and choose an effort level. These individual effort levels are subject to inert areas, which include a consideration of how individual choices affect and are likely to be affected by significant others. In other words, the group inert area is an effort range agreeable to everyone. Each employee brings to the firm not only his or her time and effort but also a set of characteristics that influences the atmosphere within the firm. One element of this atmosphere is the incentive mechanism. The incentive mechanism is an "input" that is not purchased by the firm through the market mechanism. This mechanism determines what motivates individuals and groups within the firm to put forth more or less effort, that is, to be more or less rational. This incentive mechanism depends not only on elements internal to the firm but also on elements external to the firm. In this section, we will examine some of these elements.

5.5.2. The Monopolist

Monopoly power insulates firm members from pressure to change their equilibrium effort position. The monopolist's control over price and output, and hence costs, can be shown to create this insulation. One could generate a series of numbers about prices, outputs, and unit costs in order to show that a given amount of profits can be generated with relatively high costs and prices and lower outputs. In other words, once we drop the assumption of profit-maximizing—cost-minimizing—behavior, then we would conclude that if acceptable profits are earned without the necessity of minimizing costs, then cost minimization will not be a typical behavior among monopolists. If employees have effort discretion then monopoly power will insulate the employees from any pressure to lower costs. As long as the firm satisfies its profit constraint, then there is no reason to believe, a priori, that cost minimization will be typical of monopolists. (In a later chapter, we will examine several models that include a profit constraint.) The assumption here is that if firm members can pass on their inertia to (widely distributed) owners or consumers, then they will do so. Under monopoly conditions, this is certainly possible.

5.5.2.1 Capital Markets: A Short Digression.[2] An objection is often made that even if product markets are monopolized, perfect capital markets force employees

---

2   The relation between capital markets and X-efficiency is discussed in Frantz (1984).

(managers) to minimize costs or to suffer from a takeover with a substitution of less for more cost conscious management. The existence of perfect capital markets is thus believed to make the existence of X-inefficiency highly unlikely. Variations of this argument, some of which include direct reference to XE theory, have been made by Alchian and Kessel (1962), DeLorenzo (1985), Fama(1980), and Manne (1965). Are capital markets perfect? The evidence is far from overwhelming. For example, Robert Smiley's (1976) study of 95 tender offers in the U.S. between 1956 and 1970 reported that takeovers are unlikely until the company's book value exceeds its market value by approximately 13%. Oliver Williamson (1970) reports that this "inefficiency threshold" is between 10% and 25%. Regardless of the reason(s) why such an inefficiency threshold exists, its existence reduces pressure on firm members to be X-efficient, to be alert, to be cost conscious, to reevaluate their equilibrium effort positions. Effort entropy, the phrase used by Leibenstein (1976), is not discouraged.

In addition to the existence of an inefficiency threshold, studies using both U.S. and U.K. data by Singh (1975), and Furth (1980) have reported that not only are higher postmerger profits not assured but also in the U.S. the managers and directors of the acquired firm often receive large gains. In combination, these two findings raise the interesting possibility that not only is X-inefficiency tolerated with impunity but also under some circumstances it may be "rational."

5.5.2.2. Entrepreneurship: Another Digression. The role of the entrepreneur in reducing X-inefficiency comes both by his or her direct effect on the X-inefficient firm and by the indirect effect as a competitor.

The material presented in chapter 2 implies, on the other hand, that entrepreneurship is both routine and unimportant. If markets are perfect, and if as a routine matter the firm is converting its inputs into the technologically maximum output at minimum costs, then entrepreneurship would be both a routine function and unimportant. The assumption of cost minimization in neoclassical theory is perhaps one reason why entrepreneurship has received relatively little attention. In XE theory, however, entrepreneurship is important because markets are not assumed to be perfect, and because firms are not assumed to be cost minimizing.

The term imperfect market has two meanings in this context. The first meaning is that there are obstacles to the marshaling or utilizing of inputs. Leibenstein (1978a) gives several examples. First, some inputs may be available to the firm but are currently doing other tasks. An imagination, not simply a calculator, is required to see alternative structures and arrangements with respect to these inputs. Second, inputs may exist but are not for sale at any known and specific price. Third, the value of an input may be ascertained only with respect to an entire set of inputs that could produce a hitherto unmarketed product. Fourth, some inputs, such as money, may be available to some but not to others.

The second meaning of imperfect market is that there are various types of "holes" in both input and output markets. For example, inputs such as knowledge are not always marketed. It takes incentives to convert knowledge from a feeling or idea into a form that is useful for the firm. Because production functions are not assumed to be complete, the firm may be thought of as a storehouse of experiences that are useful when properly motivated. In less developed countries, money would be added to the list of not-always- marketed inputs.

In this context, Leibenstein views the economy as a net made up of nodes and pathways. The nodes are the firms and industries, which receive inputs (and the households, which receive consumer goods). The pathway carries the inputs to the firms and the resulting output to the other firms (and households). In a well-functioning market inhabited by cost- minimizing firms, the net is complete without any holes, the pathways are well marked, and each node deals with every other node on an equal basis for the same commodity. In a more realistic situation, the day-to-day function of the entrepreneur is to be both an "input completer" and a "gap filler," improving pathways and nodes. In addition, his or her role in invention and innovations may be viewed as extending the net. Leibenstein thus concludes that in many ways entrepreneurs operate between markets.

The existence of X-inefficiency thus serves to motivate (latent) entrepreneurship both within that firm and as a competitor. The supply of entrepreneurship need not be assumed to be perfectly elastic for this conclusion to hold.

5.5.3. The Competitive Firm

Ceteris paribus, competition creates more pressure on firm members to be more rational. This effect is created through the market or price mechanism, whereby if one firm can lower its price, then all firms must follow suit or be eliminated from the industry. In the long run, firms survive by keeping costs as low as possible, not only in terms of exploiting all economies of scale but also by being able to produce on their long-run average cost function (curve). Thus, competition reduces the opportunity to engage in the various forms of discretionary behavior available to (some) employees of the monopolist, including behaving in an arbitrary, sloppy, bureaucratic, arrogant, and nonresponsive fashion. Under competitive conditions, a greater sense of obligation to other employees and to customers is a way of assuring that the firm can minimize costs while serving the market. Effort points are more thoroughly examined and more often reevaluated as pressure for survival forces such a reevaluation.

5.6. A Synthesis and an Illustration

5.6.1. The Yerkes—Dodson Law

The personality and the environment thus combine to produce X-inefficiency. In the cases of both the personality and the environment, a key concept has been that of pressure. The personality creates its own pressure because of the demands of the superego and the id. The environment creates pressure through the effects of intrafirm interpersonal relations and through market competition (or the lack of it). To illustrate the relationship between pressure and X-(in)efficiency, Leibenstein has adapted the Yerkes—Dotson law developed by experimental psycholo-

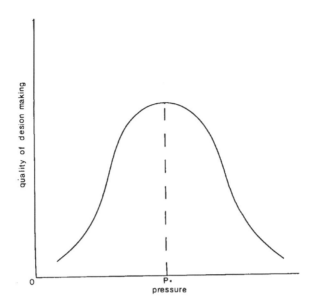

Figure 14. An adaptation of the Yerkes—Dotson law: pressure
and the quality of decision making.

gists in 1908. This "law," first written about by Robert Yerkes and John Dodson(1908), showed a relationship between the strength of a stimulus and learning (among mice). In some cases, learning increased with greater stimulus only to a certain level of stimulus, with subsequent increases in stimulus reducing learning. That is, the relationship exhibited characteristics of a quadratic relationship. In subsequent years, this relationship has been interpreted as a relationship between motivation, or arousal, and task performance. Leibenstein's (1983, 1985) own adaptation is to discuss a possible relationship between pressure and performance. His hypothesis is that this relationship is represented as a quadratic equation. That is, an individual subjected to relatively low or relatively high levels of pressure will not do as well as possible. On the other hand, there is a "medium" (optimal) level of pressure under which an individual performs best.

In figure 14, Leibenstein's adaptation of the Yerkes—Dotson law is shown as a quadratic relation between pressure and the quality of decision making. Figure 14 shows that pressure level p* evokes the maximum performance. Pressure levels less than p* represents an "easy" environment that does not provide the stimulation necessary for the individual to utilize his skills. On the other hand, pressure levels greater than p* represent pressure levels too high to evoke maximum performance. Only pressure level p* can thus be said to produce optimal or maximizing behavior. Pressure level p* will thus, ceteris paribus, minimize X-inefficiency. The word maximization is thus used in a way that at least allows for the possibility of nonmaximization to take place. Nonmaximization need not be observed. However, it is considered a possible outcome of human behavior.

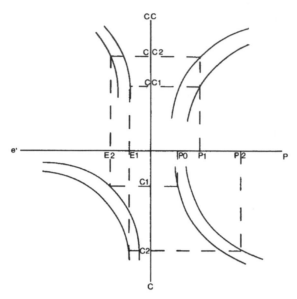

Figure 15. A synthesis: determinants of X-inefficiency.

5.6.2. Synthesis

Figure 15 attempts to show many of the ideas presented in this and the preceding chapter. In quadrant 1, pressure is the independent variable and the individual's level of constraint concern is the dependent variable. This relation has two properties. First, there is a maximum level of constraint concern, i.e., realism, that the individual can entertain regardless of how intense the pressure becomes. Second, the relation is depicted by a "fat" band rather than a line in order to represent the inert area. In this case, for any level of pressure there is a range of constraint concern that the individual can entertain, each level of constraint concern being equally satisfying as any other level within the inert area. In quadrant 2, constraint concern is the independent variable affecting effort. In other words, the decision-making attributes called constraint concerns affect job behaviors. In addition to showing an inert area—any level of constraint concern being consistent with a range of effort levels—this relation shows that as constraint concern increases, the supply of effort becomes more elastic. In other words, a level of constraint concern exists such that effort is sufficient to maximize X-efficiency.

In quadrant 3, unit cost is shown as a function of effort. Quadrant 3 shows that there always exists a level of costs—"fixed" costs—regardless of the level of effort. It also shows that costs approach infinity as effort approaches zero. Quadrant 3 shows that any level of effort will have an indeterminate affect on costs. In this case, we can understand quadrant 3 as indicating that each effort level results in a different cost function. Finally, quadrant 4 shows pressure as a function of costs. That is, as costs rise, additional pressure is placed on the firm (members) to reduce costs. In addition, as costs increase, pressure increases at an increasing rate. For the monopolist, pressure is more cost inelastic than it is for the competitive firm. In any case, for any level of cost, the individual may perceive a range of effort. That is, this relationship is shown as containing an inert area.

The sequence is thus, for example, that a certain level of pressure leads to some level of constraint concern, which in turn affects effort, which affects costs, which, in turn, affects pressure. In figure 15, we arbitrarily begin at pressure level P1. P1 creates a level of constraint concern between CC1 and CC2. In turn, this will create an effort level between E1 and E2. This range of effort creates costs between C1 and C2, which in turn creates perceived pressure on the individuals between Po and P2. As figure 15 demonstrates, the concept of the inert area in a series of simultaneous relationships means that the value of the dependent variables will be "fuzzy," containing an amount of indeterminacy. The final equilibrium level of pressure and cost will depend on the placement and elasticities of each of the curves. We have demonstrated only one of many possible dynamic structures.

5.6.3. An Illustration : Chrysler's "Detroit Trim" Plant[3]

In an April 4, 1983, edition of Fortune, "Detroit Trim," a maker of seatcovers for Chrysler Corp., was described as a "very ordinary"plant. The problems at Detroit Trim, as for other Chrysler plants in the Detroit area, became apparent in the late 1970s and early 1980s. In 1981, Chrysler lost $476 million on sales of $10 billion. In that same year Chrysler switched its budget system, which created a great deal of pressure for the employees of plants such as Detroit Trim. Rather than each plant having a budget based on its costs, the new system required that each plant compare its costs with what it would cost Chrysler to buy those same (quality) products elsewhere. While Detroit Trim's costs for the 1983 model year would have been $51.5 million, the same seatcovers could have been purchased for $30.8 million through outside vendors. (This is a reduction of approximately 40%.) A plant that was estimated to earn $1 million for Chrysler could not be kept open at the cost of such a $20 million drain. In essence, Detroit Trim was being subsidized by a company that could no longer afford to do so.

Arthur D. Little, Inc. was hired and their $85,000 fee paid equally by labor and management. Once A.D. Little confirmed the $30.8 million figure, the entire attitude of the plant employees changed: it became apparent that the plant had to become competitive or be closed. In negotiations between labor and management, it became apparent that the workers viewed the plant as being overmanned (labor), overstaffed (management and union officials), burdened by unnecessary work rules, and often failing to get more than three or four hours of work per day from its employees. A 14-person steering committee, consisting of both labor and management, was set up to improve the competitiveness of the plant. Chrysler demanded that a $6.4 million reduction in costs would be needed to save the plant.

---

3   This example is discussed in Main (1983a).

The steering committee's plan would save $5.4 million—Chrysler agreed. The plan called for a total reduction in plant employment of approximately 25% (709 to 528). The reduction in employment of "direct" (production), salaried, and "indirect" (janitors, etc.) was 21%, 25%, and 40%, respectively. The ratio of foremen to workers would rise from 1:21, to 1:30. Company-paid union officials at the plant were reduced from six to four. The size of work teams was reduced, and work rules were made more liberal. Daily output standards rose between 15% and 28% depending on the job. The increase was welcomed as a means of saving jobs, but not otherwise. On the other hand, one worker who was asked to increase the number of welts sewn on seat backs from 293 to 376—a 28% increase—had raised her output at the time of the writing of the article to 330. The increased effort, which was difficult at first, seemed less difficult the longer the increased effort level was maintained. By the time 80% of the plan had been instituted, annual savings reached $6.4 million. A.D. Little's representative was quoted as saying that many U.S. plants have as much room for improvement as Detroit Trim had. Having been kept open, the manager of Detroit Trim mused (Main, 1983a, p. 113), "To think that a plant that had so much slack in it almost closed down."

5.7. Implications And Conclusions

Some of the implications of XE theory are the firm's production function is not completely known, a firm is more than a production function (output varies for any given set of inputs), costs are not necessarily minimized, costs are a function of prices (market power), and human effort is not necessarily fully utilized, i.e., both income and job satisfaction can be enhanced if the correct stimulus is applied.

XE theory was developed in order to explain data seemingly inconsistent with the then orthodox microeconomic theory. Rather than taking the track of others such as Baumol, Marris, and Williamson, Leibenstein attempted to explain the behavior of the firm by asking the general question of what determines work effort; under what conditions would an individual direct his or her effort toward being (X) Efficient, that is, contributing to the full use of the resources at the firm's disposal? One of the outcomes of this approach was the concept that an individual need not be a maximizer in a procedural sense. This more than anything else has set XE theory at odds with neoclassical theory and has created a very strong reaction against it. This reaction will be the topic of Chapter 9.

In the next three chapters, I will present empirical studies in support of XE theory. As the reader proceeds through these chapters, he or she may find it helpful to note not only how these studies are also consistent with neoclassical theory but also what type of research design could distinguish between these two competing explanations.

6

EMPIRICAL EVIDENCE: REGULATED INDUSTRIES

6.1. Introduction

At this juncture we have presented neoclassical theory (an admitted mechanical presentation, with some justification), XE theory, and several other deviations from orthodox neoclassical theory. In several ways these deviations, including XE theory, have common elements. In several ways, each is unique. We have also presented the implications of XE theory. It is thus now time to present empirical evidence consistent with these implications of XE theory. Please keep in mind several points about the empirical evidence. First, the evidence is divided into three categories (1) studies on regulated industries, (2) studies on market structure and organizational forms, and (3) studies of input ratios, and international trade. Second, some any of these studies probes into two or more of these categories. Each study is part of the category that seemed to be its central focus, or offers the most complementarity. Third, the use of the term X-efficiency by the authors is reported here. Third, there are literally hundreds of studies whose results are consistent with XE theory. I include here only those studies that are *explicit* about XE theory.

In this chapter I review studies that cover public utilities, health care, telecommunications, airlines, school transportation, libraries, education, foreign exchange, and symphony orchestras (government funding requests). Other topics that offer complementarities are unions, and X-efficiency among players of the Boston Bruins National Hockey League team.

6.2. Empirical Studies

6.2.1. Primeaux. Economies of scale and X-inefficiency.

Costs and Competition Among Electric-Utilities If economic or technical conditions permit an industry to have only one efficient firm, then that firm is a "natural monopoly." One condition leading to the existence of a natural monopoly is positive economies of scale throughout the entire range of industry demand. Since the early 1900's the argument has been made that the government should regulate and award a monopoly franchise to producers of electricity, gas, and telephone services: public utilities.

The justification for a natural monopoly on the basis of economies of scale relies on the assumption that X-(in)efficiency—excess costs—are zero. However, the lack of competitive pressure facing these firms may also result in their costs being in excess of technologically minimum costs. If costs of production are not affected by market structure then the monopolization of public utilities is a more appropriate public policy. If, on the other hand, monopolization raises costs above competitive industry levels, then the net effect of monopolization depends upon the relative strengths of economies of scale and X-inefficiency . These relative effects were measured by Walter Primeaux in his (1977) study of US electric utility firms.

Using Federal Power Commission date, Primeaux compared average total costs among a sample of publicly owned electric utility monopolists with the average total costs among publicly-owned electric utility duopolists existing in 49 US cities. In most cases the duopolist competed against a privately-owned firm.) More specifically, the comparison was between the costs of publicly-owned duopolists, with the costs of (nearly) identical publicly-owned monopolists.

Using ordinary least squares (OLS), Primeaux controlled for sales, generating capacity utilization, fuel costs, consumption per customer, market density, internal combustion generation, 12 state dummy variables, a dummy variable for product market competition, and an interaction variable between sales and competition. Primeaux's data did indeed show that unit costs fall among the monopoly firms as output increased. That is, economies of scale among monopoly public utilities are alive and well. Second, at the average output rate for all firms in the sample (sample mean), unit costs were 10.75 percent lower for the duopolist than for the matching monopolist. Third, this difference is larger for smaller firms. That is, smaller firms are believed to be more "disciplined" by competition than were larger firms, i.e., the gains from increased X-efficiency are larger among smaller firms facing competition. Fourth at an output rate of 222 million kilowatt hours (kwh) per year the unit costs for the duopolist and monopolist are equal. The third and fourth results are shown by the fact that the cost advantage to having electricity supplied in a competitive— duopolistic—setting is reduced as output increases toward 222 million kwh, and that long run average costs are identical between the two market structures at this output rate. Fifth, for output rates higher than 222 million kwh, the monopolist has lower unit costs.

An interpretation of this data is that economies of scale. exist, but that below 222 million kwh the XE effect outweighs that of economies of scale. On the other hand, for output rates greater than 222 million kwh economies of scale outweigh the XE effect. In addition the data indicates that the XE effect is larger for smaller firms. It is worth noting that during the early 1960's only 437 (13%) of 3,190 electric utilities (eight percent of public and 27% of privately-owned firms in the sample) had annual output rates exceeding 100 million kwh. And, of the 437 whose output exceeded 100 million kwh, not all had output rates of 222 million kwh. In other words, for the period and sample under investigation the benefits of XE gained through competition outweighs the benefits of economies of scale gained through monopolization for all but the largest firms. Primeaux concludes that, "For public policy purposes, the mere existence of X-efficiency reflects a serious need for a re-examination of the regulated industries which are regulated as natural monopolies." (p.107)

Capacity Utilization and Competition Among Electric Utilities. One criticism made of the Primeaux study discussed above is the assertion that monopoly firms would have greater capacity than would the (smaller) competitive firms. It follows that the monopolist's higher unit costs may be due not to X- inefficiency but to the necessity of maintaining a greater amount of excess capacity. Do electric-utility monopolists have a larger capacity than do the combined capacity of two competing electric- utility duopolists? Primeaux tested the hypothesis that the monopolists would have greater capacity. If this hypothesis is proven incorrect then the orthodox assertion that it is excess capacity which explains the cost disadvantage among the monopoly firms would have to be rejected. This in itself would not be evidence for the existence or importance of X-(in)efficiency. However, since this hypothesis is used as a way of "explaining away" X-(in)efficiency among regulated monopoly firms, then a rejection of the capacity hypothesis would leave the X-efficiency explanation as a viable one.

Primeaux (1978) tested the capacity hypothesis using published Federal Power Commission data for the years 1964-68. Data for municipally owned electric utilities from 17 "monopoly cities" and 15 "duopoly cities" were used with the same matching procedure used as in the cost study. Again, an OLS procedure was used which controlled for sales, peak load requirements, the amount of power purchased by the utility as a percentage of their sales, the amount of hydroelectric generating capacity as a percentage of total generating capacity, sales distribution to different customer classes, state dummy variables, and a dummy variable if the firm was competitive (a duopolist).

His results include the finding that competition has *no* effect on capacity utilization. In other words, the combined capacity requirements for two competing municipally owned electric utilities is not different than the capacity requirement of a municipally owned electric utility monopolist. The capacity "explanation" for higher costs among monopolists, along with the resulting rejection of the X-efficiency explanation for higher costs is thus not consistent with the findings in this study of capacity utilization and market structure.

Are 'Natural' Monopolies Natural? In his latest work, *Direct Electric Utility Competition:The Natural Monopoly Myth*, Primeaux (1986) reports evidence inconsistent with many of the assertions made as to why public utilities are to be regarded as a natural monopoly. Since the natural monopoly argument is part of the public-interest theory of regulation, a rejection of the former would also imply a (partial) rejection of the latter. Some of his findings are reported below.

First, economies of scale have been assumed since the mid 19th. century to be to be so crucial to an electric utility as to make competition inefficient. However, as already discussed, the benefits of economies of scale have been shown to be outweighed by the benefits of competition (increased X-efficiency) for all but the largest electric utility firms in the Primeaux study.

Second, natural monopolies, including electric utilities are said to have relatively high fixed costs which allow their long run average costs to fall over the entire range of output. Primeaux tested this by comparing the capital-output (K/O) ratio for several U.S. industries in 1968. Survey of Current Business data was used. The capital measure used accounted for deprecia- tion, i.e., that the useful life of capital varies among and within industries. Thus, the capital-output ratio for each of 16 industries or sectors was calculated as (gross product or sales/depreciation). The industry ratios varied from 0.232 (farming and mining) to 0.53 (contract construction), with a 16 industry average of 0.085.

Among natural monopolies the ratios were 0.142 (all communications), 0.145 (telephone, telegraph, and related services, and all transportation), and 0.151 (railroads). These were exceeded not only by the industries listed above, but also by agriculture (0.224). In addition, all finance, insurance, and real estate had a ratio (0.151) equal to that of railroads. Finally, the Missouri Utilities Company had a (K/O) of 0.079 which placed it lower than all but three industries and lower than the 16 industry average. Primeaux concludes that the fixed costs of a public utility is not a justification for their natural monopoly status.

Third, natural monopoly conditions are said to make competition impossible. Yet, Primeaux points out that competition among duopolists have existed in regions of Missouri for 40 and 50 years. Fourth, it is believed that competition in electric-utilities will raise prices above the levels under conditions of monopoly. This is based on the assertion that costs among competitive utilities will be higher than under monopolistic conditions. Primeaux shows that prices are lower under conditions of competition, with the smallest differential being 16% (500 to 750 kwh block) and the average differential being 33%.

Another result which may be surprising is Primeaux's result for consumer awareness of price differentials. In a random (telephone) sample of 31 households in Sikeston, Missouri, Primeaux reports that 22 had service available from the cities two utility companies. Seventeen of these 22 did not know which firm charged the lower price, while only five could correctly answer this question. Five of the 22 did not even know how many firms sold electricity.

Taken together the Primeaux findings indicate that the characteristics of electric-utilities are not wholly consistent with the theory of natural monopoly. This is not to say that electric utilities should not be regulated. But if they are the decisions should be made on grounds solely than the natural monopoly argument. Finally, Primeaux's findings call into question the public-interest theory of regulation, of which the natural monopoly argument is one part. And, it offers support for the X-efficiency hypothesis.

6.2.2. Stevenson. Economies of scope and X-inefficiency.

A potential tradeoff exists not only between X-efficiency and economies of scale, but also between X-efficiency and "economies of scope" ("economies of combination"). Economies of scope exist when it is cheaper to produce two products in one firm then to produce them in separate firms. One example of economies of scope is a public utlity firm which sells both electricity, and natural gas for home heating. These "combination" utilities thus sell the two major competing products in the "home heating" market. (The economies of scope in this market is believed to come chiefly in the distribution and general administration sections of the firm, i.e., in the billing, meter reading, and management of distribution of both products.) In so doing this firm faces less competitive pressure then if it produced only one of these two products.

However, while economies of scope may serve to lower the costs of the combination utility below that of a utility which produces either electricity or natural gas—a "straight" utility —the lack of competitive pressure may raise their costs above that of the straight via the XE effect. The relative costs of combination and straight utilities will depend on the relative strengths of the effects of economies of scope and X-efficiency.

Rodney Stevenson's(1982) study examined the costs of generating electricity among a sample of 79 US utilities, 25 combination utilities and 54 straight utilities. He defined a combination utility as one which receives at least 15% of its total revenues from gas, while a straight is one which receives less than 5% of its total revenues from gas. In comparing generating costs Stevenson was not able to access the relative impacts of economies of scope and X-efficiency. He was, however, able to test for the effects of market structure—duopoly versus monopoly—on X-efficiency (costs). His data came from the Federal Power Commission and the National Association of Regulatory Utility Commissioners.

In estimating a translog cost function for all 79 utilities for 1970 and 1972, Stevenson included as independent variables input prices, output, the utilization rate of plant capacity, and regional dummy variables for the northeast, northwest, west, and south. Using 1970 data, Stevenson reports that at the sample mean (the mean values of the independent variables) the average costs of generating electricity was 6.1% lower for straight utilities than for combination utilities. Using 1972 data he reports that the average costs for straights was 8.5% less than that for combinations. Thus, "static" efficiency is higher when the firm faces greater competitive pressure.

Stevenson then tested for any "dynamic" efficiency effects of competitive pressure. Dynamic efficiency refers to the firm's ability (its actual performance) in reducing its costs over time. A greater reduction in costs over time is evidence of greater dynamic efficiency. To do this he compared cost functions among straight and combination utilities for 1964 and 1972 so as to separate out the effects of the independent variables (listed above) from a "time trend." This procedure showed that straight utilities did reduce their costs over this period faster than did the combination utilities. (Not all of the tests revealed a statistically significant differences in dynamic efficiency.) In other words, competitive pressure not only leads to lower costs at any point in time but to a larger downward shift in the cost function over time.

Stevenson concludes by stating that competition does affect costs of production (X-efficiency) and that, "While both existing utilities and regulatory commissions (with the exception of the Federal Communications Commission) have historically evidenced a distaste for competitive arrangements, new entry and increased interfirm rivalry may be a very useful regulatory tool for promoting improved utility performance."(p.64)

6.2.3. Gollop and Karlsson: Monitoring and X-inefficiency

During the early part of the 1970s, fuel prices began rising at a very rapid rate. Electric utilities, fearing that their revenues would not cover their spiraling costs, appealed to their regulatory commissions to increase electricity prices. A typical response was to allow utilities to automatically raise their prices in response only to higher fuel prices, i.e., they could not automatically increase their prices in response to higher costs of labor, capital, or nonfuel materials. This automatic adjustment mechanism is known as FAM—fuel adjustment mechanism. The potential effects of FAM are seen in figure 16. On the ordinate, we are measuring nonfuel inputs, while fuel is measured on the abscissa. The isocost curve reflecting market prices—a non-FAM world—is NF. The cost-minimizing utility would thus produce output Q at point A, using OF1 fuel and ON1 nonfuel. Given that FAM allows the utility to recover only higher fuel costs, a cost-minimizing utility would behave as if fuel prices had been reduced. In other words, FAM encourages the utility to use a more fuel-intensive input mix. The isocost curve would thus appear to shift counterclockwise to NF', and the cost-minimizing firm would adopt a more fuel-intensive input mix at point B, using OF3 fuel and ON3 non-fuel. Given FAM, point B represents a cost minimizing input mix. However, the firm shifts away from expansion path OP to a more fuel-intensive expansion path, OP1.

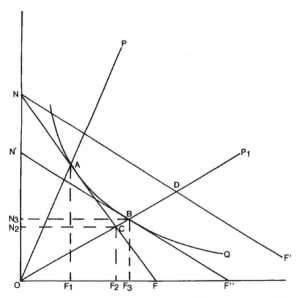

Figure 16. Allocative-price and X-inefficiency caused by
a fuel adjustment mechanism.

Evaluated at market prices, this new input mix is too fuel intensive. This is seen in figure 16 by the fact that a firm that faces market prices—isocost curve NF—cannot produce output rate Q if it produces on expansion path OP1. That is, its expenditures would not allow it to purchase enough high priced fuel in order to produce output rate Q. Given market prices, and an associated expenditure rate given by isocost curve NF, the firm producing on expansion path OP1 could only reach point C, one that clearly represents a lower output rate. It follows that in order to produce output rate Q, the firm would have to increase its expenditures or costs.

Because points A and C are on the same isocost curve, they represent the same level of expenditures. Had the firm used market prices, it would thus have produced output rate Q for a cost of OF1(Pf) + ON1(Pn) = OF2(Pf) + ON2(Pn), where Pf is the price of fuel and Pn the price of nonfuel (some weighted average of all nonfuel inputs). However, at point B the firm is spending OF3(Pf) + ON3(Pn). This is clearly a larger expenditure rate than is represented by point C. Hence the firm is spending more than necessary. In this case the firm was encouraged to do so by regulation. Be that as it may, evaluated at market prices, the firm is using too much fuel and not enough nonfuel per unit of output. That is, the firm is allocatively-price-inefficient. Allocative-price-inefficiency is measured as the distance OB/OC. Of course, given the existence of FAM, point B is a cost-minimizing point.

In addition to this allocative effect, FAM may also result in X-inefficiency. Since FAM allows firms to automatically recover higher fuel costs, it reduces the pressure for cost minimization, i.e., X-efficiency. Firms would not only shift their input mix in favor of fuel but also use more fuel than necessary. The XE effect of FAM would be shown by the firm producing output Q at point D. Evaluated at FAM prices, the firm is using the correct input mix but using too many inputs in producing output rate Q. At neither market prices NF nor FAM prices NF' is point D one of cost minimization. X-inefficiency is thus measured by the ratio OD/OB. Total inefficiency caused by FAM is thus measured as OD/OC.

Gollop and Karlson (1978) measured the effects of FAM among 105 privately owned electric utility firms in the U.S. They define FAM as the percentage of costs covered by FAM. Generally, utility commissions set a base range for fuel price (fuel costs to the utility) against which market fuel prices are evaluated. When market prices exceed this base, the utility is able to recover these higher costs. When market prices fall within the range, FAM becomes inactive. If market prices fall below the range, the utility must make a credit payment. Measuring the effects of FAM was done by estimating the net effect of FAM on a utility's costs of production (costs of generating electricity). This is done by estimating the utility's cost function, which includes as independent variables input prices, output, and FAM. This procedure was done for the Northeast, Coal Belt, and Gulf States regions of the U.S., for 1970 and 1972. This three- year interval saw a significant increase in the use of FAM.

The authors report FAM induced allocative inefficiency only in the Coal Belt in 1972. As for FAM-induced X-inefficiency, the authors report a significant effect in the Northeast and Coal Belt regions in 1970 and for the Northeast in 1972. Overall they report that a 1% increase in FAM, a 1% increase in recoverable fuel costs, leads to less than a 0.1% increase in total generating costs. However small this cost-elasticity figure seems, the effects of FAM are significant. For example, no X-inefficiency resulted from FAM in 1970 in the Northeast or the Coal Belt regions with FAM values of 0.39 and 0.51, respectively. Subsequent FAM values for the Northeast were 0.62 (1971) and 0.82 (1972) and were 0.57 for the Coal Belt in 1971. Had 1970 FAM values been maintained instead, total generating costs would have been 2% lower for the Northeast in 1971, 12% for the Northeast in 1972, and 0.4% for the Coal Belt region in 1971. However, had FAM values been 1.0, complete cost recoverability, costs would have increased by 10% for the Northeast in 1971, by 3% in 1972, and by 5% for the Coal Belt in 1971.

The authors fail to find any FAM-induced X-inefficiency for the Gulf region, where over 70% of sales are subject to FAM and whose average value is 0.73. The authors explain this by noting that Gulf States utility commissions adjust FAM values more frequently then do commissions in the Northeast or Coal Belt regions. Thus, Gulf States utility commissions are better able to keep the base prices close to market prices. Gulf States utilities thus face a greater risk than their Northeast and Coal Belt counterparts of facing either an inactive FAM or one that dictates the utility being charged to make a credit payment: both types of risks encourage X-efficient behavior. The authors thus conclude, "Continual monitoring of the fuel clause provisions may be the most effective means of preventing inefficient behavior while at the same time permitting utilities to quickly recover increasing input costs in periods of rapid inflation" (p. 583). The utility commissions in the Gulf States may thus be thought of as holding the firms more accountable for their behavior (costs).

Differential behavior among regulators is not unique to the Gollop and Karlson sample. Primeaux (1985) reviews some literature revealing a similar phenomena, that regulators often favor, for various (economic and personal) reasons, the preservation of monopoly status among public utilities.

6.2.4. Globerman and Book (Monitoring of Symphony Orchestras)

Just as federal and state branches of government provide intergovernmental aid to local government, so do they provide aid to subsidize the activities of many private groups, including performing arts organizations. These organizations would seem particularly vulnerable to market forces because, although they must pay market prices for their inputs, they often find it difficult, if not undesirable, to increase the productivity of those inputs. Services are often by their nature labor intensive and less capable of becoming capital intensive. Government and private subsidies are thus often used to close the "income gap," that is, the gap between costs and revenues.

Of course, government has a responsibility to provide subsidies wisely. (The preparation and writing of this book received no direct government subsidies!) Doing otherwise burdens the taxpayers unnecessarily by not penalizing X-inefficient behavior. Globerman and Book (1974) used a sample of 33 symphony orchestras and 23 theater groups in Canada during 1971-1972 in order to investigate whether subsidies by the Canadian government affect X-inefficiency. The dependent variable is per-performance cost. The dependent variables include the number of performances, the percentage of performances classified as "main" performances, attendance, length of performing season, input prices, and a variable measuring the effects of government subsidies. The authors choose to measure this by the age of the performing arts groups. The rationale for this measure is that older groups have more knowledge about how to fill out grant applications and are also preferred by government because of funds already "invested" in their activities. In other words, older groups are believed to be held less accountable for their costs.

OLS regressions for both symphony orchestras and theater groups shows a statistically significant relationship between age and per-performance costs. The authors conclude that X-inefficiency would be reduced if government would more closely monitor grant requests of older performing arts groups.

6.2.5. Majumdar (Deregulation of Telecommunications)

Majumdar (1993a) investigated X-efficiency among 40 local operating companies of the telecommunications industry between 1973 and 1978. Twenty-two of these firms are AT&T Bell Operating Companies, with the remaining 18 being other independent companies. The 15 year period consists of four subperiods. The first, 1973-1978, was the "prederegulatory" period. The year 1973 is a starting point for some level of competition in the industry, which was felt by 1978. The second, 1978-1981, was the "technologically driven market transition" period, so named because technology-driven product competition was its salient feature. The third, 1981-1984, was one of "political transition" because technological convergence was a recognized event and public policy designed to enhance competition was beginning to take place. Finally, 1984-1987 was the period of "consolidation" during which competition was perceived as the norm and economic forces were once again the key "strategy drivers."

The effects of competition on these 40 firms are estimated using a relatively new but very powerful econometric technique called data envelope analysis (DEA). DEA was first conceptualized by Charnes, Cooper, and Rhodes (1978), and is an extension of the work of Farrell (1957). DEA has several very attractive features. First, it is a nonparametric approach that does not require one to specify a functional form. Second, it allows one to measure the relative (x)efficiency of a "decision-making unit" (DMU)—a firm, a subgroup within a firm, or individuals within either the subgroup or the firm—against a reference group picked by the program itself. Third, it was designed to incorporate "noneconomic" or qualitative variables in order to measure the efficiency of non-profit organizations. Fourth, it was also designed to accept multiple outputs, as well as multiple inputs. Fifth, the DEA method estimates efficiency by comparing the *DMU's* output to *its* inputs. Each output and each inputs is assigned a weight by the program so that the particular circumstances of that DMU are considered and so the estimated efficiency of the DMU is maximized. Each DMU is thus put in its most favorable light.

Majumdar used DEA to estimate the effects of this deregulation period on the firm's productive or X-efficiency and on its ability to minimize its costs of production, and maximize revenues from its inputs. Estimating X-efficiency requires that the ratio of weighted outputs to weighted inputs is maximized. For revenue maximization, the linear program constrains the sum of the weighted inputs to unity and maximizes the outputs. For cost minimization, the sum of the weighted outputs is constrained to unity and the inputs are minimized.

Each of these three effects were measured in 1973, 1978, 1981, 1984, and 1987. With a maximum of 1.0, the mean scores for X-efficiency in these five years were .5038, .5032, .5770, .8269, and .8824. The lowest scores increased from .3313 (1973) to .5256 (1987), and the percentage of firms at the frontier increased from 5% (1973) to 40% (1987). Wilcoxan test statistics were used to make pairwise comparisons in these mean values between any two (measured) years. These test statistics show that X-efficiency increased significantly beginning in 1984.

With complete cost minimization given a value of 1.0, the mean score for the five years was .6644 (approximately 34% above minimum costs), .7488, .7654, .8237, and .8678 (approximately 14% above minimum costs), respectively. The percentage of firms minimizing their costs in an X-efficiency sense increased from 7.5% to 25% over the period. The Wilcoxan test statistics reveals that the attainment of cost minimization in 1973 was significantly below that for 1978-1987. And a pairwise comparison between each pair of years reveals that (p .05) firms drew closer to attaining complete cost minimization over the 14 year period. Even so, the mean value remained below 1.0 in 1987.

The five mean revenue-maximization scores were .4727 (approximately 50% below maximum revenue), .7491, .9386, .8926, and .9289, respectively. Wilcoxan test statistics reveal that firms approached their revenue frontiers over the period, the one exception being between 1981 and 1987. Overall the results reveal that deregulation in the telecommunications industry increased X-efficiency.

In a second study, Majumdar (1993b) looked at the effects of deregulation on X-efficiency via the adoption of a new technology. The sample and years are identical with those of his previous study. The technology under consideration is electronic switching. Electronic switching was developed during the early 1960s and represented a choice over the older electromechanical switching. Yet despite its superiority and low risk of conversion, the rate of adoption was far from universal. For example, in 1978 only 18% of total switches in use were the new technology with an interfirm standard deviation of 14%. By 1987, the figures were 55% and 25%, respectively.

The dependent variable, adoption of the new technology, is measured as the ratio of electronic switches to total switches. Two main classes of independent variables were used: variables capturing competitive market pressure and variables capturing intrafirm conditions. The market-pressure variables are the proportion of business access lines to total access lines, and the relative urban density of the firm's market.

Business customers are more likely to be pursued by competitors, and hence a firm with more business lines should be more X-efficient, i.e., have a larger rate of adoption of new technology. Large metropolitan areas are also a greater target for competitors, and this variable should also lead firms to be more X-efficient. The intrafirm variables are the ratio of cash flow to sales, and firm "slack." The cash-to-sales ratio measures managerial performance and wealth generation. Majumdar's assumption is that good (poor) performance reduces (increases) the incentives for further X-efficiencies and hence the adoption of technology should decrease (increase) in the future. This variable may be indicative of an "inert area." Slack is measured as the square of the ratio of the firm's installed base of switches to the total number of all switches in its operating area. The greater this ratio, the greater is the network density of a firm and the greater the potential economies of scale from adopting new switch technology. More slack should, therefore, increase X-efficiency.

The results show all variables with the expected signs, but only the intrafirm variables were statistically significant. Therefore, firm-level factors are stronger than market-level factors. Time dummies for 1981/1978, 1984/1981, and 1987/1984—using 1978/1973 as the reference time period—are all significant, indicating that adoption of the new technology increased over time. In addition, these time dummies also reflect the effect of market competition on strategic behavior and X-efficiency over time. This may be one reason why the market pressure variables fail to reach statistical significance. Be that as it may, Majumdar's results show that intrafirm variables and time affect the adoption of new technology, that is, X-efficiency.

6.2.6. Anderson and Frantz (Deregulation of the Mexican Peso)

The early part of 1982 was the end of a period during which the Mexican government's policy of buying pesos kept the price of the peso artificially high on world markets. In February 1982, 27 pesos exchanged for $1. On February 19, the value of the peso fell against the dollar since the the Mexican government stopped supporting its currency as it had under its previous policy. More subject to supply and demand conditions in the currency market, the peso began trading at 45 pesos per dollar. My colleague Joan Anderson and I (Anderson and Frantz, 1982) investigated how this would affect labor effort or X-inefficiency among piece-rate workers along the Mexican border. These workers are especially sensitive to real wage changes in that they have some control over their own wages. For residents of border towns such as Mexicali (located approximately 100 miles east of San Diego, just south of the border near Calexico, California), approximately 60% of consumer purchases in February 1982 were priced in dollars. Thus an approximately 40% devaluation in the value of the peso relative to the U.S. dollar meant an immediate real income loss of approximately 25%. (45 pesos for $1 means that 1 peso can buy 3.7 cents. After the devaluation, 1 peso could buy 2.2 cents—a 40% reduction in the purchasing power of the peso in terms of dollars.) This 25% does not include the extra inflation brought on as a result, which approached 100% by year's end.

We gathered daily output rates for each of 46 piece-rate workers in two textile plants in Mexicali. These data covered 22 weeks from November 1981 through April 1982. The period November and December 1981 served as a control period. Controlling for the demand for the firms' product, the capital stock, and the difficulty of the particular product being manufactured, we found that the effect of the devaluation was to increase weekly output by an average of 15%. In addition, a 20% wage increase granted by one of the firms in mid-March resulted in weekly output increasing another 8%.

We believe that different reasons explain these two results. The 15% increase is most likely explained by the workers' attempts to reduce the decline in real income resulting from the devaluation. Thus a decline in real wages increased work effort. This implies that these workers are satisficers with respect to money income. That is, they attempt to remain at some target income level. Also, since hours worked are fixed, the workers could not reduce the number of hours worked as real wages fell. The extra output thus did not come from less "leisure" (working more hours). The presidents of both firms confirmed this interpretation as rep- resenting the traditional and predominant attitude of their workers towards income. The effect of the 20% wage increase, we believe, was due to the increased pressure placed on management due to both the devaluation and the wage increase. These firms had loans from U.S. banks denominated in U.S. dollars, but contracts for their products from U.S. firms denominated in pesos. A "shock" effect took place and they were then between "a rock and a hard place." The result, according to the presidents of both firms, was for the management to pay more attention to the production process in order to increase output per unit of input. In this case, economic hardship served as the catalyst for both workers and management to increase effort and X-efficiency. Since our data only extended approximately two months after the devaluation, we cannot make any statement about whether this effect is a *one-time* effect or whether continued devaluations continued to improve X-efficiency.

6.2.7. Davis (Funding of Health Care)

Davis (1973) tested three theories of health care (hospital) inflation: demand-pull, labor cost-push, and cost-plus reimbursement. In her cost-plus reimbursement model, X-inefficiency enters as a "shift" parameter in the cost function. That is, average costs will be affected by the number of patients covered by a cost-reim-bursement plan (qm), the number of patients not covered (qn), and by X-ineffi-ciency, such that X-inefficiency can shift the entire cost curve upward.

However, X-inefficiency can have the effect of both shifting the cost curve upward and *increasing* the hospital's profits. This result will occur if the proportion of total patients covered by a cost-reimbursement plan exceeds the inverse of the proportion of costs reimbursed. In her notation, k is the proportion of costs reimbursed, such that if the cost-plus factor is 5%—that is, the hospital is reim-bursed $1.05 for each $1.00 of costs—then k=1.05. Therefore, X- inefficiency will increase costs and profits if qm/(qn+qm)1/k. Using one of Davis's own example, if the cost-plus factor were 5%, then more than 95% of the patients would have to be covered by the cost reimbursement plan before X-inefficiency would be profitable.

Using data for 1965, 1967, and 1968, Davis used an OLS procedure to estimate cost per patient for community hospitals from all areas of the U.S. The effect of a cost-reimbursement plan was measured by the proportion of hospital expenses covered by such a plan. In addition, Davis utilized a dummy variable for 1967 and another for 1968 (Medicare was introduced in 1966). Other variables in the equation measured hospital admissions per bed, average hospital wage rates, hospital size (number of beds), and the average length of stay. Regressions including the variable measuring the proportion of costs covered but not the dummy variable for 1967 or 1968 were run for each of the three years and for the three years combined into one regression. Only for the regression pooling the data for the three years was the cost reimbursement variable statistically significant (and positive). When the regression for the pooled data also included the time dummy variables, then the cost-reimbursement variable, while positive, was not significant. However, both time dummy variables are statistically significant, and positive.

The statistical significance of the cost-reimbursement variable is interpreted to mean that costs rise as the percentage of patients covered rises. The statistical significance of the time dummy variables is interpreted to mean that an "announcement" or *one-time* effect of Medicare on (higher) costs cannot be ruled out. While the higher costs could also have been caused by technology changes and/or product quality improvements, we wish to emphasize that the results for the cost-reimbursement and time dummy variables is consistent with XE theory. Finally, Davis's theory and results indicate that X-inefficiency may be both "voluntary" and "involuntary."

6.2.8. Silkman and Young (Funding of Public Services)

Richard Silkman and Dennis Young (1982) studied whether local government is subject to an "other people's money effect." These authors accomplished this by studying how the costs of providing local school transportation among 1317 school districts and local library services for 749 local public libraries are affected by the percentage of these costs that is paid for by local revenue sources as opposed to intergovernmental aid from either the state or federal government. To the extent that intergovernmental aid provides the revenues, the other-people's-money effect predicts that the incentive for local government to be cost (X)-efficient will be reduced. In such an environment, local government officials are less accountable to local taxpayers for expenses: local government officials become free riders. That is, they can enjoy the benefits of providing goods and services to their constituents without paying for them out of local taxes.

To answer the question about whether local governments are subjected to an other-people's-money effect, the authors first estimated the costs of providing each service for the most efficient and for the average school district and library.

Estimates of the "cost frontier" and deviations from the frontier reveal that the cost of providing school transportation per student per year is $67.07 for the most efficient provider, and $142.72 for the average school district. The most efficient local libraries provide volume-hours at $.24, while the cost for the average libraries is $.78. The authors then used both demand and supply conditions to explain deviations from the frontier. For school transportation, demand conditions include the tax-price of the service, income, and the percentage of the population of school age. Supply conditions include the percentage of the school population receiving special education (handicapped students) and the proportion of transportation services contracted out to private firms. For library services, demand conditions include the tax price of the service, income, and property values. Supply conditions include population density and number of branches. In addition, the share of local revenues in providing the service was used to measure the incentive for X-inefficiency. The authors report that when the local share for school transportation increases by 10%, the per-capita deviation from the cost frontier falls by 2.8%, or $.74. For local libraries, deviations from the frontier are reduced by 3.4%. An average school district with a population of 20,000 would find an operating cost savings of approximately 4.5% when the local share of revenues increased by 10%. Local governments appear subject to an other-people's- money effect. That is, the motivation for X-efficiency is increased when those spending public funds are to a greater extent held accountable for their behavior.

6.2.9. Craven, Dick, and Wood (Funding of Education)

Craven, Dick, and Wood (1986) investigated how changes in funding for nonuniversity higher education in Britain affected X-efficiency in one English polytechnic. As a way of reducing (presumed) government waste, the Conservative government increased the use of per-student- based funding in education.

Given this funding basis, it was felt that a reduction in available resources would lead these institutions to become more X-efficient rather than to reduce education. The authors were able to test this hypothesis for one English polytechnic for the years 1979—1984. (They provide reason to believe that their results can be generalized among non-university educational institutions.

Between 1978-1979 to 1983 -1984 expenditures in constant prices increased 8% (from 1981-82 to 1983-84 they fell by 4%), the number of full-time equivalent (FTE) students increased by 29%, the number of FTE students increased 22%, FTE expenditures fell 16%, academic staff fell 8% while nonacademic staff increased by 9%. Therefore, the quantity of education increased over this period; the quality of education—measured by the percentage of students passing their exams, the number of students graduating with honors, and faculty publications—did not fall; and, the cost per student fell. The authors interpret these results as an increase in X-efficiency motivated by a change in which income is more directly tied to X-efficiency. Finally, the authors note that it does not necessarily follow that a continuation of this (new) funding policy will continue to increase X-efficiency. In other words, the increase in X-efficiency may be a one-time effect. Two other examples of a possible one-time effects are the studies of Davis and of Anderson and Frantz (please see above).

6.2.10. Register and Grimes (Education and Unions)

Register and Grimes (1991) studied "shock effects" of unions on the educational performance of 2360 secondary school students in 61 school districts nationwide using the National Assessment of Economic Education database. Student achievement was measured by the SAT score on the college entrance exam. Independent variables included whether the faculty was unionized, school enrollment, racial mix of the students, expenditures per student, student/faculty ratio, the gender and race of the student, the number of math classes taken, student GPA, whether the students were in a college preparatory program, number of hours worked per week for pay, parents socioeconomic status, and region of residence.

Empirical results show that a unionized faculty, ceteris paribus, increases the SAT score on the college entrance exam by 46.25 points, or 4.7%. This variable is significant at the .05 level. The authors interpret this result as an increase in productivity caused by the existence of a union on campus. One of their explanations is that given tight budgets, a union creates a shock effect, forcing school administrators to increase X-efficiency as a way of controlling their budgets.

6.2.11. Register (Unions and Hospitals)

Register (1988) used a sample of 275 (mostly nonprofit) hospitals in 13 MSAs representing 15% of the U.S. population to study the wage, productivity, and hence cost or X-efficiency effects of unionization. The data come from the American Hospital Association's 1984 (conducted in 1985) survey of hospitals. In nonunionized hospitals, more than 99% of nonsupervisory, professional, and technical employees were not union members. In unionized hospitals, more than 70% percent of employees were union members. The X-efficiency connection stems from the "competitive" model of unions, that unions can offset wage increases through a union-induced productivity or X-efficiency increase. This model is in contrast to the traditional "monopoly" view, which sees unions as increasing wages in the absence of productivity gains, thus hurting the firms employing their members. With more than 90% of hospitals being non-profit, and with evidence reporting that neither trustees nor managers of nonprofit hospitals typically behave as costminimizers, the likelihood of X-inefficiency is greater. Therefore, if unions raise wages in hospitals, do they offset them by contributing to higher productivity?

Register used a semilog wage equation, with wages measured as the natural log of average annual earnings of all employees in a particular hospital. Register controlled for the percentage of employees who were medical staff, registered nurses, and licensed practical nurses, the cost-of-living, and regional dummy variables for the North, South, and Southwest. His results show that unionized hospitals pay 5.65% more than nonunion hospitals. The natural log of the average product of labor is defined as the ratio of in-patient days to total personnel. In this productivity equation, Register controlled for the capital:labor ratio, the number of full-time equivalent employees, the three regional dummy variables, and four variables reflecting "product mix," namely the ratio of out-patients to in-patients, a variable measuring the severity of patient illness, surgeries per admission, and intensive care days per in-patient. The results show that the average product of employees in union hospitals exceeds that in nonunion hospitals by approximately 16%. Finally, the average cost equation shows that this figure is approximately 10% percent lower in union hospitals. Three-stage least squares results and results for 114 hospitals in Ohio show very similar results for wages, productivity, and costs. The "shock" effect of unions is attributed to be a major cause of lower X-inefficiency among union hospitals.

6.2.12. Fiorito and Hendricks (Union Structure)

Fiorito and Hendricks (1987) remind us that unions as well as firms can be either X-efficient or X-inefficient. Barriers to replacing a union (in the short run) allow a union to formulate and carryout an inferior or X-inefficient strategy. That is, as is the case with firms, unions may operate with "slack." Fiorito and Hendricks also note that even without barriers to replacing a union, competition among unions is never so strong as to preclude X-inefficient behavior. Therefore, union X-efficiency should be related to bargaining outcomes. What are the characteristics that affect X-efficiency and hence bargaining outcomes? The authors are interested mainly in union militancy, size, centralization, and democracy on wage and nonwage bargaining outcomes.

Data about union characteristics and bargaining outcomes were derived from over 3000 union contracts in both the manufacturing and nonmanufacturing sectors between the years 1971 and 1981, and compiled from a variety of sources. The findings of Fiorito and Hendricks include the following: democracy enhances X-efficiency in nonwage outcomes but reduces wage outcomes relative to less democratic unions; smaller national unions are more X-efficient, especially in nonwage outcomes; the most X-efficient unions have a small number of large locals in several industries; militancy is weakly associated with X-efficiency but is perhaps more symptomatic of an X-inefficient union. Centralization shows no consistent impact on X-efficiency. The authors note that several measurement problems exist, including the chicken-egg problem, i.e., whether union characteristics are the cause or the effect of bargaining outcomes. Sorting this out requires further research efforts.

6.2.13. Leibenstein and Maital (Relative XE Among Hockey Players)

I am including this study at this point to illustrate the ability of the Data Envelope Analysis method to estimate X-efficiency. Majumdar's study was for an aggregate of 40 firms. Leibenstein and Maital's (1992) study is for 19 Boston Bruin hockey players—12 forwards and 7 defensemen—who played at least 30 games during the 1989-1990 season. X-efficiency was estimated by maximizing the ratio of weighted outputs to weighted inputs. Output was measured by goals per game and assists per game. Input was measured by skill (salary) and "opportunity" (shots on goal). The ratio maximized is the conversion of skill and opportunity into goals and assists. The ratio thus minimized is salary dollars and shots on goal per goal and assist.

The results of Leibenstein and Maital's study show 4 of 19 players being completely, but relatively, X-efficient, that is, maximizing goals and assists for a given salary and shots on goal. Not surprisingly, the forwards (.747) had a higher X-efficiency score than the defense-oriented players (.464). The four completely X-efficient players were all forwards while the lowest X-efficiency scores—.271 and .158—were both for defense-oriented players. Although one may argue about the measure of inputs and outputs, the power of the DEA technique for estimating X-efficiency should be clear.

6.2.14. Pustay (Relative XE Among Airlines)

Pustay (1978) measured relative airline performance yearly for 11 airlines for the period 1965-1974. Pustay believes the airline industry to be a good one for studying regulation and firm performance. First, under Civil Aeronautics Board regulations, both market prices and an industrywide rate of return based on industrywide average costs were established. Thus, regulation was pro- viding each airline with similar incentives. Second, once differences in route structures were taken into account, inputs and outputs were essentially homogenous.

However, while regulation may be providing each airline the same "carrot," it is also insulating the airlines from the "stick" of competition. Regulation may thus cause (X-)inefficiency due to either inadequate internal (carrots) incentives or inadequate external (sticks) incentives. Speaking about the behavior of regulators in general, in a statement reminiscent of the papers by Gollop and Karlson and by Joskow, Pustay comments that regulators monitor costs only to make sure that they were incurred by "honest, efficient, and economical management—a phrase which has more legal than economic significance" (pp. 49—50). The possibility of the existence of X inefficiency is his conclusion. His study attempted to measure the relative amount of X-(in)efficiency in the airlines industry, yearly, by firm for the period 1965—1974.

Pustay measured the degree of X-inefficiency of any airline in any year as the ratio of its costs to the industry average, if the "average" airline flew the same type of route as the airline in question. Three categories of costs were used: flight, capital, and passenger costs. Flight costs included expenditures for flying opera- tions, direct maintenance, and insurance. Eighty- five to ninety percent of capital costs were accounted for by the cost of the aircraft; the efficiency with which capital was used depended in part on the ratio of groundtime to flighttime. Passenger costs were measured by general services and administration expenses per revenue passenger mile.

For each of these three categories, the efficiency index was the ratio of the average industry cost to the individual firm's cost (for the same route structure). An overall efficiency index for each airline for each year was then calculated by weighting each of the three cost categories by their relative importance in airlines operations; the weights reflected the "average" importance of each cost category for the entire period 1965—74.

For the entire ten-year period, Pustay's data indicate that cost savings of 12% to 15% would have been possible had the average airline been as X-efficient as the most efficient airline. This study makes clear the "relative" nature of efficiency indices. That is, calling X-inefficient the difference between the costs of "most" efficient and those of the average assumes that the word "most" is being used in an absolute sense. Thus, had the "most" efficient been producing with costs above some technologically minimum level, then this figure of 12% to 15% would be an underestimate of the potential savings. In addition, is 12% to 15% a large or small cost savings? That is, does it prove that regulation creates a wide spread in the costs of production among firms in an industry, or does it show that regulation reduces this disparity? As Pustay points out, the answer to this latter question requires that we examine cost differences among unregulated firms.

6.2.15. Hollas and Herren (Relative Size of Allocative and XE Among Public Utilities)

Returning to more direct empirical evidence. Hollas and Herren (1982) estimated the allocative and X-(in)efficiency effects of electric utility market structures—monopoly and duopoly. To do so, they estimated *nonproduction* marginal costs among 197 publiclyowned firms, 17 of which faced direct competition in 1972. They defined nonproduction costs as expenses for customer accounts, sales, and administrative and general expenses.

Estimating a total nonproduction cost function with a dummy variable for a competitive market structure, the authors report that duopoly reduces marginal costs of serving residential customers by 0.184 cents per kilowatt hours. Second, they report that competition among this sample of electric utilities *raises* fixed nonproduction costs. Third, although the mean output for the sample was 123.6 million kwh, for output rates above 110.8 million kwh, the average nonproduction costs were lower among competitive utilities than among monopolists. Thus, for a large part of the sample, average nonproduction costs are lower with competition. In order to compare the relative sizes of allocative and X-inefficiency the authors used a subsample of 30 monopoly firms. Two marginal cost curves were used: the firm's actual marginal cost and an estimate of what it would have been if the firm had faced product market competi-tion. The various components of allocative and X-(in)efficiency estimated are shown in figure 17.

First, the summation of areas F, I, and J represent the allocative loss of the duopolist charging a price (Pd) that exceeds its marginal cost (LRMCd): PMC. If the duopolist set its price equal to its marginal cost (LRMCd), then it would produce Qc. But the monopolist has higher marginal costs (LRMCm) than does the duopolist. Thus if the monopolist sets its price equal to its marginal cost it will produce Qc'. In both cases, P=LRMC. The area J thus represents the allocative loss due to reduced output and higher prices, given that P=MC but with LRMCd < LRMCm.

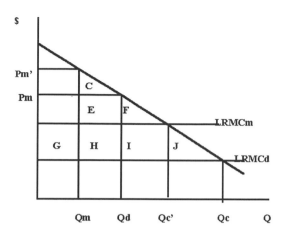

Figure 17. Components of allocative and X-inefficiency caused by a
lack of competition in the electric utility industry .

Next, if the duopolist's price (Pd) is set above LRMCd, then it produces Qd,
which is less than it would produce if Pd=LRMCm, whereby it would produce
Qc'. The area F thus represents the allocative loss because output is reduced and
Pd > LRMCm. The area I, in turn, represents that part of the allocative loss caused
by higher costs.

Area C is the deadweight loss—lost consumer surplus—due to the monopolization of the industry with the resulting PmPd and QmQd. Area E is lost profits
when output is reduced below the duopolist's output rate. Area H represents higher
costs but is part of the allocative loss due to the monopolization of the industry,
with the resulting QmQd. Last, but not least, area G represents X-inefficiency.

Several estimates were made, ranging from the assumption that Pd was only
slightly less then Pm to the assumption that Pd=LRMCd. Here I will report the
estimates for the case when Pd=LRMCm, which is the case assumed in orthodox
microeconomics: given cost minimization LRMCd=LRMCm, and given allocative
efficiency among the competitive firm, Pd=LRMCd=LRMCm. In this sample,
when Pd=LRMCm, area C—lost consumer surplus— is equal to 5% of the total
revenues for all firms in the sample; area (C+E+H) is equal to 7% of revenue; area
(F+I+J) is equal to 0.24; and area G—X-inefficiency—is equal to approximately
8.9% of revenue. The total estimated welfare loss is thus approximately 16.1% of
total revenue. As in the other estimates by these authors, the welfare losses due to
X-inefficiency were the most significant.

6.3. CONCLUSIONS

The evidence reviewed in this chapter strongly suggests that the effect of government regulation on X-efficiency is significant and multidimensional. In the next chapter, we will examine the effects of market structure.

7

EMPIRICAL EVIDENCE: MARKET STRUCTURE AND FIRM ORGANIZATION

7.1. Introduction

In this chapter, studies that address the effects of both market structure and organization of the firm on X-efficiency. Aspects of market structure and firm organization reviewed include public vs. private ownership (vs. cooperatives), the ownership form of privately-owned enterprise firms, firm size, four-firm concentration ratio, market share, and cartel and price-fixing arrangements.

Microeconomic theory traditionally assumed that firms are single-minded in the pursuit of profits and that noncompetitive market structures produce only allocative inefficiency. Accordingly, the theory implicitly assumed that every individual in the firm was either fully rational or a contributor of X-efficiency. The studies reviewed here show that the degree of X-efficiency is a variable and depends upon the motivations offered by the relevant environment both inside and outside the firm.

7.2. Owner vs. Manager-Controlled Firms

7.2.1. Medford (Management in the Production Function)

Medford's (1986) paper is not about owner vs. manager-controlled firms per se but rather about the role of management per se. This study thus sets the stage for much of the material that follows. Medford tests the role of management in influencing the firm's output by fitting three forms of a production function—Cobb-Douglas, CES, and the translog forms—to data from 30 plants in Australia, Europe, Asia, Latin America, and Canada for the years 1975—1982. The focus of the study, namely, management, was measured by the relative performance of a given's manager's plant compared with all other plants according to the ollowing criteria: meeting output goals, costs relative to budget, and quality of output (defects as a percentage of total output). For each of these three criteria, the number of standard deviations of each plant from the overall mean was calculated. These three figures were then summed to yield a management performance index. This procedure was done for each of the eight years.

Labor and capital inputs was measured in two ways, which included an adjustment for skill level and technology, respectively. Other independent variables included a time variable capturing technological progress, dummy variables for plant returns to scale, plant size, and region of plant location. The output measure is engineering based and quality adjusted. Engineers estimated the number of labor hours per unit of output so that the output of all products is measured according to "standard labor hours per unit of output."

Results for the management variable show that managerial performance enhances plant-level X-efficiency, with a performance one standard deviation better than the overall mean, increasing X-efficiency (getting the firm closer to their frontier) in the range of 10% to 17.5%.

7.2.2. Shelton (Company Managers vs. Entrepreneur—Managers)

It is not common that one gets the opportunity to study a group of firms producing the same output—the same product and the same quality of product—and using the same capital and noncapital inputs. Yet a 1967 study by John Shelton did just that. He studied the performance of a group of firms identical in these key elements but differing only with respect to ownership form. Shelton's study was of a large national fast-food restaurant chain, most of which was owned and operated by a franchisee who was independent from the parent company both legally and in terms of remuneration. There were two types of restaurants: relatively large family-eating-type restaurants and smaller quick-snack operations. Regardless of the type or the ownership form of the individual restaurant, the parent company provided details about menus, recipes, ingredients, table settings and service, and accounting procedures. Procedures were so thoroughly standardized and supervised that franchisees were selected only from individuals with no previous experience in the restaurant business; it was felt that those with previous experience would attempt to install their own procedures. From time to time, the ownership of any one of the restaurants would undergo an change from either franchisee to parent or vice versa. When the parent managed the restaurant it assigned a manager from its own staff who was very familiar and experienced in operating one of the restaurants.

The sample contained 22 such restaurants. Fifteen of the restaurants underwent one change in ownership form during the period of the study. That is, ownership changed from either a franchisee-owner (FO) to company management (CM), or vice versa. In addition, six of the restaurants experienced two changes in ownership form, while one experienced five such changes. Therefore, the study included data on 53 "restaurant units."

For the entire sample of 53, the average length of time of ownership for any FO was 38 weeks; the average length of operation under CM was 33 weeks. When the CM form followed the FO form, sales fell by 7.3%. On the other hand, when FO followed CM, the sales rate increased by 19.1%. The contrast in profit margins is even more striking. Profit margins (profits/sales) were 9.5% under FO but only 1.9% under CM. Average weekly profits under FO were $271.83 as compared with

$56.81 under CM, a difference of 478%. In addition, while only 2 of 29 FO units showed losses, 11 of 24 CM units showed losses. And, of the 22 cases where CM followed FO, profits fell 18 times, increased twice, and remained the same twice. On the other hand, when FO followed CM, profits rose seven times and fell twice. Among the smaller quick-snack units, average weekly sales were approximately 19% higher under FO. Profit margins under FO were approximately 16.2%, while for CM they were approximately 6.4%

An executive of the parent company offered an explanation for the findings in these terms: "...franchisee-owners just watch the little things closer; they utilize the cooks and waitresses better; they reduce waste" (p. 1247). Despite the close supervision and profit incentives given to company managers (profit sharing can reach 33% of salary and averaged 15%), performance was superior under independent franchisee-owners. Shelton concluded that investing one's own money and being paid only out of profits made the difference in reducing X-inefficiency.

7.2.3. Monsen, Chiu, and Cooley (Owner vs. Manager Controlled Firms)

One study of the ownership form:profits relationship using industry data was done by Monsen, Chiu, and Cooley (1968). The authors choose six firms from each of 12 manufacturing indus- tries: meat products, canning and preserving, industrial chemicals, drugs, oil refiners, iron and steel, nonferrous, electrical, motor vehicles, aircraft, industrial machines, and business machines. Each of these 72 firms was listed in the July 1964 edition of Fortune in the "Fortune 500" by 1963 sales. Data on these 72 firms were for the entire period 1952—1963.

For each industry, half (three) of the firms were owner—controlled and half were manager—controlled. An owner-controlled firm was defined as one in which either an owner who was actively engaged in the business owned at least 10% of the voting stock, or in which a nonactive owner owned at least 20% of the voting stock. A manager-controlled firm was defined as one in which no owner owned 5% of the voting stock and for which there was no evidence of recent owner control.

In estimating the profits:ownershipform relationship, the authors controlled for industry, firm size, and year. Data were obtained from Moody's *Industrial Manual* and from each company's annual reports. The total number of observations per ownership form was thus 36 (12 industries, three firms per industry) per year, or 432 for the entire 12 year period. The estimates were then gained through both analysis of variance and a balanced fixed model of a three-way analysis of covariance.

Profits, or the return on an owner's investment, were measured as the ratio of net income to net worth. For all 36 owner-controlled firms, the mean value of profits for the entire eleven year period was 12.8 %. For the 36 manager-controlled firms, this mean value was 7.3%. Furthermore, the owner-controlled group outperformed the manager-controlled group in all 12 industries. The authors feel that the best explanation is that "two quite different motivation incentive systems are at work— one for owners and another for managers" (p. 442). One implication is that the assumption of profit maximization is less applicable for manager-controlled firms.

With respect to X-inefficiency the authors state that "...Leibenstein has reported evidence indicating that motivation is considerably more important in influencing efficiency in the economy as a whole than the traditional microeconomic concern with allocative efficiency has led us to believe. Thus, the effect of the modern separation of ownership from management may have a motivational impact upon the performance of the firm—perhaps of greater consequence than allocative efficiency..."(p. 435).

7.2.4. McEachern (Owner vs. Manager vs. Externally Controlled Firms)

A somewhat different classification of ownership form is to classify firms as "owner managed," "manager controlled," or "externally controlled," and measure performance by both profits and growth. This was done by William McEachern (1978) for the period 1964—1973 using a sample of 16 firms from each of the drug, chemical, and petroleum-refining industries. The sample included eight owner managed firms, 26 manager controlled firms, and 14 externally controlled firms. McEachern defined an owner-managed firm as one in which the dominant share-holder owns at least 4% of the voting stock and is also a manager. A manager controlled firm was defined as one not having a dominant shareholder who owns at least 4% of the stock. An externally controlled firm is one in which the dominant share holder is not a manager. McEachern's model thus assumes that the motivation and behavior of a dominant owner will differ depending upon whether he is a manager.

McEachern's hypothesis is that the dominant stockholder in an externally controlled firms is less likely than either an owner-manager or a manager in a manager controlled firm to derive utility from the firm's growth. Both these latter groups are assumed to be more likely to have part of their ego tied up with the size of the firm. Therefore, externally controlled firms are less likely to actively pursue growth.

Using an OLS technique and controlling for the age and industry affiliation of the firm, McEachern showed that growth rates among both owner managed and manager controlled firms are higher than they are for externally controlled firm. However, this result is statistically significant only for the owner-managed firms. In other words, the growth rates by order of magnitude were owner managed firms, manager controlled firms, and externally controlled firms. He also reported that the drug industry had a significantly higher growth rate than did the chemical industry, while the growth rate for the petroleum industry did not differ significantly from that of the chemical industry. Finally, he reported that growth rates decline with the age of the firm.

However, growth rates do not necessarily mean that the firm is making more profits. Recall from the discussion of the Marris model in chapter 3 that growth beyond some point lowers profits by lowering the return to capital and the productivity of groups. The McEachern data, however, showed that the higher growth (owner controlled) firms were not poor investments. Data for the period 1963—1972 showed that the owner managed firms yielded a higher rate of return on stock purchased in 1963 and held until 1972 than did manager controlled firms. (Both dominant stockholder groups yielded higher rates of return than did manager controlled firms.) The implication, stated by McEachern, is that if owner managed firms are pursuing growth beyond that which maximizes the present value of profits, then they more than offsetting this loss in value by improving efficiency in other ways: "Perhaps there is less of the 'X-inefficiency' discussed by Leibenstein" (p. 264).

7.3. Market and Firm Concentration

7.3.1. Weiss and Pascoe (X-Inefficiency vs. Economies of Scale)

Weiss and Pascoe (1985) suggest that perhaps one of the better tests of XE theory is to estimate the relationship between industry concentration (independent variable) and the variance in productivity rates among firms in a given industry. Another, similar, test would be to substitute profits for productivity. Using the Federal Trade Commissions Line of Business data for 233 manufacturing industries for the years 1974-1976, the authors performed such a test, as well as tests providing some evidence about an important issue, i.e., the independent effects of X-inefficiency and economies of scale (suboptimal capacity) on costs of production. First, a diagrammatic clarification.

This distinction between X-inefficiency and suboptimal capacity (and excess capacity)[1] is shown in figure 18. On the long-run, average-total-cost curve, plant 1 (SRAC1) is the optimal size plant. Plant 2 (SRAC2) is a suboptimal plant, since it is not large enough to take advantage of all economies of scale available to the industry. If plant 2 were designed to produce Q2, then the suboptimal capacity associated with plant 2 would be measured as (ATC2-ATC1). In addition, if the firm is producing on SRAC2' rather than SRAC2, then the level of X-inefficiency associated with output Q1 is (AC3-AC2). On the other hand, if plant 2 were designed to produce Q1, then suboptimal capacity associated with plant 2 would be measured as (AC4-AC1). However, Q1 is not an efficient output rate for plant A, since a smaller plant would have been able to produce Q1 at a lower average cost. Operating plant 2 for Q1 thus involves a cost over and above that attributed to suboptimal capacity. This additional cost is referred to as excess capacity. Excess capacity not using the plant to produce at its lowest level of long-run average costs, raises costs by an amount (AC5-AC4). Finally, if the firm were producing on SRAC2' rather than on SRAC2, then the X-inefficiency associated with output Q1 would be (AC6-AC5).

Weiss and Pascoe's profit measures were the variance and standard deviation of operating income divided by sales, or by assets. The dispersion of profit rates within an industry is thus taken as a proxy measure for the existence of X-ineffi-

---

1   Siegfried and Wheeler (1981) provide a useful discussion of the issues in partition X-efficiency, excess capacity, and suboptimal capacity.

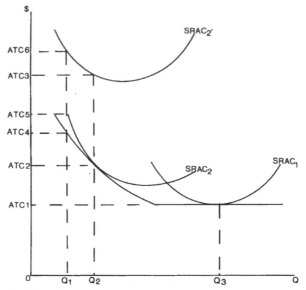

Figure 18. X-inefficiency, suboptimal capacity, and excess capacity.

ciency. The reason is that if market power shelters firm members from the pressure to be X-efficient, then more highly concentrated industries would be expected to experience a greater array of behavior patterns; i.e, a greater range in the degree of rationality will be displayed.

The independent variables in these first set of regressions were the 4FCR adjusted for noncompeting submarkets; the Herfindahl index, which measures the degree of noncompeting subproduct market fragmentation (for example, ethical drugs include vitamins, birth control pills, and antibiotics); the distance over which products are shipped, as another proxy for market fragmentation; and, the three year mean industry operating income to sales and assets ratio. The results of these OLS regressions include the consistent finding that a higher 4FCR increases the inter-industry dispersion of profits. Greater X-inefficiency in more highly concentrated industries is hypothesized.

However, this result may also be due to the fact that more highly concentrated industries may contain a relatively small number of large firms with high market shares, with the majority of firms possessing a small market share. In this case, the variance of profits would likely be high because the few large firms would earn large profits while most of the relatively small firms would earn much lower profits. On the other hand, a less concentrated industry may show a smaller dispersion of profits because all firms are more equal in size or market share. The previously reported results of Weiss and Pascoe may therefore be due to the size distribution or market shares of firms rather than to X-inefficiency.

Correcting for this possibility allows one to distinguish the effects of X-inefficiency from inefficiency due to *suboptimal capacity*, that is, inefficiency due to the fact that the firm is too small to take advantage of all economies of scale. The procedure used to make the correction was to regress profit measures on the logarithm of sales for each industry. The residuals from these regressions then became the dependent variable in the next or second set of regressions. In these new regressions, the independent variables were identical as before. The results of these regressions showed much less evidence for greater X-inefficiency among more highly concentrated industries. An interpretation is that higher dispersion of profits is due more to suboptimal capacity and an inability to take advantage of economies of scale, and to the distribution of market shares, than it is to X-inefficiency.

The authors then report that 157 of the 233 industries show a positive relationship between sales and profits, while 145 show a negative relationship. The industries exhibiting a negative relationship are believed to be in a state of disequilibrium. As such, their third set of regressions is to run the second set of regressions again but only for the industries showing a positive relationship between sales and profits. Once again, higher concentration is shown to increase the interindustry dispersion of profits. Therefore, under "normal" conditions, higher concentration increases the dispersion of profits because of X- inefficiency rather than because of suboptimal capacity.

However, the positive relationship between sales and profits could result from economies of scale, or because larger firms became larger and more profitable because they are more efficiently managed. That is, some firms are "superior" and some are "inferior." This latter view is attributed to both Demsetz (1974) and Peltzman (1977). In order to test these competing ideas, Weiss and Pascoe regressed profit levels (not their variation) and market share, using both OLS and a simultaneous system (two-staged least squares in which both profits and market shares are dependent and independent variables) against the industry's 4FCR and several other independent variables. Their results can be summarized in the following manner. First, in the OLS regressions, higher profits increases market share, and higher market share increases profits. Second, a higher 4FCR reduces profits but is not statistically significant.

Third, however, in the 2SLSQ regressions, higher market shares increase profits, but higher profits reduce market shares. Higher market shares increasing profits is consistent with the existence of and exploitation of economies of scale and market power. But higher profits reducing market shares is not consistent with the view that leading firms become large and profitable because they are efficient. This result is consistent with a more classical theory, which predicts that profits attract new firms, thereby reducing the market share of the existing firms. Fourth, a higher 4FCR *reduces* profit levels. This finding is consistent with XE theory in that the same market power that allows firms to raise their prices also reduces pressure to be cost minimizing. Lower profits could thus result when costs rise more than does revenues.

Weiss and Pascoe conclude that the first and third sets of regressions are consistent with an increase of X-inefficiency in more highly concentrated industries. While part of this result may be due to economies of scale, they believe that X-inefficiency is still a lively force in highly concentrated industries. Finally, they have no doubt that some firms are superior and others inferior, by definition. However, their study shows that inferior firms are most likely to be concentrated in more highly concentrated industries.

7.3.2. Shepherd (Market Share and X-inefficiency)

According to William Shepherd (1972a), "For given market demand conditions, the neoclassical expectation is that a higher market share...yields the firm higher profitability.... . This function may be linear; or, if X-inefficiency becomes large at high shares...,t may be curvilinear" (p. 25). Shepherd tested these ideas using 1956—1969 (a period of sustained economic growth) data from 200 firms listed in the Fortune Directory as being among the largest 500 firms. He then added another 14 firms from the next largest 500, providing a total sample of 214 firms. Firms were excluded from the sample for any one of the following reasons: they were highly diversified (thus avoiding the problems of analyzing the profits:market share relationship for a firm producing in many markets), they were part of a major merger during the period, a high percentage of their sales were to the military (Vietnam period), they were not included in the Fortune 500 list for more than one year, and either the firm or the industry experienced a major disequilibrium period.

The entire sample was divided into certain subsets, including a sample of 210 that excluded 21 firms because of special doubts about the data. Another subset consisted of 50 firms in older homogeneous-goods industries for the purpose of testing the theory that the behavior of a dominant firm tends to become passive with time such that its market share falls and/or its profits slow down or actually fall. Still another subset was 181 firms in "young" industries. The dependent variable, profits, was measured as net income after taxes as a percentage of equity (book value of equity plus retained earnings). In addition to the firm's market share, other dependent variables included the four-firm concentration ratio, the extent of barriers to entry, firm size (measured by net assets), advertising expenditures as a percentage of sales, and the growth rate of total revenues for the firm.

Shepherd's data showed that profits are higher when the firm has a larger market share, but, in general, this increase occurs at a decreasing rate. In other words, the relationship tends toward being curvilinear and is especially true for the firms in the older industries. Second, he reported that firm size and profits are inversely related, that is, larger firms are less profitable than smaller firms. About this finding he comments, "Is the negative coefficient caused by X-inefficiency? No other interpretation seems more persuasive... .Possibly size does add to market power, but it also appears (at least during 1956-1969) to add still more to costs" (p. 32). Third, for the 50-firm "old" industry group, Shepherd also reports that profits reach a maximum when the firm's market share is 27%. By contrast, maximum profits among 181 firms in "young" industries was reached at a market share of 75%. Shepherd comments, "The odds are that the observed decline in profitability above market shares of 27 percent arises at least partly from relative X-inefficiency, as other evidence about steel and meat-packing firms has cumulatively suggested" (p. 33).

In a second study, Shepherd (1972b) uses industry data for 336 industries for the period 1963—1967. His measure of profits here is deviations from marginal cost pricing or the price:cost margin, that is, (price—marginal cost) /(marginal cost). He reports that while industries with larger four-firm concentration ratios also experience larger price:cost margins, the relationship does not hold for a subset of 33 old homogeneous-goods industries. That is, for these industries, increasing market concentration or power does not increase profits. Second, as with the result for market concentration, larger firm size increases profits for all firms except those in the older industries. Shepherd concludes that these results are due at least in part to increasing X- inefficiency accompanying increasing absolute size and power.

7.3.3. Food Systems Research Group (Market Share Again)

Bruce Marion and several of his colleagues at the Food Systems Research Group (1977) at the University of Wisconsin studied the relationship between market power, prices, and profits of 17 leading U.S. food chains in 36 metropolitan areas during the period 1970.-.1974. These 17 food chains operated approximately 52% of US chain stores and 6% of U.S. grocery stores in 1974. In addition, each of these 17 food chains, which included Safeway, A & P, Winn-Dixie, Lucky, Food Fair, Grand Union, Stop & Shop, and Albertsons, were among the nations 20 largest grocery chains in 1974. Profits were measured as a percentage of sales (PR/SA).

The authors compared an index of prices for an estimated "market basket" with profits, for various levels of market concentration and the firm's market share (FMS). Four-firm concentration ratio (4FCR) levels of 40%, 50%, 60%, and 70% were used; firm market shares of 10%, 25%, 40%, and 55% were also used. The expectation is that, for a given firm market share, increasing market concentration will increase both prices and profits. Increasing prices and profits are also expected when, for a given four-firm concentration ratio, the firm's market share increases. The data confirm this general relationship. For example, given an FMS of 10, the price index is 100.0, 101.0, 103.0, and 105.3 for 4FCRs of 40, 50, 60, and 70, respectively. At the same time, PR / SA was 0.37%, 0.99%, 1.22%, and 1.28%, respectively. On the other hand, at an FMS of 55, the price index for each of the four levels of the 4FCR was 103.6, 104.5, 106.5, and 108.9, respectively. At the same time, PR / SA was 2.71%, 3.33%, 3.56%, and 3.62%, respectively. A monotonic increase in both prices and profits as FMS increased for a given 4FCR is also evident in the data.

Prices and profits clearly rise with both the firm's market share and industry concentration. However, the data also show that prices rise faster than profits. At an FMS of 10 and a 4FCR of 40, the price index is 100.0 and PR / SA is 0.37. At an FMS of 55 and a 4FCR of 70, the price index is 108.9 and PR / SA is 3.62. In other words, prices rose by 8.9%, while profits rose by only 3.25 percentage points. IIad operating costs per dollar of sales been the same for these two cxtrcmc cases, then prices and profits would have increased by the same percentage. However, the data show that higher profits accounted for only 36.5% of the increase in prices (3.25/8.90). The remaining 63.5 percent is absorbed in higher operating expenses per dollar of sales. In other words, increased market power increases costs more than it does prices such that profits rise at a decreasing rate. The authors believe that XE theory provides at least one good explanation for the data; in particular, the findings that increased market power allows for higher prices, which in turn encourage firms to allow their costs to rise unnecessarily. The difference between the increases in prices and profits is a measure of X-inefficiency.

7.3.4. Pittman (X vs. Allocative Efficiency from a Merger)

Pittman (1990) disentangles the allocative and nonallocative (cost savings, and X-inefficiency plus rent-seeking) effects of the 1983 proposed merger between the Sante Fe (ATSF) and Southern Pacific (SP) railroads. The importance of this proposed merger is that it would have reduced from three to two the number of railcarriers between California and the Midwest. Since these two railcarriers are the only ones serving the corridor between Southern California, Arizona, New Mexico, Texas, and the Gulf ports, the merger would have created a "parallel combination." The six commodities representing the largest tonnage shipped—chemical products, "piggyback" traffic, fresh fruits and vegetables, grains, automobile products, and lumber—are all subject to higher freight charges due to the reduction of competition. The merger would thus be expected to create allocative inefficiency. And to the extent that the additional revenues lead to either rent-seeking or X-inefficiency, then the merger would also create nonallocative inefficiency. On the other hand, were unit costs to drop because of the merger then a nonallocative efficiency would be the result.

Whereas Leibenstein always spoke about X-inefficiency in terms of costs, Pittman rearranges the argument and discusses X-inefficiency in terms of the higher prices that would be received by the railroads. In figure 19, the merger is expected to reduce output from Q1 to Q2, and raise price from p1 to p2. Area A is the loss to the shippers because of higher prices, while area B represents lost output that was earning more than its marginal cost and hence is a loss to the railroads. Areas A and B are welfare losses to society. Area C may be a transfer from the shippers to the railroads and hence is not a welfare loss. However, to the extent that these higher revenues create either rent-seeking or X-inefficiency, then area C is a welfare loss. Finally, area D represents the reduction in operating costs due to the merger and is thus a welfare gain. Thus, Pittman has found another "home" for X-inefficiency.

Pittman calculates the size of these four areas based on assumptions about the size of the reductions in costs, the increase in prices, and the elasticity of demand. In all cases area D is less than the combined area A + B + C. To take one example, with an elasticity of -0.75 and a price increase of 22.5%, gross deadweight losses (A + B) are $98.6 million, the transfer (area C) is $336.9 mil, and the cost savings

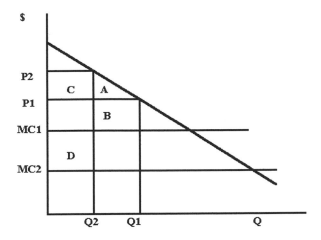

Figure 19. Railroad mergers and their welfare costs.

(area D) is $188.2 mil., or 4.3% of total variable costs. The deadweight loss *plus* the transfer (X-inefficiency and/or rent-seeking) exceeds the gains. The ICC's rejection of a merger which would create such a "large" amount of X-inefficiency/rent-seeking thus is a "rational" decision. Pittman did not attempt to identify the separate effects of X-inefficiency and rent-seeking.

7.3.5. Scherer (Cartels)

The effect of protection from international competition on X-efficiency is discussed by Frederick Scherer (1975) and his colleagues in their study of the economics of plant size and multiplant operations. One aspect of this study was comparing labor productivity in each of eight industries among firms in the U.S., United Kingdom, Canada, Sweden, France, and West Germany. For these eight industries, the authors report that, defining average U.S. labor productivity as having a value of 1.0, the average value of labor productivity for the other five countries was .47, .87, .75, .68, and .58, respectively. The explanation for these productivity differentials includes relative X-efficiency. The authors state,

> Our interviews provided considerable qualitative evidence that pure X-inefficiency was a significant cause of productivity differentials.... Executives in several British industries admitted that productivity had hovered at low levels because cartel arrangements fostered complacent attitudes. Sharp improvements were achieved in two cases after competition emerged following the cartel's dissolution.... A well-traveled American paint industry official reported that on his visits to European plants he saw 'lots of people

hanging around, unneeded,' especially in a nation with a history of carteli-
zation among paint makers (pp. 74—75).

7.3.6. Erickson (Price Fixing and X-inefficiency)

A similar story emerges in cases of price-fixing conspiracies in the gymnasium
seating and structural steel industries in the U.S. Evidence in these cases, which is
consistent with Scherer and with XE theory, is provided by W. Bruce Erickson
(1976). However, Erickson does not refer explicitly to XE theory in his article. In
gymnasium seating, price fixing under the Gymnasium Seating Council began in
1944 and lasted until 1953. In 1954 a new price-fixing arrangement was undertaken
under the direction of the Folding Gymnasium Seating Council. The Council
consisted of the six major producers of gym seating, who controlled 90% of industry
sales. The Council met monthly from April 1954 until early 1960, when it was
dissolved after an investigation by the Department of Justice. As with most cartels,
the arrangement was successful except during periods of falling demand. Prices
just prior to and just after the conspiracy period averaged $6.43 and $6.95 per
bleacher foot, respectively. During the conspiracy, the price averaged $9.06, or
30% to 40% above the other two periods. Per-foot costs during the conspiracy were
approximately 60% higher than before the conspiracy period because the conspiracy retarded innovation and cost-control programs and greatly increased wages
and salaries, especially for middle and upper-level managers. Post conspiracy costs
fell approximately 23%: the elimination of the cartel had a type of "shock effect"
on the producers.

In structural steel, a price-fixing conspiracy was operational from 1950 until the
end of 1962. The effect included prices being approximately 25% higher during
this period than two years either before or after. In addition, corporate profits were
typically twice the average for all U.S. industries during this period. Finally, costs
of producing structural steel increased by at least 10% due to the retardation of
technological change and productivity growth during this period. Inertia apparently set in and two post conspiracy entrants quickly expanded their market share
at the expense of the already established and conspirator firms.

7.3.7. Seiford, and Button and Weyman-Jones (Bureaucracy and
X-inefficiency)

Using a sample of nine empirical studies using the data envelope analysis (DEA)
method and published by Seiford (1990), Button and Weyman-Jones (1992) present
some evidence on the effect of "pressure for constraint concern" on X-efficiency.
The organizations were taken from a sample of U.S. and European financial
institutions, as well as government (public services) organizations. "High" pressure
for constraint concern was defined for those organizations described in the Seiford
paper as being either competitive, privately owned, or not severely regulated.
"Low" pressure denoted an organization described as bureaucratic or publicly
owned. For the nine studies, mean X-efficiency values ranged from .973 to .609.
For the three studies of bureaucratic organizations, the mean values were .906
(second from highest), .710 (fourth from lowest), and .609 (the lowest score).

Standard deviations of the mean scores ranged from .180 to .046. For the three bureaucratic organiza- tions the values were .180 (highest), .149 (second highest), and .144 (third highest). The minimum X-efficiency scores ranged from .840 to .180. For the three studies of bureaucratic organizations, the minimum values were .618 (third from highest), .329 (third from lowest), and .175 (second from lowest). The bureaucratic organizations thus had low mean X-efficiency values, low minimum values, and a higher dispersion of X-efficiency scores than the other organizations. The rank correlation between bureaucracy and mean X-efficiency score for the nine studies is -0.18. The evidence is consistent with what XE theory would predict.

7.3.8. Newhouse (Firm Size in Health Care)

Health care is also provided under various ownership forms. For example, while some doctors work as solo practitioners, others work in large outpatient clinics. Since the solo practitioner has the right to allocate all after-tax net revenues, he or she has obvious incentives to work longer hours and to control costs. The physician in the large outpatient clinic, however, is most likely to work under a cost-and-revenue sharing plan. As such the physician neither bears the full burden of his or her expenses nor enjoys the full benefits of his or her effort. Ceteris paribus, the physician is more likely to behave like a free-rider. In addition, large hospital out-patient clinics are more likely to receive government subsidies to cover costs, which will in turn protect the relatively high cost clinics from being "weeded out" by the market mechanism. Large outpatient clinics vis-à-vis solo practitioners are thus believed to suffer from a greater amount of X-inefficiency for two reasons: first, because the individual physician working in a large outpatient clinic has fewer incentives to minimize costs or maximize effort; and second, because inefficient clinics are less likely to be weeded out of the market. As in the Primeaux study, large outpatient clinics are believed to be able to benefit from economies of scale but to suffer from X-inefficiency.

Joseph Newhouse (1973) examined these issues using 1969 data from 20 solo practitioners or single specialty groups (private practice) and three large outpatient clinics. (The largest single specialty group consisted of five persons.) The data used for the private physicians were gathered by questionnaire, while those for the clinics were estimated by Newhouse.

While the data did show that the clinics had higher costs than did the noncost sharing physicians, the rationale for this finding often extended was that the higher costs among the clinics was due to their teaching program. The argument often presented took the following form: the only difference (an assumption) between the clinics and private practice is the existence of a teaching program; clinics are more costly to operate; and hence it follows that; teaching programs are costly to operate. Newhouse shows, however, that the higher costs among clinics had nothing to do with the clinic's teaching program. Newhouse attributes the higher costs among clinics to their relatively higher degree of X-inefficiency.

For example, Newhouse reports that overhead costs per visit for the outpatient clinics averaged $14.24, while for the private physicians it was $4.54. These overhead costs include billing, records, and clerical and nursing costs. Second, using OLS and controlling for number of office visits, and the square of the number of office visits, Newhouse reports that cost sharing increases per-office-visit salary costs by $2.55. On this basis he shows that per-office-visit salary costs are lower for a solo practitioner with 400 visits per month ($2.48) than for a cost-sharing group regardless of the number of office visits they receive per month. (For example, at 1000 visits, the per-office-visit salary cost is $2.85). In other words, the benefits of economies of scale are exhausted rather quickly, and thus the costs of X-inefficiency often exceed the benefits of economies of scale of large outpatient clinics. (This result is similar to Primeaux's finding that the gains in X-efficiency can outweigh those of economies of scale.)

Using the same model and the same OLS procedure, Newhouse estimated the effect of cost sharing on the major components of salary costs: medical records, appointment costs, billing, and rent. Thus, per-office-visit medical records increased by $0.24, per-office-appointment costs by $0.23, per-office-visit billing costs increased by $1.11, and per-visit-rent costs increased by $0.96. Third, for April 1967, solo practitioners worked an average of 218 hours, while those in large outpatient clinics worked an average of 197 hours. (Is this a case of allocative or X-in- efficiency?)

Newhouse also raises the important issue of whether the higher costs reflect higher *quality* health care. While he cannot provide a conclusive answer, he does note that 62% of the higher costs among clinics come from *paramedical* activities of obtaining a medical record, preparing a bill, and making an appointment. Thus he infers that higher cost reflect X-inefficiency and not primarily higher-quality health care.

7.4. Public vs. Private Ownership

7.4.1. Cook, Roll, and Kazakov (Privatization)

Cook, Roll, and Kazakov (1990) used the DEA method to estimate X-efficiency among 14 highway patrols in one district in Ontario, Canada. These patrols are responsible for the routine maintenance of Ontario's highways. Each patrol is responsible for a given number of lane kilometers of highway and performs more than 100 different activities. The outputs used for the 14 patrols reflect these activities. They are classified as Assignment Size Factors (ASF) and Average Traffic Serviced (ATS) indicators. ASF variables include surface and shoulder operations, right-of-way and median operations, and winter operations. ATS indicators are annual average daily traffic, as well as road length. The inputs are total expenditures and average pavement condition.

The multiple-factor output indicators mean that the DEA considers the special circumstances in which any individual patrol operates. And, by assigning weights to each output component for each patrol, it allows each patrol to be shown in its best possible light, i.e., DEA assigns weights so that each patrol receives its highest possible (relative) X-efficiency value. DEA also indicates the "peer group" to which that patrol is most similar and hence against which it should compare itself. The DEA estimates X-efficiency by solving the linear programming problem that maximizes the ratio of weighted outputs to weighted inputs and by constraining the sum of the weighted inputs to unity.

The authors specified two different models. In the "unbounded" model, the weights of both the outputs and the inputs were allowed to take any values whatsoever and to vary among the patrols (providing that the sum of the weighted inputs is unity). In the "bounded" model, the weights could only move within certain bounds. The efficiency ratings were very similar between both models. For the unbounded model, the ratings ranged between 1.0 (patrol numbers 1, 4, 8, 12, and 13) and 0.619 (patrol number 14), while for the bounded model it was 1.0 (patrol numbers 1, 4, and 8) to 0.614 (patrol number 14).

The authors then divided the patrols according to the degree of privatization, that is, the percentage of work carried out by private contractors. Private contractors are used for work that cannot be done by the regular patrol. Privatization was categorized by whether the percentage of privatization was more than (group A) or less than (group B) 20 percent. Group A had nine patrols, while group B had five. X-efficiency ratings among group A ranged from 1.0 (patrols 1, 2, and 8) to 0.646 (patrol 14), while group B values were 1.0 (patrol 4) to 0.803 (patrol 11; patrol 11's unbounded X-efficiency score was the identical 0.803). The authors thus note that grouping the 14 patrols by the degree of privatization (as in the did) made little difference to the X-efficiency ratings, and thus privatization does not significantly affect X-efficiency. A closer examination with different ways of measuring privatization is certainly warranted.

The power of DEA is further illustrated by examining the various scores for patrol 14. Its "bounded" score when compared with the other 13 patrols using common weights for all patrols was 0.586. Its bounded score when it was compared with all other 13 patrols using individual weights for each patrol was 0.614. The difference of .028 is due to the assignment of individual weights. Its bounded score when it was compared only against other group A patrols was 0.646. The difference between 0.646 and 0.614—.032—is explained by privatization. Finally, its maximum possible score is 1.0. The difference—0.354—is the "unexplained" residual. Clearly, in this case much more work needs to be done in order to explain X-efficiency among Ontario's highway patrols.

7.4.2. Bruggink (Public vs. Privately—Owned Water Companies)

Water utilities, whether private or publicly owned, are regulated and subject to rate-of-return regulation. These regulations, as we have alluded to before, have at least two effects that will hamper cost control. First, the control of profits by the regulatory agency reduces the incentive for the owners to monitor costs. Since the owners cannot wholly capture the profits, it is expected that they will not strive to produce them. Second, the cost-plus nature of rate-of-return regulation reduces the manager's incentives to minimize costs.

Managers of either private or publicly owned utilities also face pressure to be X-efficient. Managers of a privately owned utility must achieve some level of X-efficiency (profits) or face the threat of a job loss. Managers of a publicly owned utility face the same threat if their decisions visibly hamper service to the public. However, the owners (taxpayers) of publicly owned utilities may not have the same incentive to monitor management as would private- sector owners. Several researchers, including Thomas Bruggink, believe that managers of a publicly owned utility face another incentive for X-efficiency, That is, operating in an "unfriendly private enterprise environment," these managers must prove their skills as managers and the benefits of public ownership by managing efficiently operated utilities.

Bruggink tested this idea using a sample of 77 public and nine privately owned water utilities in 1960. Costs were measured as operating costs per million gallons of water produced. The data were supplied by the American Water Works Association. In testing for the effects of ownership form, Bruggink controlled for production, environmental, distribution, factor cost, and regula -tory factors. These factors include quantity of water produced, source of water and amount of treatments used, type of customer served, population density, wage rates, whether regulation is lax or stringent, and whether or not the publicly owned utility is regulated by the same agency that regulates the privately owned firm. The results of his regression analysis showed that the net effect of public ownership is to reduce average variable costs by an average of 24%. His data also showed that ownership form did not affect the slope of the cost curves. In other words, while the slope of both the average variable and marginal cost curves are identical for the public and privately owned firm, the cost curves for the publicly owned firms would be lower than that for the private firms. Despite the fact that Bruggink offers no evidence that publicly owned firms face more pressure to be X-efficient, his data are consistent with his hypothesis.

7.4.3. Tyler (Public vs. Private Again)

Tyler (1979) estimated an industry production frontier for 16 plastics and 22 steel firms in Brazil in 1971. Both industries at the time enjoyed a relatively large amount of effective protection from foreign competition. As a result, one would predict that (X-)inefficient firms would be able to remain in business. Tyler's sample of plastics firms included 11 domestically owned firms and five foreign owned firms. Among his 22 steel firms, 15 were domestically owned of which five were publicly owned, and seven were foreign owned.

Deviations from the industry production frontier were large in both industries. In the plastics industry, the average efficiency rating for the 16 firms was 0.48, while for the five foreign firms it was 0.58. Thus, on average each plastics firm could produce about twice as much as it did with its own inputs if it were as (X-)efficient as the most efficient firms in the industry. For the 22 steel firms, the average efficiency rating was 0.62. For the five publicly owned firms, the average figure was 0.56. For the seven foreign firms the figure was 0.72. In 1971, publicly owned steel firms accounted for 54% of steel production. One of Tyler's interpretations of the data is, "This can be considered as evidence of substantial X-inefficiency" (p. 486). These X-inefficiencies are larger for both domestic and publicly owned firms, vis-à-vis foreign firms.

7.4.4. Gillis (Public vs. Private Again)

Malcolm Gillis (1982) also found a relatively large amount of X-inefficiency among publicly owned tin-mining firms in both Bolivia and Indonesia. Gillis's evidence, however, consists of first hand reports of activities within these firms. His examples of X-inefficiency include the resistance to known and economically efficient technology for six years because "...things have never been done this way" (p. 160). Another example followed a reduction in export taxes for low-concentrate tin in 1973. In 1973 low-concentrate tin accounted for 45% of output among publicly owned firms and 43% among privately owned firms. One year later, the private firms increased their share of low-concentrate tin to 94% while the public firms reduced their share to 17%. Gillis reports that the public firms simply continued to carryout previous plans with out regard to the new tax incentives, while private firms did not regard these incentives. The public firms were caught in an "inert area." Public firms also suffered from relatively obscure accounting techniques that were based more on "ex-post income determination" than on generating information for current decision making, as well as a lack of delegated authority, which resulted in extensive downtime. Strict limits on compensation based on performance and "social responsibility" stated in ambiguous terms also contributed to costs in excess of minimum levels and above those privately owned firms.

Gillis contrasts these examples with cases of allocative inefficiency. The latter is felt when, for example, price controls on energy in Indonesia and Bolivia resulted in investment projects that were overly energy intensive when evaluated at world, not subsidized, energy prices. Another example arises when the value of domestic currency is kept artificially high, which encourages a consumption and capital mix favoring imports. In the case of allocative inefficiency, there is a change in output or input mix along a production frontier. With X-inefficiency, the firm is producing inside its frontier.

7.5. Other Ownership Studies

7.5.1 Bradley and Gelb (Cooperatives vs. Noncoops)

A somewhat different type of study from those already presented was a comparison of privately owned cooperatives, known as Mondragon, in the Basque region of northern Spain, with non- cooperatives in the same region. While Bradley and Gelb (1981) do not report the relative economic performance of the cooperatives and noncooperatives, they do cite the work of Thomas and Logan (1982), who have reported data showing that the cooperatives have generally outperformed the noncooperatives of the region when measured by productivity, growth of sales, and profits. I will simply assume the Thomas and Logan results and proceed to report some related results from the Bradley and Gelb study.

This study is one of only a very small number that distinguished "external" from "internal" factors affecting firm performance. In their study external factors refer to the level of payments and job security, while internal factors include the "Basqueness" of the enterprise, its cooperative nature per se, and working conditions. One difference between employee-owners of the Mondragon cooperatives and employees of the more traditional private enterprise firms (control group) is that while only 15% of cooperative employee-owners ranked payments as either first or second in their priorities, 37% of the control group indicated this about wage payments. The cooperative nature of the firm ranked easily as the most important characteristic among cooperative employee-owners, while among the control group, job security ranked number one and working conditions number two.

Bradley and Gelb also report that, vis-à-vis the control group, the employee-owners perceive a much smaller gulf between management and labor (supportive vertical relations), show much less support for trade unions, have a much greater sense of participating in important firm decisions, feel more strongly that the success of their enterprise depends upon the work effort of the individual employees, and feel that peer group pressure (horizontal relations) favors hard work. In conclusion, Bradley and Gelb find the environment of the cooperatives to have enhanced X-efficiency (as measured by the various performance measures discussed in Thomas and Logan). As might be expected from this, cooperative employee-owners indicated a much greater reluctance to change jobs because of wages, vis-à-vis the control group.

7.5.2. Altman, and Kiyokawa on Wages and X-(in)efficiency

Altman's (1988) paper focuses on the effect of wage levels on the economic development of Quebec and Ontario between 1870 and 1910. The issue is whether high wages are a hindrance to development, income growth, and employment—the "high wage/slow growth" thesis first argued by Arthur Lewis (1954). Altman builds on XE theory to build an alternative thesis, that high wages encourage firms to enhance X-efficiency as a way of offsetting high wages. In effect, high wages encourage higher X-efficiency, thus lowering unit labor costs to the level of the low- wage firm, region, or country.

Data from the manufacturing sector of high-wage Ontario and low-wage Quebec support this "high wage—high X-efficiency" thesis. First, a comparison of current dollar manufacturing value-added per capita shows Quebec producing 87.5% of Ontario's level in 1870 but only 75.3% in 1910. Second, in constant-dollars, the figures were 86.9%, and 72.5%, respectively. Third, the growth of constant-dollar manufacturing value-added was higher in Ontario (3.42 vs. 3.14), as was per-capita growth (2.28 vs. 1.80). Fourth, despite higher wages, manufacturing- employment growth was higher in Ontario (2.57 vs. 2.24). Fifth, unit labor costs in Quebec were 89.7% of Ontario's in 1870 but 104.6% of Ontario's by 1910. Sixth, despite lower wages in Quebec, constant-dollar savings per employee in Quebec was 90.7% of that of Ontario in 1870 and 84.4% of Ontario's by 1910. Ontario's superior performance despite its relatively high wages is possible because labor effort—X-efficiency—must often be induced. The need to stay competitive in the face of high wages is one such inducement.

Kiyokawa (1991) identified three aspects of the silk-reeling industry in Japan as having been crucial to its development: the (piece-rate) wage system, the training system, and the dormitory system. The majority of employees in this industry were young, single, unmarried females from rural areas. Transforming these unskilled workers into semiskilled workers was a function of six factors: individual aptitude, length of service, education, production control, training, and coercion. The latter five factors can be influenced by management; X-efficiency in this industry will be the outcome of the success of shaping these five factors.

Every worker's performance was measured daily according to the quantity and quality of reeled silk, and then converted into a productivity score that measured the individual's output as a deviation from the average of all workers' output. In this way the total wage bill could be kept constant, with workers "fighting" for their share of the "wages fund." Management encouraged competition and even held "production races" among the workers. Eventually, a minimum guaranteed wage replaced the straight piece-rate system. The wage system "encouraged" X-efficiency. The dormitory system also encouraged X-efficiency by fostering group cohesion and discipline, by reducing the inertia of rural life, and by helping to bridge the gap between principles and agents. However, the system accomplished this at the cost of personal freedom and privacy. By contrast, Leibenstein never envisioned increases in welfare-enhancing X-efficiency as coming at the cost of either freedom and privacy or one's personal health (via the straight piece-rate system).

7.5.3. Vining and Boardman (Cooperatives vs. Noncooperatives.)

Is competition per se more important than whether a firm is publicly owned or privately owned? Vining and Boardman (1992) show that ownership form is an important determinant of both X-efficiency and allocative efficiency. The authors come to this conclusion by estimating a structure—performance relationship using 1986 data on the 500 largest nonfinancial Canadian corporations. Ownership is measured as either state owned, mixed enterprises, cooperatives, or private companies. Other independent variables control for industry characteristics and concentration, market share, assets, sales, and number of employees (firm size). Performance is measured as both X-efficiency (or technical efficiency) and profits. In turn, X-efficiency is measured as both sales per employee and sales per asset, while profits are measured as return on assets and sales and net income.

With regard to both X-efficiency and return on assets, the authors report that cooperatives are the most X-efficient and the most profitable, followed by private companies, mixed enterprises, and finally state owned enterprises. On the other hand, industry concentration measured by the four-firm concentration ratio was not related to either X-efficiency or profitability. Unfortunately, the authors do not seem to offer much of an explanation for these results. Needless to say the findings are consistent with those of Bradley and Gelb.

7.5.4. Junankar (Ownership vs. Leasing Farm Land)

The desire to increase the performance of farmers, especially in less developed countries, has evoked two different responses or proposed solutions: socialization of land and placing ceilings on land holdings and transferring ownership rights to tenant farmers. On the one hand, large farms are sometimes believed to be more disciplined toward profit maximization. In addition, the owners of large farms may have better information and hence are more likely to employ the latest technology; they may also have better access to the often imperfect and undeveloped capital markets. On the other hand, placing a ceiling on farm size assumes that, beyond some point, further increases in the size of the farm does not increase either productivity or other measures of performance. Transferring ownership rights to tenants assumes that ownership of the land being worked improves the performance of the farmer. Not being able to capture the full returns to their own effort, and having greater uncertainty about the future use of the land, tenants are likely to invest less in more productive capital but that requires a longer gestation period before the farmer realizes any returns.

Junankar (1976) examined the question of farm size and ownership form on X-efficiency for farms in Punjab, India for the period 1968—1970. Ownership form was measured by the amount of land leased as a percentage of total land size. Thus, a farmer owning more of the land on which he or she works represents "more" ownership. (X)-inefficiency was measured by the difference in the value of the main crop—wheat— produced from given inputs by owners and tenants. Junankar thus measured the effects of ownership by comparing output on farms using a similar amount of labor (hours), fertilizer, tractors and oxen. His statistical analysis was done for small (less than 25 acres) and large (more than 25 acres) farms. His results showed that farm size per se does not affect X-efficiency. That is, large farms do not produce more output per unit of input than small farms. However, among large farms, greater ownership increases X-efficiency. That is, on large farms, greater ownership increases output from a given quantity of inputs.

7.5.5. Lin (Collective vs. Individual Land Ownership)

Lin (1992) examined the effect of decollectivization on Chinese agricultural growth among 28 of 29 Chinese provinces (Tibet excluded) over the period 1970—1987. The period 1978—1984 witnessed dramatic growth and coincided with the change from the collective farm system to the "individual household-based farming system" or "household responsibility system." To test the effects of this change and others on agricultural growth, Lin utilizes a Cobb—Douglas function with four conventional inputs—land, labor, capital, and fertilizer—and six to capture the period's reforms, including the change in ownership form. OLS, GLS, and stochastic frontier specifications all show a positive and statistically significant effect of the change from collective to individual ownership on the constant-dollar value of agricultural output. Lin concludes that production is not an engineering relationship whereby inputs are automatically converted into maximum outputs, but that factors such as ownership form affect the intensity with which inputs are used, and hence affect technical or X-efficiency.

Lin also estimates the contribution of various factors to agricultural growth for the periods 1978—1984 and 1984—1987. For the first period the growth was 42.23%. Of this, inputs accounted for 19.34% (46% of 42.23%), productivity accounted for 20.54% (49%), and the residual accounted for 2.35% (5% of 42.23%). Of the increase in productivity of 20.54%, the change in ownership form accounted for 19.80%, larger than the contribution of the four conventional inputs. For the latter period, the total growth was only 4.21%; the change in ownership program had already occurred and hence did not contribute to growth. The four conventional inputs contributed -0.42%, productivity 2.05%, and the residual 2.58%. Overall, the data support the X-efficiency hypothesis.

7.5.6. Schieve (Land Ownership by Government Monopoly)

Schieve's (1988) study of X-efficiency focuses on the 23 sugar mills in the Taiwan sugar industry from 1976 to 1983, and more specifically the role that the Taiwan Sugar Company (TSC) has played in the industry. TSC is a fully owned government monopoly, accounted for more than 50% of Taiwan's exports and the county's largest corporation during the 1950s. Since the mid- 1970s higher costs and lower sugar prices have led to consistent losses, reduced output, and a diversification into nonsugar products. In fact, by 1984 sugar production was no longer TSC's main product.

To measure X-efficiency among TSC's 23 mills, Schieve fit a frontier production using direct labor, indirect labor, and fixed capital as inputs. This measure yields the ratio of (actual / maximum) output for each mill. Of the 23 mills, one mill operated at 80% to 90% efficiency, seven at 70% to 79%, four at 60% to 69%, four at 50% to 59%, and seven between 40% to 49%. Approximately one third of the mills operated at an X-efficiency level of 70% or above, while another one third operated at below 50%. Schieve then used the mill's efficiency rating as a dependent variable in a regression equation. The independent variables include the percentage of land owned by TSC, the educational background of the plant manager, the mix of raw and refined sugar being produced (refined sugar requires more time and control), the region of the mill (affects soil conditions and climate), the quality of sugarcane, the utilization rate of the mill, its output capacity, and an exogenous technological-change variable.

His results show that a greater percentage of land owned by the government monopoly reduces X-efficiency. Schieve interprets this finding to mean that individual incentives improve X-efficiency, whereas government enterprise allows inertia and X-inefficient mills to continue to operate. Second, managers with an education in either agronomy or business are associated with more X-efficient mills. This finding is similar to ones reported by Anderson and Frantz (1985), and Page (1980). Third, the closer a mill operates to capacity, the higher is its level of

X-efficiency. In particular, a mill operating at 80% of capacity is 25 percentage points more X-efficient than a mill operating at 40%. Fourth, raw sugar mills average approximately 13 percentage points more X-efficient than the more troublesome refined sugar mills.

7.5.7. Timmer (Owner vs. Tenant Farmers)

Timmer (1971) estimated a Cobb—Douglas frontier production frontier for U.S. agriculture by *state*, where output was measured as the dollar value of agriculture production for the period 1960—1967. Capital was measured as current farm operating expense deflated by a price index. Land was measured by its sales value, differences in the productivity of land were assumed to be reflected in market prices. Labor was measured as total farm employment, i.e., family and hired workers.

Eliminating the most efficient 2% of firms in each state in order to reduce the bias inherent in measuring efficiency by using "outliers" as the basis upon which to measure inefficiency, Timmer reports that South Dakota had the highest efficiency (Q/Q^*) ranking at .991, while West Virginia had the lowest ranking at .810. The average X, or technical efficiency[2] ranking was 93.4. That is, on average, each state was only 6.6% below the production frontier.

Adjusting for measurement problems, this figure is believed to be reduced to 3%—4%. Of course, aggregating the data by state does not allow observation of intrastate, interfarm differences in technical or X-efficiency. Timmer recognizes both this possibility and the inability of the data to reflect X-inefficiency within states.

Timmer then used these efficiency rankings as the dependent variable regressed against several independent variables in order to predict efficiency. One of the independent variables was the number of tenant farmers as a percentage of all farmers. The results of the regression analysis showed that the state's efficiency ranking increased when the percentage of tenant farmers increased. Timmer commented that this might "...be associated with the extra effort and motivation of the young farmers in the non-southern states who are attempting to save enough to buy their own farms" (p. 791). Increased X-efficiency among tenant farmers due to their effort and motivation is thus a conclusion of the study. While many other factors could cause deviations from the production frontier, Timmer choose to give the data an X-efficiency interpretation.

Timmer also estimated the industry production function using an OLS regression technique. This technique provides an "average" production function rather than the frontier production function. These results differed from those for the frontier production function in several interesting ways. First, the capital coefficient on the frontier function is up to 30% higher thanover that reported by the

---

2   For similarities and differences between the concepts of X and technical efficiency, see
     Leibenstein (1977).

average function. Second, the labor coefficient on the frontier function rises between 40% and 70% over that reported by the average function. Timmer interprets this to mean that the best farms use relatively less labor and hence experience a higher marginal productivity of labor. This, in turn, may be due to good management adopting relatively high capital intense technologies.

(These results seem inconsistent with those of Junankar. However, in the U.S. where capital markets are more highly developed, where both land owners and tenant farmers have more equal access to those markets, and where upward mobility is more commonplace, tenants are more likely to be motivated to save in order to purchase their own farm. India, with its more traditional society and less well-developed capital markets may not make such opportunities available to tenant farmers. In addition, Junankar noted in his article that tenants are moved from time to time in order to prevent the possibility of their receiving ownership rights. The unwillingness of the tenant in India to give as much effort as the owner may thus be as under- standable as the willingness of the tenant farmer in the Timmer sample to give more effort than an owner. Different opportunities available to tenants in the U.S. and India may thus help produce different incentive systems favoring the former group.)

7.5.8. Anderson and Frantz (Foreign vs. Domestic Ownership)

Joan Anderson and I (1985) estimated an industry production frontier for 24 textile firms from Tijuana and Mexicalli, Mexico. The average level of X-efficiency, measured by the ratio of actual to potential value-added, for the entire sample was 0.469, with a standard deviation of 0.332 and maximum and minimum values of 1.0 and 0.013, respectively. The firm's X-efficiency score was then used as a dependent variable, yielded several major results. First, the ownership variable—the percentage of capital owned by Mexican nationals—shows that Mexican owned firms are less X-efficient than US-owned firms. Second, firms that pay higher wages to their technicians are more X-efficient. Because technicians are a very scarce resource, firms that pay them significantly more than unskilled workers are able to secure their services and thereby produce closer to their production frontier. Third, X-efficiency increases as the age of the firm increases through approximately none years, and then decreases. Fourth, firms that experience larger fluctuations in the month-to-month demand for their products are more X-efficient. Consistent with the concept of the "inert area," firms with larger fluctuations are forced to manage themselves more closely, whereas firms with steady demand are more likely to sink into their inert area or comfort zone.

7.6. Conclusions

The studies reviewed in this chapter seem to reveal differential motivation toward X-efficiency according to both market structure and organizational form. While most of the studies report findings that would be predicted by XE theory, some—for example, Bruggink—(implicitly) raise the important issue of capturing all the pressures on employees for X-efficient behavior. This issue will be taken up again in chapter 9. In the next chapter, we will review studies of input ratios, and international trade on X-efficiency.

8

EMPIRICAL EVIDENCE: INPUT RATIOS AND INTERNATIONAL TRADE

8.1. Introduction

Our final chapter on the empirical evidence for XE theory will be concerned with the firm's use of capital and labor and the effects of international trade—exports and protection from foreign competition—on X-efficiency. Data from these studies cover numerous countries including Australia, Bangladesh, Brazil, Canada, Ghana, Great Britain, India, Kenya, Korea, Malaysia, Mexico, Norway, Pakistan, the Philippines, Sweden, Tanzania, and Thailand.

8.2. Input Ratios

The choice of appropriate technology is particularly relevant for many less developed countries in which both high unemployment and the use of capital-intensive technologies coexist. Appropriate technology and the distinction between allocative-price-inefficiency and X-(in)efficiency are reviewed briefly in figure 20. Given isocost curve CC' and isoquant Q1, a firm would be allocatively-price-efficient if it produced at point A where relative factor prices (W/R) were equal to relative marginal products (MPl/MPk). At point A, the firm is also X-efficient because it is producing Q1 on the isoquant or production frontier. That is, it is using a minimum amount of inputs to produce Q1.

At point B, however, the firm is allocatively-price-inefficient because although it is on the frontier, it is not equating relative factor prices with relative factor marginal productivities. We can measure allocative-price-inefficiency as OB/OF. On the other hand, at point D, the firm is allocatively-price-efficient but X-inefficient because, although it is using the correct factor combination (points A and D define the same capital/labor ratio, since are both located along the same "ray"), it is using more inputs than are technologically necessary in order to produce output Q1. The degree of X-inefficiency at point D is OD/OA. At point E, the firm is both allocatively-price, OG/OH, and X-inefficient, OE/OG.

8.2.1. Lecraw (K/L in Thailand Manufacturing)

How extensive are price (allocative) and X-inefficiencies in less developed countries (LDCs)? Don Lecraw (1977, 1979) provides estimates of both types of

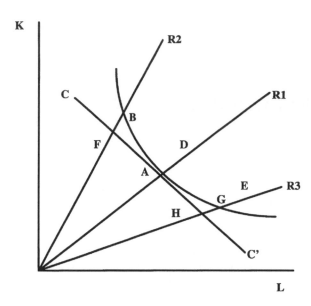

Figure 20. Appropriate technology, allocative-price inefficiency
and X-inefficiency.

inefficiencies for a sample of 400 light manufacturing firms in 12 four-digit
industries in Thailand for the period 1962—1974. All the firms in his sample had
recently made a substantial new investment in Thailand during this period. Therefore, some of the data are based on *projected* - ex ante—values, i.e., capital, labor,
and the projected profits from the investment. These and the other data used were
collected during an interview with each firm, in which an extensive questionnaire
was administered to 200 of these firms while a shorter questionnaire was administered to the remaining 200 firms. Lecraw's estimate's for X-inefficiency were
gained by estimating a constant elasticity of substitution (CES) production function. A nonlinear form of the CES production function was used that does not
require assuming profit-maximizing behavior. Once the parameters of the CES
function are known, a comparison can be made between each of the following:
actual and potential outputs, the actual and the cost-minimizing capital:labor (K/L)
ratios (which requires knowledge of the input prices), and the actual and the
cost-minimizing level of total costs.

Using the CES production function, Lecraw estimated the potential output (Q*)
for each firm and then compared it to actual output(Q). This ratio (Q/Q*) he called
D1. He then aggregated over all firms in the industry to arrive at an industry value
for D1. A value of D1 less than 1.0 indicates that the firm is producing less than
the maximum possible output with given inputs. In figure 20, this is shown by a
firm being at a point such as D. Since point D represents a firm using an amount
of inputs in excess of what is technologically required in order to produce a given
amount of output, it also must represent a firm producing less than the maximum

possible output from those inputs represented by that point D. Values of D1 less than 1.0 thus measures the extent of technical (X)inefficiency.

Allocative-price-inefficiency was estimated by taking the ratio of the actual capital to labor ratio (K/L) to the capital:labor ratio that would minimize costs (K*/L*). This ratio— (K/L) / (K*/L*)—he called D2. If D2 is greater than 1.0, then the firm's capital-labor ratio is excessively capital intensive. That is, its actual K/L ratio is in excess of that which, given input prices, would minimize costs. Recall that, because these data are ex ante, a value of D2 different from 1.0 does not indicate allocative-price-inefficiency due to changing input prices. Since the data are ex ante any deviations from a cost-minimizing input ratio must have come from some other source. In Figure 20, the resulting allocative-price-inefficiency is measured by the ratio OB/OF. If D2 is less than 1.0, then the K/L ratio is excessively labor intensive. In figure 20, allocative-price-inefficiency due to excessive labor intensity is represented by the ratio OG/OH.

Finally, allocative-price and X-inefficiency were combined by taking the ratio of actual total costs for the technology utilized to the minimum total costs that would be incurred if the most efficient technology were chosen. This ratio he called D3. If a firm chooses appropriate technology (point A in figure 20) then D1, D2, and D3 would each have a value of 1.0.

Firms in Thailand clearly had a choice of which K/L ratio to use, as evidenced by the fact that the most capital-intensive firms in any industry had a K/L ratio almost four times greater than the least capital intensive firms. The values of D1, D2, and D3 also indicate the existence of significant amounts of both allocative-price and X-inefficiency. For example, the average value of D1 across the 12 industries was 0.74. That is, on average, each firm was producing approximately 25% less than it could have with its existing inputs. The lowest value recorded for any firm was 0.44. The range of industry averages was 0.62 to 0.88.

The average value for D2 across the 12 industries was 1.71, indicating that overly capital- intensive technologies were employed on average. The lowest and highest values recorded for any firm were 0.38 and 3.75, respectively. The range of industry averages was 1.25 to 2.02. The average value for D3 across the 12 industries was 1.60. That is, costs exceeded technologically minimum levels by 60%. The highest value recorded for any firm was 2.42, while the range of industry values were 1.41 to 1.82.

Lecraw then attempted to explain the values of D1, D2, and D3 with a set of (independent) variables that included expected profits from an investment at the time the investment was made; the number of firms in the industry, reflecting product market competition; whether the firm was owner managed or managed by a hired manager; the degree to which the firm was owned locally; and whether the manager had experience in an LDC.

The results of Lecraw's regression analysis for D1 shows that each of the following increases the value of D1, that is, brings the firm closer to its production frontier or increases X-efficiency: lower expected profits, a larger number of competing firms, a firm whose manager is NOT the owner, and a manager with experience in an LDC. Lecraw's results for D2 show that each of the following increases the value of D2, that is, results in the use of a more excessive capital-intensive technology: higher expected profits, less product market competition, a firm that is owner managed, and a firm whose manager lacks experience in an LDC. Not surprisingly, the results for D3 are almost identical with those of D2 and show that each of the following increased the value of D3, that is, increases total costs above minimum levels: higher expected profits, less product market competition, a firm that is owner managed, and a firm whose manager lacks experience in an LDC. Local ownership was shown to reduce the value of D1 and to increase the values of D2 and D3, but not in a statistically significant manner.

The effect of an increased number of firms—that is, for more competitive environments to increase X-efficiency—is not surprising. Neither is the result that lower expected profits increases X-efficiency: lower expected profits force the firm's employees out of their inert areas and require them to place more attention on minimizing costs and producing closer to the production frontier. The result that is not predicted a priori by XE theory is the one showing that owner-managed firms are *less* X-efficient. Lecraw's explanation of this result was derived from his interviews with company managers. It seems that owner-managers were not only interested in profits, and hence in being X-efficient, but also in the satisfaction derived from using modern Western technology, which entails some cost disadvantages. This effect has come to be known as engineering-man satisfactions, a term coined by Louis Wells (1973). Thus, although the owner knew that he or she was interested in more than profits, the hired manager did not know this and tended to assume that the owner's interest was merely to maximize profits. In fact, according to Lecraw, "absentee" owners were less interested in engineering-man satisfactions than were owner-managers. Despite the fact that the hired manager may receive engineering-man satisfactions, his or her performance was being judged by an absentee owner whose interests were otherwise. Overall, the data indicate that the gains from increased X-efficiency are substantial.

Capacity Utilization Once Again. Don Lecraw (1978) estimated the effects of competition, ownership form, expected profits, and other variables not only on (Q/Q^*) and deviations of the K/L ratio and total costs from their minimum values, but also on capacity utilization. Lecraw measured capacity utilization as the percentage of 8760 hours during which the plant was operated each year (8760 being the total number of hours in a year). The object of this study was to understand how the factors discussed above affected desired (D) capacity utilization rates so that he could compare this rate with both the actual (A) and profit maximizing (P) rates. For the entire sample of 200 firms the desired, actual, and profit-maximizing capacity utilization rates were 30%, 27%, and 67%, respectively.

Lecraw then used the difference (P-D) as a proxy measure for X-inefficiency. He reports that although "economic"variables such as technology, input prices, wage differentials for second and third shift, and output rates are more than adequate to explain the profit-maximizing rate of capacity utilization, they are not as powerful in explaining the desired rate. To explain both D and (P-D), Lecraw makes use of XE theory and utilizes many of the variables discussed above. Results from his regression analysis shows that among "low"profit firms (those with a return on equity less than 25%), D is lower when expected profits from a one-shift operation are higher and when the firm is owned either by a Thai or by a non-LDC citizen. For these firms, (P-D) is larger when expected profits from a one-shift operation are higher. Among "high" profit firms (return on equity greater than 25%), D is lower when expected profits are higher, when there are fewer firms (less competition) in the industry, when the perceived risk of multishift operations is higher, when the firm is owner managed, and when the firm is owned by either a Thai or a non-LDC citizen. For these firms, (P-D) is larger when expected profits are larger, when there are more firms in the industry, when the perceived risk of multishift operation is greater, when the firm is owner managed, and when the firm is owned by either a Thai or non-LDC citizen.

In addition, "noneconomic" variables play a larger role in both D and (P-D) among high-profit firms than among low-profit firms. Earning high profits, the former firms would seem to have the discretion to allow such factors to be more influential in their decisions. Based on our discussion of Lecraw's other study, the result that deviations from profit maximization are higher when expected profits are higher and competition is less is not surprising.

8.2.2. Gregory and James. (Vintage Capital Model in Australia)

The effect of embodied technical progress on estimates of X and technical efficiency is certainly an important one. However, this consideration of embodied technical progress already implies not only that technical change is embodied in the latest technology but also that this technology is being used to its capacity. At the least, this consideration implies that the newest capital should be accompanied by higher labor productivity than that accompanying older capital. This is the assumption of these "vintage" capital models. These models imply that X-inefficiency is zero, that is, labor productivity is generated in a machinelike manner, and is almost "predetermined" once the quantity and vintage of the capital stock is known. Once again, we return to the neoclassical production function where the actual output is assumed to be the maximum output and is determined by labor, capial inputs, and technology.

Gregory and James (1973) tested the vintage capital model with a sample of 116 new factories from 46 Australian industries. These factories began operation between 1953 and 1958; Gregory and James' analysis of the vintage capital model concentrated on 1957—1958, but included only factories operating during 1956—1957. New factories were defined as those built on new sites. Data were collected by a questionnaire that was returned at the discretion of the appropriate employee of the factory. As in the case of the Shapiro and Muller paper, while the Gregory and James paper is not about ownership form it is concerned with one of the topics at hand: the relative contribution of physical capital and X-efficiency factors in productivity differentials.

The vintage model was tested by comparing, within each industry, the labor productivity figures in new factories with those of the existing factories. Labor productivity was measured as value added per worker. Because of multiproduct factories, the more preferred measure—physical productivity per worker—could not be estimated.

Gregory and James' first test of the vintage capital model was done by comparing variations in labor productivity across new factories within each industry. Variations in labor productivity is always to be expected because of (rational) differences in the capital:labor ratio due to, for example, different (rational) expectations in future prices, misspecifications in the industry, or different product mixes within different factories. Given these considerations, however, the vintage capital model would still predict that variations in labor productivity across new factories would be relatively small as compared to variations in labor productivity across all factories.

Such comparisons could be made in 25 industries. In half of these the labor productivity in the most productive new factory was more than three times that in the least productive new factory. Although a comparison with variations in older factories could not be made, the authors conclude that this range is probably greater than what one would expect from the vintage model. An explanation of these results is perhaps made clearer when the reader considers that, because only new factories are being compared, the variation in labor productivity is being "standardized" for the vintage of the factory. As a result these variations reflect, according to the authors, several nonvintage factors including X-efficiency.

Gregory and James' second test was done by comparing labor productivity in new factories with that of the industry average. The prediction of the vintage model is that labor productivity in the new factories should exceed the industry average. The more important is the contribution of capital vintage vis-à-vis nonvintage factors to labor productivity, the greater should be the disparity between labor productivity in new factories as opposed to the industry average. The authors thus divided new factory productivity by the industry average. Of the 46 industry groups, new factory productivity exceeded the industry average 24 times while in 22 of the industries the reverse was reported. Furthermore, of the 116 factories, 59 reported labor productivity exceeding the industry average. Therefore, new factory productivity exceeds the industry average in approximately half the cases. For all 46 industries, the ratio (new-factory labor productivity / industry-average labor productivity) was 1.103, suggesting that vintage effects are operative.

Gregory and James also tested for the possibility that strong vintage effects in a few select (large) industries could make the vintage effects for the economy as a whole more significant than the 1.103 figure cited above. They performed this test by taking a weighted average of the ratio (new-factory labor productivity / industry-average labor productivity), where the weights reflect the relative size (employment and output) of the industry. For the entire 46-industry sample, the ratio is 1.15 (employment-based weights) and 1.18 (output-based weights). Since economies of scale are expected to be relatively more important in large industries, this figure probably overestimates the effects of vintage capital. However, regard-less of this factor, proponents of the vintage model such as Salter (1966) suggest that labor productivity differentials of 50% to 100% in favor of new factories should typically be found.

Two other considerations should be mentioned. First, it is possible that new factory productivity is less than the industry average because of learning and "settling-in" time requirements before maximum efficiency is reached. The authors tested this possibility by calculating the ratio (productivity *growth* of new factories / industry- average productivity growth) between 1956—1957 and 1957—1958. If learning and settling-in are not significant factors in relative productivity growth among new factories, then this ratio should be randomly distributed around 1.0. Among the 37 industries for which such a ratio could be calculated, 18 reported this ratio to be less than 1.0. Among the 116 factories, 48% reported productivity growth less than the industry average. Thus, for this sample, learning and settling-in do not appear to be significant obstacles for a new factory to overcome.

The second consideration is that differences in capacity utilization between new and older factories may make any comparisons difficult to interpret. The authors report that capacity utilization among new factories was approximately 80%. For this time period, this figure is either typical or larger than expected. In other words, capacity utilization was not seen as a factor tht would bias the results. The authors thus conclude that new factories do not embody the best technology and/or that other nonvintage factors such as X-efficiency are as important if not more so in determining factory productivity.

8.2.4. Shen (Technological Diffusion and X-efficiency)

Shen (1973) sought to explain changes in output, capital, and labor as a result of firm size, technological diffusion, technological change, input substitution, and X-efficiency. His sample was 1947—1959 data on 4000 manufacturing plants in Massachusetts. Results show that the "best-practice" plants have both a higher Q/L and K/L than other plants of the same size. Shen demonstrates that X-efficiency raises Q/L more than K/L, while increases in the latter are more the product of technological change. Factor substitution is shown to be of limited significance. Thus, technological diffusion takes place but only the X-efficient firms take maximum advantage of it. Shen concludes that his results are consistent with a model of technological diffusion that includes the X-efficiency factor. Finally, Shen calls for a reconsideration of the concept of a production function to one that includes *behavioral* as well as technical factors.

8.2.5. Lee (K/L in Korea)

Lee (1986) estimated the determinants of X-efficiency (which he also refers to as technical efficiency) among a group of 51 Korean manufacturing industries using 1970 Bank of Korea Financial Statements Analysis, and tried to disentangle the identities of X-inefficiency from rent-seeking behavior. The dependent variable,

X-efficiency, is measured as value added at world market prices divided by the value of inputs valued at shadow prices. Independent variables include the effective rate of protection of domestic industries from import competition; difference in effective subsidy rate between exports and domestic sales (incentive for exporting and hence exposure to international competition); relative economies of scale, measured as the average size of large Korean manufacturing plants relative to their size in Japan; access to subsidized credit (incentive to waste borrowed funds); and relative capital intensity (with Japan) as a measure of excessive capital intensity and perhaps the engagement of engineering-person satisfactions. Results show that protected industries, those with greater access to subsidized credit, and those that are excessively capital intensive are less X-efficient, while those with greater exposure to international competition are more X-efficient. Lee also estimated a profits equation and found that greater protection from foreign competition is a significant source of profits for Korean industries. The conclusion is thus that protected industries are more profitable only to the extent that the same protection does not increase their X-inefficiency. He reports not being able to identify the unique effects of X-inefficiency vis-à-vis rent-seeking.

8.2.6. Shapiro and Muller (K/L in the Push for Modernization)

Shapiro and Muller (1977) used a technique similar to that of Timmer in estimating the relationship between X-(in)efficiency and "modernization" among a group of Tanzania farmers. (They use the terms X-(in)efficiency and technical (in)efficiency interchangeably.) Shapiro and Muller's data are taken from 26 cotton farms (10% of the population) in a 55 -square-mile political ward in Tanzania for the period 1970—1971. Data on labor (hours worked), land (acres of cotton planted), and output (value of cotton sales in Tanzania cents, or senti) were collected twice a week for one year. Capital was not included because little capital is used and most farmers using fertilizers or insecticides do not use these products properly. The authors felt that the necessary corrections to standardize for these problems would have been too complex and, obviously, not worth the cost. (Otherwise they would have done it.)

Data on modernization were collected through the use of questionnaires and interviews. These techniques generated data on 85 variables reflecting the relative extent to which the farmer adopted the *available* modern items of business management. Guttman scaling techniques were then used to create nine modernization scales consisting of a total of 45 items. Each farmer's modernization score for each of these nine scales was thus calculated as the number of items in that category that he or she had adopted. These nine scales measured knowledge of cotton-growing recommendations, knowledge of input and output prices, knowledge of local agricultural officials, seeking agricultural information, crops grown, farm in puts employed, (7) farm possessions, household appliances and furnishings, and permanent parts of the house and compound.

The authors estimated a (Cobb—Douglas) frontier production function including only labor and land as independent variables. This generated potential output

(Q*) for each farm and thus provided the basis for estimating the degree of X-inefficiency (Q/Q*) with which any farm was operating. The authors then reported the correlation between X-efficiency and both the general or overall degree of modernization, as well as each of the nine Guttman scales generated. The correlation on the overall measure and each of the nine scales were positively correlated with the overall measure, which possessed a correlation of .566, statistically significant at the 1% level. Other scales significant at the 1% level were scales number 2, 3, 8, and 9. Scales significant at the 10% level were numbers 1, 5, 6, and 7. (Scale 4 was significant at the 20% level.)

Shapiro and Mueller's estimated frontier production function yielded the equation (in logs), $Q = 5.343 + 0.050K + 0.803L$. Estimating this same (log) equation using OLS yielded an average production function (the production function for the average firm), $Q = 5.470 + 0.291K + 0.690L$. In other words, comparing the results of the two production functions leads one to postulate that the best firms, as opposed to the average, achieve greater X-efficiency through higher labor productivity but not through higher capital productivity or through a "neutral" shift in the production function. (A neutral shift would be captured in the constant. Since the constants in both equations are virtually identical, the conclusion is that a neutral shift did not occur.)

The authors then report their results of estimating an average production function containing the modernization variable. The modernization variable was placed both in the constant and interacting with both labor and land. When placed in the constant, modernization is hypothesized to affect the intercept of the production function but not the productivity of either factor. The intercept thus captures the across the board effect of modernization. That is, modernization creates externalities that at some point simply raise the output rate of the farm. On the other hand, while interacting with an input, *changes* in modernization are hypothesized to raise the marginal productivity of a given amount of that input.

The results of eight different regressions—each representing a different use (combination) of the modernization variable— were reported. Overall, these results can be summerized as follows. First, the marginal productivity of both land and labor are positive and generally significant at the 10% level. Second, when placed in the intercept, modernization is generally shown to create a positive across-the-board effect, with a statistical significance of .10. Third, increases in modernization are generally shown to reduce the marginal productivity of land. Fourth, increases in modernization are generally shown to increase the marginal productivity of labor. In other words, modernization—a willingness to be efficient, not merely the existence of knowledge— is primarily "labor augmenting" and is an important determinant explaining productivity differences among this sample of farms.

Shapiro and Muller reported that the differences in farm performance were due to a willingness to adopt available modern items related to production, or a willingness to be, in the authors' words, "technically efficient." Because these items were available it seems that this is a case of X-efficiency. Therefore, recall that one of the nine scales was knowledge of input and output prices. Does a lack of knowledge of these prices result in allocative inefficiency? For example, if the firm does not know the relative input prices, then it is not likely to use the cost-minimizing capital/labor ratio. That is, even if the firm were producing on its isoquant, it would probably not be producing at the point on this isoquant for which MPl/MPk=Pl/Pk. In this case, the firm would be X-efficient yet allocatively inefficient. Yet, to the extent that its lack of knowledge of input prices is due to inattentiveness to market conditions, we might conclude that this is an X-inefficiency appearing as a form of allocative inefficiency. These issues are, without doubt, very sticky.

8.3. Exports and Effective Protection from Competition

8.3.1. Page

Page (1980) estimated economic efficiency, X (or technical) efficiency, and price efficiency within the logging, sawmilling, and furniture manufacturing industries in Ghana for the period 1972—1973. Page defines the degree of economic efficiency as the ratio of the social opportunity costs of factor inputs to their value-added at world prices. A ratio less than one indicates efficiency in that value-added exceeds opportunity; the firm with the lowest ratio is thus the most efficient. Minimizing this ratio is also equivalent to maximizing value-added at world prices per unit of input. Among the three industries, logging is the most efficient, followed closely by sawmilling. However, furniture manufacturing was both relatively and absolutely economically inefficient.

For the logging industry the mean value for economic efficiency was .700, with a range among the 28 firms (accounting for 54 percent of industry output) of .336 to 1.123. Thus for the "representative firm" value-added exceeded social opportunity costs by approximately 30 percent. For sawmilling, the mean was .811 with a range among the 36 firms (accounting for 80 percent of industry output) of .6132 to 1.244. However the mean value for eleven firms (accounting for 64 percent of industry output) in the furniture manufacturing was 1.142, with a range of .670 to 2.010. Page states that the results are not surprising in as much as logging and sawmilling products are produced mainly for export, have negative rates of nominal and effective tariff protection, and produced close to their capacity output during the years 1972-1973. On the other hand, furniture is mainly an import substitution product protected by tariffs and quotas, and the firms operated with much more excess capacity during these years.

X-efficiency estimates were derived by fitting a Cobb-Douglas production function using both linear programming (frontier function) and OLS residuals (average function). Page reports that the representative firm was approximately 30 percent from the frontier in both logging and sawmilling, and approximately 26 percent from the frontier in furniture. Using OLS, firms in all three industries had more than 90 percent of predicted output. His explanation of the relatively high levels of average efficiency in both the logging and sawmilling industries is that they are among the oldest Ghanian industries, and given its competitive conditions it is reasonable to expect inefficient firms to be eliminated. Regarding the furniture industry, although it is an import substitution industry, the firms in the sample compete against a large number of small producers. (Many of these small firms did not complete Page's questionnaire and hence his sample was biased towards the larger more efficient firms.)

Price efficiency was calculated as the ratio of (projected factor costs for the firm's optimum input ratio and its level of output / its actual factor costs). A price efficient firm—one using the optimal factor proportions—has an index value of one. Price inefficient firm's have index values less than one. Estimates using OLS show that the logging industry, which receives government subsidies on its capital expenditures has an average index value of .775, with firm's in the range of .537 to .938. In other words, the representative firm in the logging industry could reduce its factor costs by approximately 23 percent if it switched to the optimal input ratio, or the appropriate technology. In sawmilling and furniture the reduction in costs to the representative firm are approximately three percent and one percent, respectively. In these two industries firm values range from .899 to .991, and .943 to .996, respectively. Although not X-efficiency per-se, decision makers in all three industries, especially in logging, are making sub-optimal decisions. Comparing potential gains in X and price efficiency, the potential gains in X-efficiency are larger.

Factors correlated with sub-optimal decisions and X-inefficiency is gleaned by Page's results using an OLS regression, the firm's X-efficiency index as the dependent variable, and four independent variables. These are: (1) a dummy variable for manager's with prior industry training and experience ("education"), (2) the number of production workers per supervisor, (3) the ratio of expatriate managers to total managers, and (4) registered age of the firm. The results show that managerial training and experience, a greater percentage of managers who are expatriates, and a smaller number of production workers per supervisor are associated with higher X-efficiency in all three industries. Newer firms are significant only for sawmilling and here the effect is a higher level of X-efficiency. Foreign or domestic *ownership*, however, was not correlated with X-efficiency. Expatriate managers are correlated with greater X-efficiency because: (1) they have more training and experience than Ghanian born managers, (2) they are most often employed in single-proprietor owner-managed firms, and these manager/entrepreneurs are known to expend more effort than other managers. On the other hand, foreign (or Ghanian) *ownership* does not affect X-efficiency. In other words, X-efficiency "reflects the important influence of an excluded variable, management, from the production function." (p. 335)

8.3.2. Hossein

Hossein (1987) used many of the same independent variables as did Page in his study of allocative and X-efficiency among 1,207 firms in rural Bangladesh between 1979 and 1980. These industrial firms were divided into three groups: (1) cottage industries requiring between 0 and 1000 taka per worker, (2) cottage industries requiring between 1,001 and 4,000 taka per worker, and small industries requiring more than 4,000 taka per worker. Hossein uses two measures for allocative efficiency. First, the ratio of valued added or actual output to how much the firm *could* produce with its inputs if the marginal productivity of its inputs were equal to that of the rural industrial sector as a whole. This ratio is the relative efficiency of inputs employed, and is similar to what Leibenstein would call X-efficiency. A ratio greater (less) than one means that the firm is more (less) efficient with its inputs than is the rural industrial sector as a whole. Second, economic profits.

The data on the relative efficiency of inputs employed shows that the *least* efficient firms are those which use either very little capital or are very capital intensive. For example, jute baling with 49,909 takas of capital per worker has a ratio of 0.43, hosiery with 33,235 takas per worker has a ratio of 0.44, and job printing with 31,254 takas per worker has a ratio of 0.34. At the other extreme there is coir rope and cordage with 4 takas per worker and a ratio of 0.61, cane and bamboo fishing equipment with 29 takas per worker and a ratio of 0.47, and paper and paper products with 181 takas per worker and a ratio of 0.62. On the other hand, the *most* efficient firms ranked in the middle with respect to capital intensity. For example there is jewelry with 1,751 takas and a ratio of 1.64, footwear making with 1,070 takas and a ratio of 1.86, and dairy products with 2,876 takas and a ratio of 1.45.

To summarize his other findings on allocative efficiency: profit rates are lowest for firms with either low or high capital intensity, and they are highest for firms whose capital intensity is in the middle. Thus there is no conflict between static efficiency (relative efficiency of inputs employed) and dynamic efficiency (profits). Finally, the marginal propensity to save is lowest for firms with either low or high capital intensity, and they are highest for firms whose capital intensity is in the middle.

Deriving estimates of X-efficiency from the coefficients of the frontier production function and then using them as a dependent variable in an OLS regression, Hossein reports that formal education among proprietors is correlated with increased X-efficiency only among small industries which are relatively capital intensive. Other finding are: (1) proprietors with education and experience in financial record keeping is correlated with increased X-efficiency among cottage industries with medium capital intensity, and small industries with relatively high capital intensity, and; (2) proprietors with formal training is correlated with increased X-efficiency among cottage industries with little capital intensity, and among small industries with relatively high capital intensity. In other cases the coefficients are of the expected sign but fail to reach statistical significance at the 1% level.

8.3.3. Pack

The role of managers in maximizing X-efficiency includes the ability and willingness to search for the optimal K/L. According to Howard Pack (1974, 1976), searching is important even in LDCs and under conditions in which the conventional wisdom often assumes that searching is fruitless because substitution among inputs is very limited. Using firm-level data gathered by the UN from both MDCs and LDCs, Pack (1974) reports elasticity of substitution values ranging from 3.7 to 0.24, with 8 of 12 values being 1.5 or greater. Surprisingly, substitution is "alive and well." Also of surprise is the fact that the inefficient firms—those using the most capital and per unit of output—tend to use *capital*-intensive technologies. How inefficient are the firms in this sample? The gain in output from adopting the optimal K/L and maximizing output from a given K/L ranges from 41% (bicycles) to 270% (paint production). Increases in employment range from 15% (cotton spinning) to 445% (wool processing). The numbers are large, and according to Pack, there is no tradeoff between output and employment growth. Pack is not surprised at these numbers, given "distorted foreign trade structures (including tariffs and quotas)..." (p. 402).

In his study of 42 plants among the manufacturing sector of Kenya, Pack (1976) reports considerable ex ante choice about the K/L and that most managers choose the labor-intensive options. While the cost of labor is important in these choices, the *deus ex machina* of neoclassical theory—adopting the K/L that minimizes costs of production—does not adequately explain managerial choices. Managers with technical training are overrepresented among those choosing the labor-intensive options, whereas managers with sales or finance backgrounds are more willing to accept the advice/advertising of Western consultants and salespeople. Surprisingly, foreign-owned firms were more likely to adopt labor-intensive methods because they searched the used-machinery market and other labor-intensive options.

In effect, Pack illustrates this difference by stating that managers with technical training take their firm along an isoquant to a lower isocost curve. In other words, the entire isoquant, although technically feasible, "exists" only for those managers who can search and take advantage of it. "This implies that the textbook isoquant has little meaning—the range of real world options is nowhere conveniently laid out" (p. 54).

Another implication of search behavior is that a large untapped source of productivity growth is disembodied technical progress, i.e., firm reorganization and better supervision. In other words, X-efficiency gains are a large untapped source of productivity (or efficiency) growth.

8.3.4. Carlsson

Estimating the effects of competition on X-inefficiency (Q/Q^*) was also done by Bo Carlsson (1972) using plant data for firms in 26 Swedish manufacturing industries for the year 1968. A Cobb-Douglas frontier production function was estimated for each industry, with output measured by value-added. Capital was measured alternatively by the horsepower capacity used in production; consumption of electric power; the fire insurance value of the buildings, machinery, and equipment; and the fire insurance value excluding the buildings. Labor seems to have been measured by number of workers, separated by technical personnel and foremen, and direct labor.

Carlsson estimated the frontier production function using the variables described above and then derived the ratio Q/Q* for each industry from it. He then used each industry's (Q/Q*) as the dependent variable in OLS regression in order to explain interindustry differences. His choice of independent variables was designed to test his major hypothesis, namelt, that a lack of competitive pressure is the main cause of X-inefficiency. His independent variables thus included the industry's four-firm concentration ratio (4FCR), the nominal tariff rate, the export / output ratio, and the import / consumption ratio. Because economies of scale are expected to increase efficiency, Carlsson used two measures for 4FCR in the expectation of separating out the effects of X-inefficiency and economies of scale. His two measures were the unweighted industrywide ratio and a weighted ratio of the major commodity groups within the industry Foreign competition was captured by the remaining three variables.

Carlsson's independent variables also included the number of commodities produced by the industry, a measure of the heterogeneity of output. The number of observations for each industry (which ranged from 12 to 154) was included to adjust for the fact that only so many plants can appear on the frontier. Hence, for any *given* distribution away from the frontier, an industry with more observations will appear to be less X-efficient. The sum of the coefficients obtained from estimating the frontier production function was included in order to provide another correction of the 4FCR for economies of scale.

Finally (and this variable is important), he included a variable constructed as the change in industry assets over 1968 multiplied by the capital / output ratio. This variable was used as a proxy for capital utilization. However, it also may be used as a proxy for the efficiency effects of new investments. That is, do some firms and/or industries appear inefficient simply because they are still "breaking-in" new capital? This is the issue raised in the Gregory and James paper from the previous chapter.

Carlsson then ran several regressions so as to include each of his 4FCR variables and his several capital measures. His results may be summarized in the following way. First, both measures of the 4FCR are positive and significant. His interpretation is that in a relatively small and open economy such as Sweden, the 4FCR reflects economies of scale more than it does market power, and hence increased industry concentration is shown to increase industry efficiency. Second, higher nominal tariff rates lower the industry's efficiency ratio. Third, participation in foreign trade as measured by either the imports / consumption ratio or the exports / output ratio did not prove to have a significant effect on industry efficiency. Finally, the variable designed to measure the effect of new investments on efficiency showed a negative sign but is statistically *insignificant*.

Another way in which Carlsson attempted to glean the effects of foreign competition on efficiency was to adjust each industry's efficiency index for the "technical" factors: number of commodities, number of observations, and capital utilization. Having done this, he reports that the average industry efficiency index for the 26 industries was .78, with a range of .9053 (machine and engine manufacturing) to .5770 (print shops). Furthermore, the ten least efficient industries all were heavily protected from foreign competition through relatively high tariff or other restrictions on imports (textiles and apparels, breweries, and dairies) or because of language barriers (print shops). On the other hand, the three most efficient industries— machine and engine manufacturing, auto and body manufacturing, and ship and boat building—were among the largest exporters of Swedish manufacturing goods: their export shares were 54%, 43%, and 69%, respectively. These results are consistent with Carlsson's main hypothesis: "that the lack of competition is the main theoretical cause of X-inefficiency" (p. 479).

8.3.5. Kalirajan and Tse

Kalirajan and Tse (1989) measure X-efficiency—referred to interchangeably as technical efficiency—among 115 Malaysian food manufacturing firms using Malaysia's Survey of Manufacturing Industries data for 1974—1976. The authors emphasize that X-efficiency reflects entrepreneurial skills and talents within the firm and that this factor, perhaps more so than "material" factors, is vital to the performance of firms. X-Efficiency is measured by fitting a translog production function with output measured as gross output and the conventional inputs of land, labor, and fixed capital. The production function also yields the total variability among the firms around the (assumed common) production frontier, the variability due to deviations in firm-specific performance, and statistically random variability. Of importance here is that the firm-specific variable as a percentage of total variability is positive and statistically significant at the 1% percent level, meaning that measured differences in X-efficiency among firms are due to differences in firm-specific performance—X-efficiency—and not to statistically random variability.

Among the 18 categories composing the food manufacturing industry, technical efficiency ranges from .82 (cocoa manufacturing) to .60 (rice mills), with a mean grade of .73. The mean grade is interpreted to mean that food manufacturing firms on the average produce with 73% of their "technical abilities." Of particular interest is the authors' comment that the first and third (tapioca and saga) most X-efficient groups are heavily engaged in international trade and face stiff competition from foreign competitors.

8.3.6. Green and Mayes

Levels and determinants of X-efficiency (equated with technical efficiency by Green and Mayes (1991)) are presented for 72 British manufacturing industries using Annual Census of Production data for 1977. Fitting a translog stochastic frontier production function, Green and Mayes report that the ten most X-efficient industries range from cement (industry average equal to .885 of a possible 1.0) to weaving (.810) and polishes (.810). At the other end of the spectrum are the ten least X-efficient industries, which include aluminum (.595) and broadcast and receiving equipment (.394). The authors report that, overall, industries that compete in the product market and industries that engage more in international trade are likely to have higher industry average values of X-efficiency. (A five-firm concentration ratio of 40% is correlated with the most X-efficiency.) Finally, they report that their results are similar using U.S., Japanese, and Australian data.

8.3.7. Heitger

Heitger (1987) investigated the effect of exports and protection of domestic industry on GDP growth and on the I/GDP ratio for about 50 countries during the period 1950—1980. His underlying assumption is that competition through trade is the "best antimonopoly policy" to prevent X-inefficiency. With respect to exports, more exactly X/GDP, he reports that a higher X/GDP does not affect the growth of GDP at the 5% level of significance. However, a higher export share does significantly increase (I/GDP), which in turn significantly increases GDP growth. Regarding the overall effective rate of protection of domestic industry (ERP), he reports that it significantly retards GDP growth. But the ERP also varied among industries giving some industries and products a greater degree of domestic monopoly power. And this degree of monopoly power is also shown to significantly retard GDP growth. The loss of GDP growth due to protectionist policies ranged in the neighborhood of 1.5% to 3.1% per year. Over a ten-year period, this loss has reduced worldwide living standards by 20%. The social costs of X-inefficiency— which make up part of this 20% figure—are significant.

8.3.8. White

The effects of both domestic and foreign competition, as well as engineering-person satisfactions on capital / labor ratios in 31 Pakistani industries during 1967—1968 was studied by Lawrence White (1979). White examined the effects of engineering-person satisfactions by assuming that Pakistani entrepreneurs wanted to emulate U.S. entrepreneurs' capital / labor (technology) choices. In order to test specifically whether changes in the U.S. capital / labor) ratio affected the ratio in Pakistan, White utilized data from 31 similarly defined industries in both Pakistan and the U.S. To test for the effects of competition on the capital / labor ratio, he used both the Pakistani 4FCR and the percentage of industry output exported by Pakistani industries. White measured the latter as a dichotomous variable. That is, industries exporting at least 10% of their output were classified as facing the pressure of foreign competition, while those industries exporting less than 10% were considered sheltered from foreign competition. (Ten percent is admittedly an somewhat arbitrary criterion.) His other independent variable was a dummy variable to identify whether the industry was a chemical or process-related industry. Either is relatively rigid and hence less able to substitute inputs for each other. The capital / labor ratio was defined in three separate ways, each utilizing a different definition of labor: total labor, production labor, and nonproduction labor.

His statistical procedure was OLS. For all three variants of the capital/labor ratio, the results of his regression analysis reveal the following. First, higher capital/labor ratios in the U.S. lead to higher capital/labor ratios in Pakistan. However, as the ratio increases in the U.S., the ratio in Pakistan falls progressively further behind that of its U.S. counterpart. Thus, he concludes that engineering-person satisfactions exist among his sample of Pakistani entrepreneurs. Second, the capital/labor ratio in Pakistan increases as the four-firm concentration ratio increases. Third, the capital/labor ratio in Pakistan is higher if less than 10% of industry output is exported. These results are consistent with his hypothesis that competition forces firms to be more X-efficient, or cost conscious. In the case of Pakistan, cost-consciousness means using more labor-intensive technologies. While White's data are consistent with those reported by Lecraw and Carlsson, the reader should be aware that, unlike Lecraw's data, White's data cannot tell us whether the higher capital/labor ratio is a reflection of allocative-price and/or X-inefficiency.

8.3.9. Bergsman

Still another study of the relationship between market power and protection from foreign competition and X-inefficiency was done by Joel Bergsman (1974). Bergsman's estimated both allocative-market and X-inefficiency (plus "monopoly returns") as a percent of Gross National Product for Brazil, Malaysia, Mexico, Norway, Pakistan, and the Philipines. In all cases, protection entails costs because it allows domestically produced goods to be produced at higher prices than would otherwise be the case. However, protection creates allocative- market-inefficiency when the minimum possible cost among domestic firms exceeds that of foreign firms. Bergsman refers to these as "unavoidable" higher costs. By protecting domestic firms from foreign competition under these circumstances, the price of the foreign good is raised and consumers select a consumption bundle different from what would be selected under free trade.

Second, protection results in X-inefficiency when domestic costs of production could be lowered but are not because the pressure for cost control is reduced by those trade barriers. These higher costs he calls "avoidable." Finally, protection results in "monopoly returns" when domestic and foreign costs are kept close despite protection but when protection is still used to raise wages and/or profits. Bergsman admits that distinguishing X-inefficiency from monopoly returns is a very formidable task, and thus he lumps X-inefficiency and monopoly returns together in his estimates.

His estimates of the cost of protection (as a percentage of gross national product) in terms of allocative-market-inefficiency for the six countries listed above are 0.3%, -1.2%, 0.3%, -0.2%, 0.5%, and 1.0%, respectively. On the other hand, the cost in terms of X-inefficiency (plus monopoly returns) are 6.8%, 0.4%, 2.2%, 2.0%, 5.4%, and 2.6%, respectively. As in Leibenstein's original treatment of X-efficiency, Bergsman finds X-inefficiency considerably larger than allocative-market-inefficiency.

Bergsman then compared both effects for three types of economies: small, relatively open ones, represented by Malaya and Norway; large, relatively industrialized ones, represented by Brazil and Mexico; and small, and heavily protected ones, represented by Pakistan and the Philipines. The average level of allocative-market-inefficiency in each of these three groups is -0.7%, 0.3%, and 0.75%, respectively. The average level of X-inefficiency in each of these three groups is 1.2%, 4.5%, and 4.0%, respectively. The results showing smaller effects for small and open economies are not surprising. The result that X-inefficiency is larger than allocative inefficiency is consistent with other results reported in this book. As Bergsman states, however, results showing the X-inefficiency effects of protection are surprising within the context of a model which assumes that firms are cost minimizers. He states,

> Every such estimate I have found assumes that the inefficiencies attributable to protection are only the result of misallocations induced by the effect of protection of relative prices. The assumption is usually explicit, and sometimes only implicit, but is always there: protection causes welfare losses because it induces a country to produce a different mix of products than it would under free trade conditions and further because it reduces consumers' surplus" (p. 410).

Clearly, his data are not consistent with this assumption.

8.3.10. McFetridge

Donald McFetridge (1973) began a study of 43 Canadian industries for the period 1965—1969 by stating, "The approach taken here provides only a partial analysis of market performance in so far as attention is focused on static allocative efficiency while other aspects of market performance such as cost minimization...are neglected. These may well exert a more profound effect on social welfare than does allocative efficiency. Unfortunately they are also less amenable to analysis and are therefore left for future investigation" (p. 345). McFetridge measured (P-C) by the gross profit margin, that is, by (P-AVC)Q/(VA), where P is the price of the final product, AVC is average variable cost, Q is output, and VA is the value added. Assuming constant cost, this equation measures the deviation of price and marginal cost expressed as a percentage of value added. He then regressed (P-C) on a variety of variables, including measures of the concentration ratio for both firms and plants, asset size, growth rates, whether the industry produces consumer or producer goods, advertising intensity measuring product differentiation, and the effective tariff rate. McFetridge's expectation was that higher concentration ratios and higher effective tariffs would increase (P-C). The latter, by reducing foreign competition, would allow domestic firms to raise prices with less fear of losing their competitive position. His results show that higher tariffs result in *lower* (P-C), but not in a statistically significant manner. McFetridge comments on this surprising result by stating that, "A possible reason for this is that the effective tariff protection is associated with suboptimal capacity and excessive cost rather than excess profits" (p. 351).

McFetridge began by investigating the effects of market power on allocative (in)efficiency but concluded his study by stating, "Knowledge of the degree of allocative inefficiency associated with a given market structure is necessary for the evaluation of alternative market structures. A complete evaluation would also take into account...the degree of X-inefficiency...associated with each of the alternative market structures" (p. 353).

8.3.11. Katrak

Price-cost margins were also used by Homi Katrak (1980) in his study of Indian manufacturing. Katrak's measure of (P-C) is (P-W-M) / P, where P is the product price, W is wages, and M is materials costs. With constant returns to scale this is identical with (P-MC) / P. Katrak attempted to explain interindustry variations in P-C using not only measures of seller concentration and capital intensity but also variables measuring foreign trade. Concentration was measured as the percentage of industry assets accounted for by the industry's four largest factories. Capital intensity was measured both by the capital:labor and capital:output ratios. Foreign trade variables included imports as a percentage of industry output, exports as a percentage of industry output, and "implicit" tariff rates on both imported goods and inputs. (Implicit tariffs include not only the tariff rate per se but also other nontariff restrictions on imports.) Theory, according to Katrak, predicts that a higher level of seller concentration, fewer exports, and fewer imports as a percentage of industry output will increase (P-C) because each increases the ability for domestic firms to collude and raise prices.

The results of Katrak's regression analysis showed that (P-C) increased under the protection of higher implicit tariffs. His results also showed (P-C) increasing until concentration ratios reach 50%, and declining thereafter. He asks whether this latter result is the result of lower prices or higher costs at concentration ratios in excess of 50%. If X-inefficiency becomes prevalent at these higher concentration ratios, then this could manifest itself, according to Katrak, in both higher unit labor (w) and unit materials (m) costs, but especially the former. Furthermore, if w/m increased sufficiently, it would offset any price reductions that may occur, thus reducing (P-C).

Katrak thus regressed w/m on seller concentration and capital intensity (capital / labor). The results of this regression show that w/m increases with increased seller concentration. Specifically, a 1% increase in seller concentration increases w/m by 0.5%. Because seller concentration ratios ranged from 0.1 to 0.9, Katrak concluded that the potential increase in w/m could be large enough to cause a decline in (P-C) when concentration ratios exceed 50%. In other words, the reduction in (P-C) may be due to X-inefficiency cost increases rather than to lower prices. (Katrak points out that increases in w/m might also be caused by union-induced higher wages in the more concentrated industries.)

8.4. Conclusions

As in the two previous chapters, the evidence presented in this chapter has shown itself to be consistent with XE theory. Inefficiency in the use of capital and labor have been shown related to X-inefficient behavior. And openness to international trade has been shown to be related to X-efficiency among firms.

These three chapters have presented a large number of studies on a wide variety of issues for a large number of countries. I have argued that the evidence presented is consistent with XE theory. I now turn to another interpretation of this evidence, that given by the critics of XE theory. In the course of the discussion I will respond to these criticisms point by point.

9

X-EFFICIENCY, ITS CRITICS, AND A REPLY

9.1. Introduction

The literature on X-efficiency, both in its theoretical and empirical aspects, has been voluminous since Leibenstein's 1966 article. In fact, between 1969 and 1980, Leibenstein's article was the third most frequently referenced article in the Social Science Citation Index.[1] And, as work on X-efficiency has developed and grown, it has evoked different identifiable "schools" of criticisms. In this chapter I shall

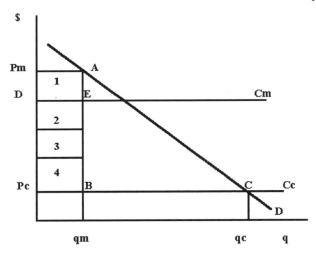

Figure 21. Partitioning the higher costs of monopoly power: profits, wages, job perquisites, and X-inefficiency.

---

[1] The Social Science Citation Index includes a publication called "Current Contents" that reviews often-referenced articles. The review of Leibenstein's work on XE theory appears in Number 33, August 16, 1982, p. 20. Mark Perlman, in the Forward to the Second Edition of this book, cites the number of references since 1980.

explore these criticisms and provide a response. This discussion will be aided with the use of figure 21.

In figure 21, the competitive firm produces Qc, charges price Pc, and has long-run costs Cc. The monopolist would produce output Qm, charge price Pm, and have costs Cm. Allocative inefficiency due to monopoly power is thus the area ABC. Area PmABPc has four components to it. Area 1 represents profits; area 2 represents higher wages and salaries; area 3 represents job perks, but would also include higher costs due to factors such as suboptimal and/or excess capacity; and area 4 represents pure X-inefficiency. However, areas 2 and 3 may also contain X-inefficiency. Higher costs due to wages and salaries may reflect X-inefficiency if these higher costs are not the outcome of "rational" wage policies. Area 4 may contain X-inefficiency if, for example, the costs of perks exceeds the value of these perks to its recipients. (Employees may prefer cash but tax laws encourage the firm to provide perks.)

Using figure 21, I will identify four schools of criticism, some of which we have already discussed. These schools are rent-seeking, leisure as output, management utility under competition, and property-rights.

9.2. Rent-Seeking

In chapter 3, we discussed Tullock's assertion that rent-seeking expenditures are rational private investments that create social waste and that account for any increase in (observed) costs. Two other studies will now be discussed: Crain and Zardkoohi (1980) and Schap (1985).

9.2.1. Crain and Zardkoohi

Crain and Zardkoohi take the position that the existence of X-inefficiency in production, by reducing available rent-seeking investment funds, involves an opportunity cost of lower profits. Therefore, they hypothesize that in a "rent-seeking society," firms are (strongly) motivated to be X-efficient so that their supply of rent-seeking investment funds is adequate in order that they may be able to influence government so as to meet their profit needs. X-inefficiency is thus not a free good. Furthermore, greater X-inefficiency simply means less of another type of inefficiency, namely rent-seeking. Society thus faces a tradeoff between two types of inefficiencies.

On the other hand, a firm that is more X-efficient generates the funds to engage in the other type of inefficiency, namely rent-seeking. This is shown in figure 21, which divides the area PmABPc into three categories: area 1—PmAB'Pm'—is profits, area 2—Pm'B'B''Pm''—represents rent-seeking expenditures, and area 3—Pm''B''BPc—pure X-inefficiency. The reader should consider in addition, that area 2 may contain X-inefficiency to the extent that, for example, the cost of rent-seeking expenditures exceeds their value to the firm (or group).

In their analysis of X-inefficiency and rent-seeking (and leaving the details of their empirical results to a reading of their article), the authors conclude that pure

X-inefficiency (area 3) can exist, changes in X-inefficiency are assumed to be offset by equal changes in rent-seeking expenditures (area 2), and what follows is that X-inefficiency, even if does exist, does not result in any net change in total welfare. In other words, even if it exists, it is assumed not to be of any consequence.

9.2.2. Schap

David Schap (1985) provides an argument similar to the writing of others on the topic of rent-seeking. Schap's argument is based on the assumption that the higher costs of a monopoly are due to the rent-seeking, rent-dissipation process. His argument is shown in figure 22. Assuming that the costs of the competitive and monopolist firm are the same, Cc, then the output, price, and costs of the X-efficient competitive and X-efficient monopolist firm are Qc, Pc, and Cc, and Qm, Pm, and Cc, respectively. The lost surplus is the familiar PmACPc, of which ABC is allocative inefficiency. Schap then asserts that the area PmABPc is due to the rent-seeking, rent-dissipation process and, as such, rules out the possibility for X-inefficiency to exist.

If the monopolist is X-inefficient, then it would exhibit unit costs Cm, and produce Qm' at a price Pm'. Comparing the X-inefficient monopolist with the X-efficient competitive firm shows that the lost surplus is the area Pm'DCPc. Of this total, the area DFC is allocative-market-inefficiency, GHFPc is the higher costs incurred by the monopolist producing Qm', and DHGPm' is the higher costs due to the rent-seeking, rent-dissipation process.

Schap then shows, with the use of figure 22 the welfare effects attributable to an X-inefficient monopolist. First, the area ABFJ represents the additional alloca-

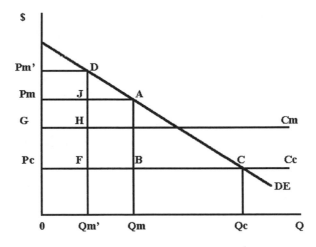

Figure 22. Rent-seeking, allocative-market inefficiency and X-inefficiency.

tive-market-inefficiency due to the X-inefficient monopolist. Schap points out correctly, I believe, that whereas Leibenstein speaks about X-inefficiency in terms of costs of production and as a nonallocative form of inefficiency, these higher costs themselves create an allocative inefficiency. Second, the area GHFPc represents the X-inefficient monopolists' higher costs of producing Qm'. Third, the area PmJHG represents rent-seeking expenditures. In other words, the area ABPcGHJ is a welfare loss regardless of whether the monopolist is X-efficient or X-inefficient. What would have been spent on rent-seeking if the monopolist were X-efficient— ABPcPm—is, under an X-inefficient monopolist, an allocative-market loss (ABFJ) and X-inefficiency (GHFPc). The welfare loss due solely to the X-inefficient monopolist is thus the area Pm'DAPm.

Schap makes another important assumption, that a monopolist firm's higher costs are intrinsic to the firm and hence unavoidable. Under this assumption, the area GHFPc—X-inefficiency—is irrelevant to the producer, since it cannot be removed. As a result, the ownership rights to the inherently X-inefficient monopolist are less valuable. The rational owner thus engages in less rent-seeking, which is just equal to the higher costs represented by X-inefficiency. We are, in short, back into the world of Crain and Zardkoohi. And the welfare loss due solely to X-inefficiency is the area Pm'DJPm.

Finally, if the X-inefficient monopolist produced Qm rather than Qm', then ABC represents allocative-market-inefficiency and ABPcQm represents rent-seeking expenditures. It "follows" that the net welfare costs of X-inefficiency are zero. (In other words, if you begin with the assertion that X-inefficiency does not exist, you can always conclude that X-inefficiency does not exist!)

9.2.3. Reply to Rent-Seekers

Tullock's departure from the then neoclassical orthodoxy was similar in spirit to Leibenstein's. Yet, this similar departure leads to different expressed concerns and theories. Leibenstein explored nonmaximization as a source for the cost and productivity changes that were observed and reported in his original treatment of X-efficiency. Tullock cited some of these same data, yet went on to discuss rent-seeking as a source of welfare losses. Leibenstein looked at costs above minimum levels and called them X-inefficiency. Tullock found nothing inefficient about these higher costs. He surmised that they represented a rational response to an incentive created by government. It seems interesting how such similar beginnings lead to such differences in emphasis. It is also interesting that Bierman and Tollison (1970) cited Leibenstein's original article in support of Tullock's theory of rent-seeking.

Rent-seeking and XE theory are not easily comparable. Rent-seeking is a form of maximizing behavior. Rent-seeking behavior is purposeful and directed; it is a highly calculated response to a profit incentive. Furthermore, the firm is perceived to be a production function. That is, all employees are directed, presumably by management, to achieve a common goal that is achieved. Thus, the firm expends scarce resources on rent-seeking until the marginal benefit is equal to the marginal cost, and hence, given its rent-seeking expenditures, the firm is a cost minimizer.

Does a firm actually calculate its rent-seeking budget as closely as the theory of rent-seeking implies? One reason for believing that their budgets are not as finely calculated as the theory implies is that some portion, perhaps a significant portion, of the firm's "rent-seeking budget" is expressed as dues to trade associations. In other words, firms often do not make marginal calculations as to the benefits and costs of rent-seeking expenditures. In these cases, they simply pay into an association that then carries out activities. Many times these activities are of a very general nature, more informational than "arm-twisting."[2]

Finally, it is difficult to evaluate a concept (X-(in)efficiency) if it is evaluated by a theory (orthodox microeconomics) whose assumptions (including maximization) themselves do not allow that concept to have real meaning and/or significance.

9.3. Leisure as Output

Several writers have used the leisure-as-output approach, most notably George Stigler. With respect to figure 21, this approach either denies that pure X-inefficiency (area 4) exists or asserts that area 3 represents on-the-job leisure and hence is wholly a transfer. The latter argument means that on-the-job leisure is valued at least to its full cost.

This approach rests on the notion that a firm produces two types of commodities. First, it produces commodities that are sold, that is, it produces what is ordinarily thought of as the firm's output. Second, it produces "nontraded" commodities such as on-the-job leisure, the quiet life, friendship, rest and relaxation, and other commodities that are similar in content. The higher unit costs that the firm might incur if it is a monopolist thus represent employees' utility, and as such, are benefits rather than social costs of monopoly. Assuming rational or maximizing behavior means that an individual will help "produce" these nontraded commodities until the marginal benefit is just equal to the marginal cost. In other words, if a firm is not minimizing its costs because employees are accepting on-the-job leisure, then the employees must prefer on-the-job leisure to the profits (income) that they knowingly forgo.

A response to Leibenstein's theory that higher-than-minimum costs are a form of inefficiency is that this statement is only true if the utility gained from on-the-job leisure is heavily discounted. But, of course, if individual's "choose" leisure, then how can it be discounted? Leibenstein, therefore, must be arbitrarily defining inefficiency according to his preferred definition rather than according to the preferences of others.

---

2   This information was conveyed to me in a conversation with John Danielson, a Vice-President with Pacific Gas and Electric.

9.3.1. Parish and Ng

Parish and Ng (1972) were among the first to make this general line of argument. They state that higher costs are a form of allocative inefficiency, not X-inefficiency. If entrepreneurs act rationally, say Parish and Ng, then X-inefficiency does not produce any net social costs, because the leisure of the entrepreneur is part of the social product not part of social cost. Social costs arise in this context only when, for example, there is some inefficiency in the pricing of leisure. When this inefficiency occurs, then the person substituting leisure for income does not bear the full cost of his or her decision. The undertaxation of leisure is, in their view, the most "obvious" example of a price, or allocative, inefficiency that raises unit costs of production.

9.3.2. Levin, Peel, and Pasour

After Parish and Ng, use of the leisure argument appeared often. For example, Levin (1974) argued that the production of goods and services behaves according to the laws of physics—specifically, to the laws of mass and energy, which teach us that "nothing is ever lost." Levin interprets this to mean that if the firm is producing less of its traded commodities than is possible, then it must be producing more of its nontraded commodities. After all, the energy expended in a fixed work day must be expended in some form, and if it doesn't manifest as traded commodities it must manifest as nontraded commodities. One form that energy takes when it manifests as a non-traded commodity is on-the-job leisure.

Peel (1974) offered the argument that a "lazy" work force is X-efficient if its production level maximizes the output per its own (lazy) level of effort. Furthermore, he believes that it is "operationally more convenient" to consider the actual output to be the maximum output. In addition, he considers noncost minimization to be consistent with X-efficiency when these costs increase the motivations of the employees. Expenditures on piped music and bonuses are two examples of such costs.

Pasour (1982) offers the similar argument that less output and more leisure is not necessarily a sign of any type of inefficiency. Since the leisure is chosen, it obviously must be worth more than the income forgone by those individuals. Finally, Pasour defines inefficient actions as the outcome of a situation in which an opportunity for net gain has not yet been noticed. Accordingly, inefficiency creates market disequilibrium; by definition, therefore, all inefficiencies are allocative. Since unobserved opportunities are totally subjective, they cannot be observed by anyone other than the individual. The conclusion is that no one can define when another person is being inefficient.

9.3.3. Martin

Martin (1978) discussed effort—leisure tradeoffs in the context of the efficiency effects of protection from international trade. Martin defined X-efficiency in terms of managerial effort. The effect of higher protection is not necessarily to increase X-inefficiency. The effect depends upon the relative strengths of the income and substitution effects of such protection. One possible scenario is that an increase in protection, by increasing the firm's product prices, increases the price of leisure. An increase in effort—the substitution effect—would be expected. On the other hand, the income effect of higher prices would be to reduce effort. Martin concludes that protection will increase X-inefficiency when, among other things, the income effect is more influential than the substitution effect.

Martin also cautions us to consider both the static and dynamic effects of protection. Thus, while protection may increase X-inefficiency in the import sector (the "warm sun" effect), it may also decrease X-inefficiency in the export sector (the "cold shower" effect). Martin considers the work of Bergsman, discussed in chapter 7, to be static and hence probably overestimating the effects of protection on X-inefficiency.

Martin follows Parish and Ng in stating that less effort means that more leisure is being "produced," but believes that this leisure is a benefit of protection rather than a cost. Furthermore, since individual behavior is assumed to be rational, then the leisure is increased until its marginal benefits are equal to its cost. In other words, the producer is fully absorbing the entire rise in unit costs through a substitution of leisure for income. Higher costs—call them X-inefficiency if you choose—thus entail no social cost.

Finally, Martin holds that all welfare costs of protection are allocative. This result occurs because, for example, the price of leisure is too low relative to the price of commodities while at the same time society values hard work and regards the quiet life as undesirable. In terms of figure 21, area 3 is wholly a transfer. Area 4 either does not exist, or exists but involves no welfare losses, or involves welfare losses that are actually allocative in nature. In other words, either X-inefficiency doesn't exist or it exists but is actually allocative inefficiency.

9.3.4. Stigler

The leisure—effort criticism of XE theory was perhaps most forcefully presented by George Stigler. When Stigler asks, "What is output?" his answer is that the "product" of the firm is what it sells plus "commodities" such as the health and leisure of its employees. Assuming rational, utility-maximizing behavior, he states that when more effort increases "traded" output but reduces "nontraded" output— leisure—then this increase does represents a change in output rather than an increase in efficiency. To judge this as an increase in efficiency is to adopt a tunnel vision of output and to impose one's own goals on others who have never accepted ththose goals. Higher costs do not involve waste; ex post waste arises because ex ante plans were developed in the presence of uncertainty. This type of waste is unavoidable but controllable. Ex post waste can also arise if individuals are not maximizers. This possibility Stigler refuses to accept until we have a theory of errors. Finally, Stigler, like the other authors writing about leisure as output, asserts that once all the firm's inputs (and outputs) have been properly defined, then all firms can be shown to produce on "their" production function. In terms of figure 21, area 4 represents the utility of the firm's "nontraded" output.

9.3.5. Reply to Leisure-as-Output Arguments

The leisure-as-output argument denies the existence of X-inefficiency on the assumption that rational decision makers would never choose leisure if its value were less than its (opportunity) cost. The choice of leisure is thus a revealed preference for leisure vis-à-vis (money) income. The higher unit costs resulting from leisure are thus absorbed by the employees. However, Crew (1975) has argued that employees are most likely to fully absorb these higher costs if they are employed in the "old neoclassical entrepreneurial firm" (p. 158). By this he means a relatively small, competitive, owner-managed firm. Among modern firms possessing market power, this situation is less likely to be the case for several reasons. First, "dog-in-the-manger"—type labor—management relations leave the group's welfare (on both sides) less than it could be. Second, Crew considered X-inefficiency to be an "insidious disease" that affects behavior without announcing its presence. Third, institutional arrangements, rather than (rational) choice, often dictate the amount of leisure an employee will receive or his or her ability to trade off leisure for income.

A second argument that all inefficiencies are allocative rests on the assumption that every manifestation of human energy can be treated as if it were traded in a market and hence involves prices. These prices, if not explicit, must be implicit. This argument thus rests on the assertion that there is both a market for and a price of leisure, that every employee knows of the existence of this market and that every employee knows the current and past prices as well as having some expectations as to future prices of leisure. (Past and expected future prices would seem necessary for a buyer to make an informed judgment as to when and how much leisure to purchase.) Of course, assuming that all inefficiencies are allocative means that (implicit) prices and markets for effort must exist. These arguments are difficult either to prove or to refute, as is the argument that firms produce both traded and nontraded commodities. Do employees behave as if peer relations or a slow walk to the water cooler are commodities? Do they know the price of peer relations, or slow walks? For these reasons, I will refer to this form of allocative inefficiency as implicit-price-allocative-inefficiency.

These arguments put forth by the critics of XE theory are tautological. Leibenstein (1982b, p. 461) comments in the following way:

> An example of this interpretation is the approach which argues that everyone maximizes utility, and instances that appear to falsify the theory occur because the objective function is not understood by the observer. The essence of this interpretation is bull's-eye painting. The analyst seems to be saying, "give me an observed result and I can state an objective function for which the result fits." Although this approach is frequently used by defenders of neoclassical theory, such defenders cannot really be genuine friends of the theory. In the long run such an approach must appear nothing else but foolish.

Can we say that people are ever X-inefficient? I believe we can. First, we start with the interpretation that X-inefficiency is possible. We must then state, for some specific instance, the set of procedures that an individual would have to engage in if efficiency is to result. If all the procedures are carried out, then the outcome would be efficient; but if some 'necessary' procedures are not carried out, then we would view it as inefficient.

Forsund, Lovell, and Schmidt (1980) have enumerated the difficulties of measuring and interpreting X-(in)efficiency estimates gained through an industry production function but have nevertheless argued that nonallocative (in)efficiencies do exist. Their response to this neoclassical critique of the XE concept and to Stigler in particular is similar to Leibenstein's. They state (p. 21):

> Stigler basically takes the view that all perceived inefficiency is allocative inefficiency, and even this is perceived because of a failure on the part of the observer—e.g., a failure to measure all relevant inputs, or to correctly perceive what is being maximized or to account for all of the constraints on the maximization process, etc.
>
> This kind of argument seems to be accepted by most economists. However, this is really an act of faith, since the dogma being proposed is not amenable to empirical proof or disproof.

There seem to be two cases of "leisure as output." The first would be when the owners of the firm (directly or through their agents) knowingly sacrifice profits in order to operate the firm so that the workers enjoy on-the-job leisure, and when the workers prefer the leisure to the income that may also be sacrificed. This case probably does not involve any X-inefficiency. The second case is all other cases. For example, when the employees do not know the tradeoffs involved (which I assert that they probably do not unless their jobs are in serious jeopardy) and the owners expect a "fair day's work for a fair day's pay." Because employees are paid to work, the concept of on-the-job leisure seems a strange one. If employees are asked to work for their wage, then the fact that they must exert more effort does not seem like a loss of their welfare but rather an exertion of effort to earn their wage. I am in no way making a value judgment here as to how hard employees do or should work. What I am saying, however, is that when someone is being paid to work then that contractual agreement is the element of most importance. To discuss on-the-job leisure as a welfare-yielding "commodity" in this context is to take an anarchistic view of welfare. That is, whatever makes you happy is good, and more is preferred to less.

A third point raised by these critics is the definition of inefficiency used by Pasour, namely that inefficiency is "not yet noticed opportunities for gain." Accordingly, all inefficiencies are allocative caused by, for example, uncertainty, or incomplete information. This is, to say the least, an unusual definition of the term "inefficiency." The difficulty with using it is not its unusualness, but that it implies that individuals are always doing as well as they can. It implies that individuals are primed to pounce upon opportunities for gain but do not recognize all of them because of some genuine lack of information that is created, not by their unwillingness to avail themselves of opportunities that require effort to find and bring to fruition but by their external environment, e.g., no one can be aware of all or even most opportunities that exist. In other words, Pasour's definition of inefficiency implies that X-inefficiency is zero.

A fourth point concerns Martin's paper. Martin is correct in stating that protection need not always increase X-inefficiency. In reading Martin's paper, the reader should be aware that he assumes that the firm is a well-defined production function, is perfectly competitive, displays utility-maximizing behavior, and prefers diminishing utility to effort. XE theory, on the other hand, applies best to imperfect competition, assumes that production functions are not well defined, and holds that behavior may exhibit both maximizing and nonmaximizing characteristics, In other words, Martin uses a more traditional neoclassical model to evaluate a nonneoclassical model.

Finally, there is a literature in industrial psychology (Locke, 1976) and economics (Scitovsky, 1976) demonstrating that the relation between effort and job satisfaction is parabolic, not linear. That is, employees are often found to dislike both too little effort and too much. To treat on-the-job leisure as a desirable part of a job, per se, is thus an incorrect assumption leading to incorrect conclusions.

9.4. Management Utility under Competition

9.4.1. DiLorenzo

Thomas DiLorenzo (1981) has argued that competitive capital markets and the fact that private-sector managers are "residual claimants" who must compete for jobs make the concept of X-inefficiency a "highly suspect notion" (p. 122). Furthermore, he considers his analysis applicable for both competitive and monopolistic firms, since in both environ-ments managers' rewards are tied to profitability. It follows that the rational-utility maximizing private-sector manager will best be able to increase his utility not by enjoying the quiet life, but by being X-efficient and increasing the firm's profits. Although one could argue that managers in monopolistic firms enjoy sufficient shelter from competitive pressure so as to allow them to be X-inefficient with impunity, DiLorenzo's argument is that so long as capital markets are perfect, an X-inefficient manager faces the threat of his firm being taken over, with a subsequent loss of his or her own job. The key to this argument is the existence of perfect capital markets. In term of figure 21, DiLorenzo concludes that X-inefficiency in area 3 or 4 could exist but will be forced to zero by perfect capital markets and, utility-maximizing managers will increase their utility by reducing area 3 and 4 to a minimum and thus increasing profits (area 1).

9.4.2. Reply to DiLorenzo

The existence of perfect capital markets in the U.S. is a suspect notion. I have already reviewed the evidence for perfect capital markets in chapter 4 of this book and in a previous article (Frantz, 1984).

9.5. Property Rights

9.5.1. DeAlessi

DeAlessi (1983) argues against XE theory by presenting generalized neoclassical theory and showing that the assumptions, implications, and empirical evidence presented for XE theory are consistent with generalized neoclassical theory. His preference for generalized neoclassical theory is based on at least the fact that it studies individual choice made under constraints on the assumption that the individual is a utility maximizer. By identifying arguments in a utility function, generalized neoclassical theory is thus able to identify potentially observable preference relations.

On the other hand, he discounts XE theory because it rejects the notion of maximizing behavior, because it does not consider the effects of property rights on behavior, because it denies that (wealth) maximization ever occurs, and because it focuses on unobservable preference relations requiring the use of the concept of the personality.

Using the concepts of property rights and transactions costs, DeAlessi feels that generalized neoclassical theory is better able to explain the central postulates of XE theory but with fewer assumptions. Consider, for example, the effect of positive transactions costs. Transactions costs have been defined by Kenneth Arrow (1969, p. 48) as the "costs of running the economic system." These costs are not costs of production as usually defined, but the costs of the "friction" that characterize human (economic) transactions. These transactions costs have both ex ante and ex post components. The ex ante component includes the drafting, negotiating, and safeguarding of a contract. The ex post component includes the setup and operation of a system of dispute resolution, as well as bonding and haggling costs.

These transactions costs can explain why a firm's production function is not well specified, why labor contracts are incomplete, why some inputs are not marketed, and why individuals work within an inert area or are selectively rational. Thus, inert areas exist because the benefits of change are less than the costs (transactions and adjustment costs). The existence of inert areas thus does not require an explanation that uses an immensely complex notions such as a personality. A simpler explanation is that the benefits are less than the costs.

Evidence presented for XE theory is also more "efficiently" explained by generalized neoclassical theory. For example, positive transactions costs explain why firms are not producing on their expansion path. Furthermore, noncost minimization is not necessarily inefficient, since inefficiency must be defined in terms of the constraints facing that firm. What XE theory identifies as inefficiency is done in part to compare the performance of actual firms against an unattainable (competitive) ideal. XE theory thus commits the "nirvana fallacy." As other critics maintain, when a (rational) person chooses on-the-job leisure rather then extra income, then his work behavior is efficient. To quote DeAlessi, "The equilibrium solution associated with a given set of constraints is efficient" (1983, p. 73).

9.5.2. Holtmann

Holtmann (1983), like DeAlessi, maintains that both XE theory and empirical evidence are consistent with generalized neoclassical theory, which includes the concepts of uncertainty and utility maximization. For example, because uncertainty lowers expected profits, then uncertainty can explain why the owner-managed firms in the Shelton study had higher profits than did the company-managed firms. Holtmann's reasoning is that owner-managers face less uncertainty in the effort of their employees than do company managers, and hence will have higher profits.

Another example is that Shepherd's (1972) finding that market share and profits are not linearly related to each other is due to the absolute risk aversion among managers of larger firms. A third example is that Primeaux's (1977) finding that duopolists have lower costs than monopolists is due to greater variability in demand (more excess capacity utilization) among the monopolists. In terms of figure 21, this fourth school of criticism denies that pure X-inefficiency—area 4—exists. Furthermore, X-inefficiency may exist in area 3 because the benefit of perks to the recipients are not worth the cost. However, these perks would be "produced" due to factors such as positive transactions costs, uncertainty, or attenuated property rights. Regardless of the cause, these factors represent constraints on the behavior of the individual and hence represent not X-inefficiency but rather constrained utility maximization. Area 3 inefficiencies are thus allocative inefficiencies.

9.5.3. Reply to Property Rightists

Several comments are very relevant here. First, and contrary to DeAlessi's statement, Leibenstein has spoken about ownership form in his book, *General X-Efficiency Theory and Economic Development*. Ownership form has also been discussed by several writers and reviewed in this book in chapter 6. Second, and contrary to DeAlessi's statement, Liebenstein (1976, 1983, 1986) has clearly stated that he does not deny maximization. However, he allows for the possibility of both maximizing and nonmaximizing behavior and has attempted to explain under what conditions each type of behavior is most likely to be forthcoming. For DeAlessi, maximization is an article of faith. For Leibenstein, maximization should be the outcome of certain decision-making procedures and hence should be observable and potentially refutable. Third, it is difficult to assess DeAlessi's objection to the use of the concept of personality. DeAlessi's explanation for individual behavior includes the concept of utility (maximization), and hence, implicitly, of the concept of the personality. DeAlessi, like McCormick et al., prefers the simple explanation—in this case, one not requiring the concept of a personality.

Is it really simpler to use terms such as transactions costs or property rights in an ex post manner so as to make any observed behavior appear efficient? I think not. With regard to transactions costs, Oliver Williamson (1985, pp. 20—21) has pointed out that these costs cannot be measured directly. As a result, transactions costs are assessed by comparing various corporate forms and making ordinal judgments as to their magnitude, i.e., transactions costs will be greater in organizational form A vis-à-vis organizational form B. If these costs can't be measured directly—they are not subject to any standard bookkeping procedures—then it is difficult to know whether and to what extent they can explain differences in work effort and hence in costs among firms.

The use of property rights is also troublesome. In general, arguments about property rights have been concerned with the property rights of managers. The implication is that the firm is considered to be a production function, subject to the prevailing system of property rights. Thus, once this system is known, the managers have their incentives and the remainder of the employees "fall in line" to accomplish the goals that the managers design. We have already discussed that XE theory does not view the firm as a production function. To view the firm as such is to assume away X-(in)efficiency.

Fourth, most evidence that is consistent with the implications of XE theory is not a "nirvana fallacy." Most of the studies presented in chapters 6—8 make comparisons between two or more real firms rather than between a real firm and a competitive ideal. In these cases, the authors have attempted to compare similar firms that differ by ownership form or market power. Is there an alternative explanation to the empirical results presented in this book? Of course. In a very extensive literature review on property rights presented by DeAlessi (1980) in 1980 he reviewed over 100 studies. At least 20 of the these studies consistent with the implications of XE theory.

How can we decide which explanation is preferred? Should we count the number of assumptions used by each theory? This would be, I believe, a pointless exercise because both theories make the same number of assumptions. For example, in not making any assumptions about the (dual nature of) the personality, DeAlessi is assuming that personalitydoes not affect production is any meaningful way. Surely, we are not going to limit ourselves to explicit assumptions!

Fifth, DeAlessi maintains that the central postulates of XE theory are consistent with generalized neoclassical theory. Likewise, noncost minimization in the face of transactions costs is not per se evidence of inefficiency. The question in both cases is, are the concepts used by generalized neoclassical theory being used in an ex ante or an ex post sense? Leibenstein's concern in this regard is that they are used in an ex post, "bulls-eye painting" 3 manner.

In addition, DeAlessi and Leibenstein are, according to DeAlessi, concerned with different questions. DeAlessi (1983, p. 845, fn. 2) states, "Leibenstein seems to be concerned with the rationality of the individual and how particular individuals might behave in particular circumstances. My concern, on the other hand, is with the rationality (logic) of the theory and its ability to explain real world phenomena." In fact, Leibenstein developed XE theory to explain real-world data which seemed inconsistent with neoclassical theory. In some ways, DeAlessi has countered these arguments with concepts that have been used in a tautological manner, but that are consistent with neoclassical theory.

Sixth, Holtmann argues that the empirical evidence offered for XE theory is consistent with (generalized) neoclassical theory. For example, uncertainty explains Shelton's findings. However, the owner-managers "watched" the operation more closely than did the company managers and made higher profits. This result is not contingent upon uncertainty. The parent company may have been completely certain about the effort of the hired managers but were profit satisficers rather than profit maximizers. And, we need not assume that the owner-managers were profit maximizers. What they did was to generate higher profits, mostly by keeping costs lower.

Finally, were the managers of the larger firms in Shepherd's study risk averse, as Holtmann suggests? As for the Primeaux study, I have presented evidence in chapter 6 showing that the monopoly firms did not have greater excess-capacity utilization. Therefore, greater excess-capacity utilization could not explain the higher costs of the monopoly firms. One problem with using the concepts of utility, uncertainty, or transactions costs to explain intrafirm behavior is that none of them enjoys the benefits of being measured by any standard bookkeeping procedures. Each can be used in a tautological or nontautological manner. By changing the use of the term "allocative inefficiency" from allocative-market to implicit-price-allocative, these critics have seemingly created a definition of inefficiency that does not allow for X-inefficiency.

9.6. Some General Comments

There are several other interesting aspects of these criticisms. First, if individuals make choices, then why can't they make an inferior choice? If inferior choices cannot be made, does this reduce the meaningfulness of the word choice? Second, the critics have seemed content merely to be able to "state" an argument against nonmaximizing behavior consistent with the neoclassical framework. That is, it seems that stating that nontraded products are produced, or that rent-seeking behavior accounts for higher costs, or that individuals are maximizing their utility by purchasing leisure, is sufficient proof against XE theory.

However, proof by assertion is not proof. And, while these critics assert the existence of factors that can question the existence of X-inefficiency, nowhere do they use these same arguments to prove the existence of maximizing decisions.

Third, the critics seems to be making the interesting argument that individuals are maximizers subject to their distaste for maximization. Firms are X-efficient—cost minimizers—given the fact that the employees do not want to put forth the effort to minimize costs. An individual is X-efficient given his or her unwillingness to think through the available options before making a decision. Maximizing behavior becomes whatever is chosen, and the meaningfulness of the word maximization is severely reduced. Finally, if all behavior can be "shown" to be efficient, then is the concept of efficiency important? And are these writers really interested in efficiency? When Harberger reported his small estimates for allocative-market-inefficiency Leibenstein and Tullock and others were concerned that this might give the impression that economics itself is not important. Leibenstein has tried to show that there is another type of inefficiency that may be more significant than allocative inefficiency. Many of his critics continue to give the impression that efficiency is not an important concept.

9.7. X-Efficiency and Allocative Efficiency: What Have We Learned?

Let me assume that the critics are correct. Now let me draw some conclusions from their correctness—conclusions that range from the ridiculous to the sublime.

9.7.1. Leisure and the Welfare Effects of a Subsidy

Let's assume that the critics are correct and that on-the-job "leisure" is a benefit of monopoly power rather than a cost. In figure 23, the impact of monopoly power is thus allocative inefficiency, ABC, plus and the higher costs of production caused by on-the-job-leisure, PmABPc. These higher costs are not an inefficiency in any meaningful sense. Rather they are a transfer of "income" from the owners of the company to the "owners" of leisure. Similar to monopoly profits, leisure does not reduce economic welfare.

Assuming that firms use marginal cost pricing, and assuming the monopolist's position of Qm, Pm, and Cm, policy makers could eliminate allocative inefficiency by providing a per-unit output subsidy. Under our current framework, this means subsidizing leisure. The subsidy would lower the firm's price from Pm to Pc as it lowers its marginal cost from Cm to Cc. The subsidy would increase the monopolist's output from Qm to Qc, the socially optimum rate. The costs of the subsidy would be PmECPc. All of this is standard economic analysis.

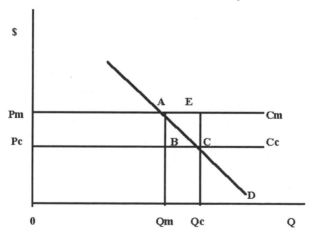

Figure 23. On-the-job leisure, and the welfare costs of a subsidy.

What are the benefits of the subsidy? The fact that leisure is a benefit changes both the calculation of the benefits and the desirability of this subsidy. Standard analysis measures the benefits as PmACPc, which is the increase in consumer surplus caused by the lower price and higher output rate of the subsidized monopolist. On this basis, standard analysis concludes that the benefits of the subsidy, PmACPc, are less than the costs, PmECPc. In other words the subsidy lowers welfare by the area AEC.

But assuming that PmABPc is leisure, a benefit, then we measure the benefits of a subsidy as PmACPc + AECB. First, it is correct to state that the consumer surplus will increase by PmACPc. There is, however, an additional benefit. Leisure being a benefit, any additional employees hired to increase output from Qm to Qc can reasonably be assumed to also experience leisure. If leisure is a benefit, then we must account for two sets of "consumers"—consumers of the commodity produced by the subsidy-assisted employees, and consumers of the leisure produced by the subsidy itself.

In other words, if PmABPc is a benefit, then so is AECB. The area ACB is thus enjoyed by both the employees of the subsidized firm and the consumer at large. The benefits of the subsidy, PmABPc + (2AECB—AEC), thus exceed the cost of the subsidy, PmECPc, by the amount ACB. The subsidy thus increases economic welfare. The perverse implication is that allocative efficiency and welfare can be increased by subsidizing X-inefficiency or leisure.

9.7.2. Rent-Seeking and the Welfare Costs of X-Inefficiency

Rent-seeking arguments have tended to assume that X-inefficiency can exist but entails no welfare loss. The reasoning is that rent-seeking and X-inefficiency are perfect substitutes for each other such that a dollar "allocated" to X-inefficiency is not available for rent-seeking. If leisure is a benefit, then X-inefficiency can affect economic welfare.

If a zero-sum game exists between X-inefficiency and rent-seeking, then we argue that it only exists in a static environment. In a dynamic environment, and beginning in figure 24 at Pm, Qm, and Cm, assume that rent-seeking expenditures, PmADE, secure the firm a government subsidy. The firm's cost curve falls to Cc, and the firm produces at Qc. The consumers pay Pc while the firm receives Pm. In standard analysis, the benefits of the subsidy are PmABPc while the costs are PmFBPc. The subsidy thus lowers economic welfare by ABC.

But if leisure is a benefit, then the benefits accrue to the consumers of the commodity and consumers of leisure. Consumers of the commodity benefit from an increase in their surplus, PmABPc. Consumers of on-the-job leisure benefit by DGBC. Again, if EDCPc is a benefit, then so is DGBC. The firm's excess profits, which are captured as rent-seeking expenditures, increase by AFGD. The total benefits of the surplus are thus PmACPc + (2AFBC—AFB). In this case, rent-seeking increases net social welfare by AFB.

Furthermore, the benefits of the subsidy include both more rent-seeking and more X-inefficiency. Both increase because both have the characteristic of being a

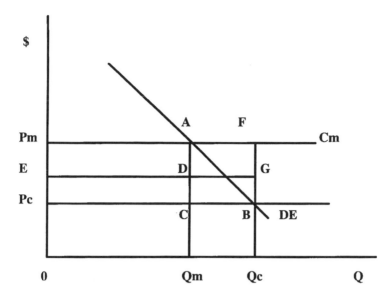

Figure 24. Rent-seeking, on-the-job leisure, and the welfare costs of a subsidy.

public good. That is, either is a benefit accruing to someone without there being a cost to anyone else. Again, there is a perverse implication: subsidizing leisure or X-inefficiency enhances economic welfare.

9.7.3. From the Ridiculous to the Sublime

With tongue in cheek, I will now extend some of the tortured logic of the critics of XE theory.

(1) Allocative inefficiency *cannot* exist. The socially optimum rate of output must take both commodities and leisure into account. As compared with a monopoly, competitive industries produce *more* commodity output but *less* leisure output. Since leisure is a benefit of monopoly, there is no a priori reason to believe that individuals prefer the competitive bundle. In other words, a priori, the monopoly bundle is not inefficient in any meaningful way. To claim otherwise is to apply a type of nirvana criterion to the definition of inefficiency. That is, it is a mistake to apply one's own discounting of leisure to the population at large. The implication is that if X-inefficiency cannot exist because it is merely beneficial leisure, then allocative inefficiency also cannot exist because it too is actually beneficial leisure. Mundell may have been correct after all!

(2) Productivity growth is of no importance. So long as wages reflect marginal products, then, in the long run, workers who demand on-the-job leisure will accept lower wages. Lower productivity is thus balanced by lower wages. The firm does not pay for on-the-job leisure that becomes an externality. The implication is thus that management should not care about long-run productivity growth.

(3) U.S. productivity has never fallen. In recent years there has been shifts from producing commodity output to producing leisure output. The implication is that there isn't any productivity "puzzle" to solve.

(4) Neither preferences nor choice matter. A worker producing less market output *must* be producing more leisure because, according to the laws of physics, "nothing is ever lost." The form taken by mass and energy — commodity output or leisure —does not matter: form is insignificant. The implication is that neither preferences nor choice matter.

9.8. Conclusions

If individuals make choices, then why can't we make an inferior choice? If we cannot, then what is the meaning of the word *choice*? Is the ability to *state* an argument against non-maximizing behavior sufficient proof that nonmaximizing behavior does not exist? The critics have proceeded'as if it is sufficient. They have proceeded *as if* nontraded products are traded, as if leisure is purchased while the individual is at work, and as if every type of cost—be it real or derived—is incurred in the correct quantity at the correct time so as to make nonmaximizing behavior an illusion.

They have proceeded as if individuals maximize subject to their—apparently observable—taste for nonmaximization. Thus firms are X-efficient and are cost minimizers, given their employees' taste for putting forth little mental and physical effort and hence driving costs above minimum levels. An individual is X-efficient given his or her unwillingness to put forth the effort to consider available options and costs and benefits. If only I could convince the Administration at San Diego State University that I am most deserving of yearly merit pay increases, given my unwillingness to work more than the expected *minimum*!

What becomes of the word *maximize* if nonmaximize is not possible? Is the concept of *efficiency* important if the possibility of inefficiency is ruled out a priori? When Harberger reported his small estimates for allocative-market-inefficiency, Leibenstein, Tullock and others were concerned that he might give the impression that economics itself is not important. Leibenstein, Tullock, and others have shown that there is a nonallocative inefficiency that is more important than allocative-mar-ket-inefficiency. In their hands, economics remains important. Harvey's critics continue to give the impression that efficiency, and perhaps economics itself, is not important.

10

IMPLICATIONS AND CONCLUSIONS

10.1. X and Allocative Efficiency

Do economic systems operate with inefficiencies not caused by market prices? In this book, I have presented one such type of (in)efficiency: X-(in)efficiency. X-inefficiency is not an inefficiency of the *market;* it is an intrafirm inefficiency.

The concept of X-efficiency was developed in the first place because the concept of allocative-efficiency did not account for important intrafirm activities that are a source of economic advantage to firms and/or industries. Clearly, the source of this economic advantage is different from the type caused by a competitive market generating the socially optimum rate of output, but it is an important source of economic advantage nonetheless. This type of advantage was ignored by traditional economic analysis but served as a motivator for Leibenstein's pursuit of its existence and nature.

In attempting to understand it, Leibenstein used the concepts of internal and external pressure, and selective rationality. These concept allowed Leibenstein to convey the idea that individual behavior, and with it the firm's functioning, often varies with its environment. The emphasis was on working out the implications for economic theory of environments that allow and tolerate noncost-minimizing behavior. The emphasis was *not* on theorizing about how a set of "implicit" prices influence the decisions of maximizing agents and create a unique price-output combination that defines implicit-allocative-efficiency. Leibenstein's approach, in short, was not to develop a theory that would "save" orthodox theory from empirical evidence.

Does orthodox theory need saving? Or are individuals and groups in fact always maximizing their goals, given the constraints they face? In order to evaluate these questions, data would have to be gathered on the motive and strategy of the managers. A firm-by-firm series of case studies would be required. Empirical studies using the data envelope method (DEA) have allowed researchers to enter the "black box" of the firm and hence approach this goal. The studies discussed in this book using the DEA method have presented data interpreted as showing the existence of X-inefficiencies.

On the other hand, expressing the intrafirm behavioral components as optimal reactions to implicit prices (as a utility function) too often only results in a tautology being presented as an explanation. One manifestation of this is the use of what I have referred to as implicit-price-allocative-inefficiency. The use of this definition of allocative inefficiency obviously does not prove that X-inefficiency does not exist.

10.2. X-Efficiency Theory as a Research Design

Empirical evidence supporting the existence of X-(in)efficiency were reported in chapters 6—8. These studies attempted to explain the (relative) efficiency of individuals, firms, or industries where performance was measured by relative profits, costs, or productivity. The evidence is varied and substantial enough, and lends support for XE theory.

The performance of the firm, however measured, is constrained by various factors. The issue that I believe needs some elaboration is which constraints were considered. In chapter 9, we considered the criticisms of both XE theory and the empirical evidence. These criticisms either explicitly or implicitly also considered certain constraints on the firm's performance. Again, which constraints were considered?

Let me argue that we might consider two types of constraints: external and internal. Let me also state the obvious, that productivity is affected by both external and internal constraints. The boundary between external and internal is, admittedly, vague. With this in mind, external constraints are those constraints that are part of the (external) environment within which the firm operates, and would include the structure of regulation, the structure of the market, and the structure of property rights, as well as the ownership form.

Internal constraints are those we could think of as being inherent in the behavior of an individual, or in the intrafirm interactions among individuals. Internal constraints would include personality traits, work norms, (internal) motivational factors, and transactions costs. Neoclassical theory chooses (but not exclusively so) to analyze the effect of external constraints on performance because of a belief that they are relatively easier to measure and analyze. In this regard, a difference between XE theory and neoclassical theory is stated succinctly by DeAlessi (1983, p.71 fn. 13):

> As Leibenstein argues, individuals no doubt differ regarding the way they feel they ought to behave and the way they would like to behave. They also differ in a variety of other characteristics (psychological, intellectual, physical) too numerous to list, and these differences presumably affect the extent and the intensity with which individuals respond to various changes in circumstances. What is at issue, therefore, is the usefulness of the theory used to choose and organize the variables that matter.

In other words, neoclassical theory chooses to focus on external constraints, at least in part because the internal constraints represent a "Pandora's box" that need not be opened. The internal constraints, although important, are "held constant" by the ceteris paribus clause. What neoclassical theory considers to be one of its strengths is also one of its major weaknesses. That is, by focusing on external constraints, neoclassical theory cannot correctly explain interfirm variations in productivity due to intrafirm activity. Considering only external constraints, neoclassical theory is forced to face a "specification" problem; that is, the net impact of the external variables is difficult to access. Due to the classic problem of "missing variables," the coefficients of the external variables will be both biased and inefficient.

To compound the problem, these external constraints were chosen in the first place because they are believed easier to measure. In any study, some variables must be measured and other controlled for, that is, not measured. In terms of an effective research design or strategy, it may be more appropriate to control for the external, more easily measurable constraints and to grapple with the more difficult-to-measure internal constraints. One advantage of this approach is that it increases the probability that appropriate controls are being implemented. Second, it forces the researchers to grapple with the difficult measurement issues raised by the inclusion of the internal constraints. And, while this approach is very challenging, the potential rewards are high, i.e., success allows one the ability to carry out more complete, and much needed, tests on the causes of interfirm productivity differences.

Many of the studies presented in chapters 6—8 focused on external constraints. Despite the fact that XE theory emphasizes both the external (environment) and internal (superego and id functions) pressures, most of the research has focused on the former. (The external pressures or constraints are easier to measure!) These studies present data interpreted to show the existence and magnitude of X-(in)efficiency and how it is affected by external pressures.

At the same time, several of the studies presented here make inroads into identifying and discussing internal constraints. These studies include those by Anderson and Frantz; Bradley and Gelb; Button and Weyman-Jones; Cook, Roll, and Kazakov; Fiorito and Hendricks; Gillis; Gollop and Karlson; Junankar; Kiyokawa; Lecraw; Maital and Leibenstein; Majumdar; Pack; Shapiro and Muller; Shelton; and; Timmer. More work is needed, and the DEA method offers great assistance, but the research on X-efficiency has already made a contribution to this endeavor.

10.3. X-Efficiency and Its Critics

Criticisms against the empirical work on XE theory have often focused on either an external and internal pressure that the author omitted from the study and that, were it included, would "save" the critic's interpretation of neoclassical theory. In some cases, the critics are either not aware of all the evidence or else doubt the reported results. For example, one criticism of Primeaux's finding that the monopolized industry has higher costs is explained by the critic with the assertion that the monopolist has more excess capacity. Primeaux has shown that the monopolist does not have greater excess capacity. And Weiss and Pascoe have presented data showing that X-efficiency can be separated from suboptimal capacity (economies of scale) and shown to have an independent effect on costs.

The other line of approach is for the critics to assert the existence of an internal pressure or constraint that has not been measured, i.e., utility-maximizing behavior, transactions costs, or implicit prices. The argument is usually that, given this internal constraint, the evidence is consistent with neoclassical theory. The difficulty with this criticism is that the constraint is always specified ex post. This approach, in other words, has been advanced for the purpose of assuming, ex ante, that X-(in)efficiency does not exist. The anarchistic nature of the "leisure as output" argument and the difficulties with using the concept of ex post transaction costs have already been discussed in chapter 9.

Another aspect of this consideration is given in Leibenstein's (1985) example of an individual who prefers commodity A to commodity B. On day 1 his consumption experience confirms his preference ranking. But on the following day, he takes a pill that clouds his judgment; he purchases commodity B and regrets the decision. Does the pill represent a "constraint"? Did this individual make optimal decisions both days, given this constraint? Does this example mean that XE theory does allow for optimizing decisions?

If the pill represents a constraint, then it represents a constraint that cannot be specified (identified) ex ante. It probably cannot be identified ex ante by an economist. In other words, either the pill must be used only in an ex post, tautological sense or else the example argues forcefully for interdisciplinary research efforts (in this case between economics and the biological sciences).

However, I would argue (as did Leibenstein) that the pill is the reason why a suboptimal decision was made. Individuals do not always make the best decision possible. Sometimes we are tired, sometimes we are angry, jealous, afraid. We often (speaking personally) look back and regret the decisions we make. And, looking back, we realize that a better decision could have been made only if....we had done something that we knew was correct at the time but did not carry out. Are we to consider our emotional states as constraints? Do we make optimal decisions given our anger, or does our anger prevent us from making optimal decisions?

10.4. X-Efficiency Theory and Neoclassical Theory: Some Final Thoughts

To say that an individual makes an optimizing decision given constraints is not a very helpful statement in the sense that there must always be some reason(s) why we do things. For example, suppose a person spends almost his or her entire paycheck buying clothes that he or she does not want but purchases anyway because he or she is depressed. After the depression ceases, the individual takes some of the clothes back and allow some of them to waste away in the closet. Was this person optimizing, given their constraint (his or her depression), or did the depression prevent him or her from allocating time and money in an optimal way?

Therefore I would ask the reader to consider the following: to assert that human behavior is optimal given constraints means that the economics profession is committed to discovering these external and internal constraints. If this is our intention, then we may want to consider abandoning the approach that all human behavior can be adequately analyzed as if were a market transaction, i.e., a transaction motivated by a market price.

When we analyze (real) market transactions we are on solid ground, i.e., we understand that people respond to market prices given the income and technology constraints and allow much of the remainder of the world to be "controlled" for with the ceteris paribus assumption. And this ceteris paribus assumption is appropriate, because we are interested in analyzing market behavior, i.e., reactions to prices. However, when our interest is in nonmarket behavior, then the critical constraints facing the individual become the world surrounding him or her. Since these constraints are the critical ones, then we cannot set aside the world and the individual's interaction with it through the ceteris paribus assumption.

These constraints come within the boundary of many other disciplines. It would seem, therefore, that the process of economic models specifying the constraints facing human behavior is in a very early stage. Therefore, it does not seem efficient to limit our models to those in which human behavior is assumed everywhere to be market behavior, i.e., aggressive and tightly calculating.

In 1966, when Leibenstein formulated XE theory, the concept of intrafirm behavior was relatively new to the economics profession. Leibenstein developed XE theory in order to provide an explanation for intrafirm behavior that was seemingly noncost minimizing. Because economics was mostly concerned with market behavior, the constraints were relatively straight- forward. The attempt to explain intrafirm behavior led many economists to assert optimization under constraints. (As I mentioned earlier, this was not Leibenstein's approach.) This required the specification of many more constraints.

For whatever reason, these constraints were specified both ex ante and ex post. Any serious look at the critics of XE theory would have to conclude that this has been the case. The critics of XE theory have not proved their case because they have had to specify their constraints ex post. Perhaps this should lead us to rethink our belief that economic theory is an intellectual tool so powerful that it can analyze all behavior, regardless of whether behavior is called, sociological, psychological, political, marital, or spiritual.

And this observation is perhaps one of the major contributions of XE theory. That is, XE theory presents us with the prospect that economic theory has currently undertaken more than it can deliver. By putting forth the concept of X-efficiency—a form of inefficiency not caused by market prices deviating from marginal cost— and including the concept of suboptimal behavior, Leibenstein has caused the most jealous defenders of neoclassical theory to come forth and argue their case by assertion. One can conclude, that these assumptions are what micro-economic theory now rests on, then the push into intrafirm behavior has temporarily thrown microeconomics into a state of disequilibrium. That is, in attempting to explain intrafirm, not market, behavior, microeconomics has delved into an area that it is not now equipped to handle efficiently. And, there is no reason to believe that it could make the transition from market to nonmarket behavior automatically.

To return to the pill example: does this example mean that XE theory does not allow for optimizing decisions? Furubotn (1987), while sympathetic to some aspects of Leibenstein's arguments and to XE theory in general, tries to argue that it does. I would argue that the pill example simply makes the point that suboptimal decisions are possible. That is, there are reasons why a suboptimal decision is made. It does not mean that optimal decisions cannot or are not made—only that suboptimal decisions are possible. While Furubotn is not meant to be the object of this statement, I would ask the reader to consider that the idea of maximization is so central to the work of academic economists that the concept of nonmaximization evokes a type of "gut" response that is not efficient.

Looking at this issue another way, we can say that to assert that behavior is optimizing for given constraints implies that undesirable outcomes are the result of an environment that is creating these outcomes. At the same time, the individual is considered to be doing his or her best for this given environment. The policy implication is that we should change the environment such that the individual is able to respond to a more (socially) desirable set of incentives, but at the same time make no attempt at interfering directly with the individual. (Of course, the environment was created by individuals.)

Let me argue briefly why the existence of suboptimal behavior would be important. To assert optimal behavior can and has been interpreted to mean that whatever is, is best for both the firm and the employees. To allow for suboptimal behavior would change this perspective. This is perhaps especially true when two parties enter into a contractual arrangement where one party is more prone to suboptimality than is the other. For example, if employees are more subject to making suboptimal decisions than is the firm, then perhaps one very useful function of the union is to protect their members from such suboptimal decisions, which they might later regret. Perhaps this is one way to interpret the positive impact of unions reported by Freeman and Medoff (1984). (I am fully aware that this concept of protecting ourselves from ourselves raises extremely serious and broad-ranging issues that obviously are not being taken up in this book.)

A second example is perhaps the impact of advertising. If consumers are more subject to suboptimal decision making than are the advertisers (as advertisers), then a more compelling case can be made that advertising is more than simply dispersing information. A more compelling case could be made that advertising has some adverse effects of which the consumer may not even be aware at the time. In general, the concept of suboptimal decisions could lead us to change our perspective of any contractual relations.

There are two separate points here that need to be clarified. One is that X-inefficiency is nonmarket inefficiency. It is caused by an environment—external and/or internal—that does not result in procedurally rational decisions and that affects the utilization of resources within the firm. Leibenstein has been a voice for making the economics profession aware of the need to establish (structural) behavioral relations that affect intrafirm behavior.

I will assert that behavior inside of the firm vis-a-vis inside the market is involved to a greater extent with less objective and less quantifiable situational variables. Whereas markets provide signals in the form of prices, firms do not provide such clear, unambiguous signals to employees. On this basis, complete rationality is less likely to occur inside firms.

Second, suboptimal decisions have been defined as nonprocedurally rational decisions. I would ask the reader to consider that X-inefficiency occurs regardless of whether suboptimal decisions occur, because an individual works for a firm in which the norms discourage high levels of effort, or because terminating an employee is very difficult (which is often a fact of life in both the private and public sectors), or because the individual is not given proper instructions, or because individuals are afraid to seek available information (because, for example, they fear that they are not competent and do not want to know it). Perhaps some suboptimal decisions are unavoidable. Others are avoidable. It would clearer be useful to be able to identify the components of both categories. Regardless of the reasons, (avoidable) suboptimal decisions are being made that results in an unnecessary loss of productivity.

REFERENCES

Alchian, A., and Kessel, R., 1962, "Competition, Monopoly and the Pursuit of Money," in Aspects of Labor Economics, edited by the National Bureau of Economic Research, Princeton, N.J.: Princeton University Press.

Altman, M., 1988, "Economic Development with High Wages: An Historical Perspective," Explorations in Economic History, vol. 25, pp. 198-224. Anderson, J., and Frantz, R., 1982, "The Response of Labor Effort to Falling Real Wages: The Mexican Peso Devaluation of February 1982," World Development, vol. 12, July, pp. 759-766.

Anderson & Frantz, 19X5, "Production Efficiency among Mexican Apparel Assembly Plants," Journal of Developing Areas. vol. 19, no. 3. pp. 369-378.

Arrow, K., 1969, "The Organization of Economic Activity: Issues Pertinent to the Choice of Market versus Nonmarket Allocation," in The Analysis and Evaluation of Public Expenditure: The PPB System, vol. 1, U.S. Joint Economic Committee, 91st. Congress, Ist. Session, Washington D.C.: U.S. Government Printing Office.

Atkinson, S., and Halvorsen, R., 1986, "The Relative Efficiency of Public and Private Firms in a Regulated Environment: The Case of U.S. Electric Utilities," Journal of Public Economics, vol. 29, no. 3, pp. 281-294.

Aukrust, O., 1959, "Investment and Economic Growth," Productivity Measurement Review, vol. 16, Feb., pp. 35-53.

Babilot, G.. Frantz, R., and Green, L., 1987, "Natural Monopolies and Rent: A Georgist Remedy for X-lnefficiency Among Regulated Firms," American Journal of Sociology, Vol. 46, April 1987, pp. 205-216 .

Banker, R., Chang, H, and Majumdar, S., 1992, "Economies of Scale in U.S. Local Exchange Telecommunications: Evidence and Implications," Unpublished Manuscript, Graduiate School of Business, University of Michigan, Ann Arbor.

Barnard, C., 193X, The Functions of the Executive, Cambridge: Harvard Univ. Press.

Baron, D., 1974, 'A Study of Hospital Cost Inflation," Journal of Human Resources, vol. 9, Winter, pp. 33-49.

Baumol, W., 1959, "The Revenue Maximization Hypothesis,' in Busincss Behavior, Value, and Growth, New York: Macmillan, pp. 45-53.

Baumol, W., 1965, The Stock Market and Economic Efficiency. New York: Fordham Univ. Press.

Bergsman, J., 1974, "Commercial Policy, Allocative Efficiency and 'X-Efficiency'," Western Economic Review, vol. 8, Dec., pp. 409-433.

Berle, A., and Means. G., 1932, The Modern Corporation and Private Property, New York: Macmillan.

Bierman, H., and Tollison, R., 1970, "Monopoly Rent Capitalization and Antitrust Policy," Western Economic Journal, vol. 8, Dec., pp. 385-389.

Boddy, R., Frantz, R., and Poe-Tierney, B., 1986, "The Marginal Productivity Theory: Production Line and Machine Level by Work Shift and Time of Day," Journal of Behavioral Economics, vol. 15, Spring/Summer, pp. 1-24.

Bradley, K., and Gelb. A., 1981, "Motivation and Control in the Mondragon Experiment," British Journal of Industrial Relations, vol. 19, July, pp. 211-231.

Bruggink, T., 1982, "Public versus Private Enterprise in the Municipal Water Industry: A Comparison of Operating Costs," Quarterly Review of Economics and Business, vol. 22, Spring, pp. 111-125.

Button, K., 1985, "Potential Differences in the Degree of X-Inefficiency Between Industrial Sectors in the United Kingdom," Quarterly Review of Economics and Business," vol. 25, Autumn, pp. vol. 85-95.

_____, and Weyman-Jones, T., 1992, "Ownership Structure, Institutional Organization and Measured X-Efficiency," American Economic Review, Papers & Proceedings, vol. 82, May, pp. 439-445.

Carlsson, B., 1972, "The Measurement of Efficiency in Production: An Application to Swedish Manufacturing Industries, 1968," Swedish Journal of Economics, vol. 74, Dec., pp. 468-485.

Charnes, A., Cooper, W.W., and Rhodes, E, 1978, "Measuring the Efficiency of Decision-making Units," European Journal of Operations Research, vol. 2, November, pp. 429-444.

Cook, W., Kazakov, A., Roll, Y., and L. Seiford, 1991, "A Data Envelope Approach to Measuring Efficiency: The Case of Highway Maintenance Patrols, " Journal of Socio-Economics, vol. 20, No. 1, pp. 83-103.

Cole, A., 1959, Business Enterprise in Its Social Setting, Cambridge: Harvard Univ. Press.

Crain, M., and Zardkoohi, A., 1980, "X-Efficiency and Nonpecuniary Rewards in a Rent Seeking Society: A Neglected Issue in the Property Rights Theory of the Firm," American Economic Rev., vol. 70, Sept., pp. 784-792.

Craven, B., Dick, B., and Wood, B., 1986, "The Behavior of a Resource Reducing Bureau. A Case Study of an English Polytechnic," Applied Economics, vol. 18, pp. 87-99.

Cyert, R.M., and March, J.G., 1963, A Behavioral Theory of the Firm, Englewood Cliffs: Prentice-Hall.

Davis, K., 1973 "Theories of Hospital Inflation: Some Empirical Evidence," Journal of Human Resources, vol. 8, Spring, pp. 181-201.

DeAlessi, L., 1980, "The Economics of Property Rights: A Review of the Evidence," in Research in Law and Economics, vol. 2, edited by R. Zerbe, Greenwich: JAI Press.

De Alessi, 1983, "Property Rights, Transactions Costs, and X-Efficiency: An Essay in Economic Theory," American Economic Review, vol. 75, March, pp. 64-81.

DeBono, E., 1982, DeBono's Thinking Course, New York: Facts on File Publications.

DiLorenzo, T., 1981, "Corporate Management, Property Rights, and the X-istence of X-Inefficiency," Southern Economic Journal, vol. 48, July, pp. 116-123.

Erickson, W., 1976, "Price-Fixing Conspiracies: Their Long Term Impact," Journal of Industrial Relations, vol. 24, March, pp. 189-202.

Estes, W., 1980, "Comments on Directions and Limitations of Current Efforts Toward Theories of Decision Making," in Cognitive Processes in Choice and Decision Behavior," edited by T. Wallsten, Hillsdale, N. J.: Lawrence Erlbaum Assoc.

Farrell, M.J., 1957, "The Measurement of Productive Efficiency," Journal of Royal Statistical Society, Series A, vol. 120, no. 3, pp. 253-282.

Fechner, G., 1860, Elemente der Psychophysik, Leibzig: Breitkopf & Hartel.

Fiorito, J., and Hendricks, W., 1987, "Union Characteristics and Bargaining Outcomes," Industrial and Labor Relations Review, vol. 40, June, pp. 569-584.

Food Systems Research Group, 1977, "The Profit and Price Performance of Leading Food Chains, 1970-1974," in U.S. Congress, Joint Economic Comm., 95th. Congress, Ist. Sess., April 12, 1977.

Forsund, F., and Hjalmarsson, P., 1974, "On the Measurement of Productive Efficiency," Swedish Journal of Economics, vol. 76, June, pp. 141-154.

Forsund, Lovell, C., and Schmidt, P., 1980, "A Survey of Frontier Production Functions and of their Relationship to Efficiency Measurement," Journal of Econometrics, vol. 13, May, pp. 5-25.

Frank, Robert, Microeconomics and Behavior, New York, McGraw Hill, 1991.

Frantz, R., 1980, "On the Existence of X-Efficiency," Journal of Post Keynesian Economics, vol. 4, Summer, pp., 509-527.

————, 1982, "Worker Motivation and X-Efficiency Theory: A Comment." Journal of Economic Issues, vol. 16, Sept., pp. 864-868.

————, 1984, "Corporate Management, Property Rights and the Existence of X-Efficiency Once More," Southern Economic Journal, vol. 50, April, pp. 1204-1208.

————, 1985, "X-Efficiency Theory and Its Critics," Quarterly Review of Economics and Business, vol. 25, no. 4, pp. 38-58.

————, 1986, 'X-Efficiency in Behavioral Economics," in Handhook of Behavioral Economics, vol. A, edited by B. Gilad, and S. Kaish, Greenwich, Ct.

————, 1992, "X-Efficiency and Allocative Efficiency: What Have We Learned? American Economic Review, Papers & Proceedings., vol. 82, # 2, May, pp. 434-438.

————, and Galloway, F., 1985, "A Theory of Multidimensional Effort Decisions," Journal of Behavioral Economics, vol. 14, Winter, pp. 69-82.

————, and Green, L., 1982, "Prejudice, Mistrust, and Labor Effort: Social Infuences on Productivity," Journal of Behavioral Economics, vol. 11, Summer, pp. 101- 131.

Freeman, R., and Medoff, J., 1984, What-Do Unions Do?, New York: Basic Books.

Furubotn, E., 1986, "Efficiency and the Maximization Postulate: Another Interpretation," Journal Behavioral Economics., vol. 15, Winter, pp. 41-48.

Furth, M., 1980, "Takeovers, Shareholder Returns, and the Theory of the Firm, Quarterly Journal of Economics, vol. 94, March, pp. 235-260.

Geldard, F.A., 1972, The Human Senses, New York: Wiley & Sons.

Gillis, M., 1982, "Allocative and X-Efficiency in State Owned Mining Enterprises: Comparisons Between Bolivia and Indonesia," Journal of Comparative Economics., vol. 6, March, pp. 1-23.

Globerman, S., and Book, S., 1974, "Statistical Cost Functions for Performing Arts Organizations," Southern Economic Journal, vol. 40, April, pp. 668-671.

Gollop, F., and Karlson, S., 1978, "The Impact of the Fuel Adjustment Mechanism on Economic Efficiency," Review of Economics and Statistics., vol. 60, Nov., pp. 574-584.

Gordon, R.A., 1961, Business Leadership in the Large Corporation, Berkeley: Univ. Cal. Press.

Green, A., and Mayes, D., 1991, "Technical Inefficiency in Manufacturing Industries," The Economic Journal, vol. 101, May, pp. 523-538.

Gregory, R.G., and James, Denis, 1973, "Do New Factories Embody Best Practice Technology?," Economic Journal, vol. 83, December, pp. 1133-1155.

Harbison, F.H., 1965, "Entrepreneurial Organization as a Factor in Economic Development," Quarterly Journal of Economics," vol. 70, August, p. 373.

Hayakawa, H., and Venieris, Y., 1973, "Consumer Interdependence via Reference Groups," Journal of Political Economics, vol. 85, May/June, pp. 599-615.

Heitger, Bernard, 1987, "Import Protection and Export Performance - Their Impact on Economic Growth," Weltwirtschaftliches Archiv., vol. 123, # 2, pp. 249-261.

Hicks, J. R., 1935, "Annual Survey of Economic Theory: The Theory of Monopoly," Econometrica, vol. 3, Jan., pp. 1-20.

Hillman, A., and Katz, E., 1984, "Risk-Averse Rent Seekers and the Social Cost of Monopoly Power," Economic Journal, vol. 94, March, pp. 104-110.

Hitch, C., and Hall, R., 1939, "Price Theory and Business Behavior," Oxford Economic Papers, vol. 2, May, pp. 12-45.

Hollas, D., and Hereen, R., 1982, "An Estimate of the Deadweight and XEfficiency Losses in the Municipal Electric Industry," Journal of Economics and Business, vol. 34, pp. 269-281.

Holtermann, S., 1973, "Market Structure and Economic Performance in the U. K. Manufacturing Industry," Journal of Industrial Economics, vol. 22, Dec., pp. 119-139.

Holtman, A., 1983, "Uncertainty, Organizational Form, and X-Efficiency," Journal of Economics and Business, vol. 35, pp. 131-137.

Hossain, S., 1987, "Allocative and Technical Efficiency: A Study of Rural Enterprises in Bangladesh," The Developing Economies, vol. 25, March, pp. 56-72.

Junanker, P., 1976, "Land Tenure and Indian Agricultural Productivity," Journal of Development Studies, vol. 13, Oct., pp. 42-60. Kalirajan, K.P., and Tse, Y.K., 1989, "Technical Efficiency Measures for the Malaysian Food Manufacturing Industries," The Developing Economies, vol 37, June, pp. 174-184.

Katrak, H., 1980, "Industry Structure, Foreign Trade and Price-Cost Margins in Indian Manufacturing Industries," Journal of Development Studies, vol. 17, Oct., pp. 62-79.

Keynes, J.M., 1935, Essays in Persuasion, London: Macmillan.

Kilby, Peter, 1962, "Organization and Productivity in Backward Economies," Quarterly Journal of Economics, vol. 76, May, pp. 303-310.

Kiyokawa, Y., 1991, "The Transformation of Young Rural Women into Disciplined Labor Under Competition-Oriented Management: The Experience of the Silk-Reeling Industry in Japan," Hitotsubashi Journal of Economics, vol. 32, December, pp. 49-69.

Kohler, H., 1986, Intermediate Microeconomics. Theory and Applications, Glenview, Illinois: Scott Foresman.

Krueger, A., 1974, "The Political Economy of the Rent-Seeking Society," American Economic Review, vol. 64, June, pp. 291-303.

Lecraw, D., 1977, "Empirical Tests for X-lnefficiency," Kyklos, vol. 30, no. 1, pp. 116-120.

_____, 1978, "Determinants of Capacity Utilization by Firms in LDC's," Journal of Development Studies, vol. 5, June, pp. 139-153.

Lecraw, D., 1979, "Choice of Technology in Low-Wage Countries: A Non Neoclassical Approach," Quarterly Journal of Economics, vol. 93, Nov., pp. 631-654.

Lee, J, 1986, "Market Performance in an Open Developing Economy: Technical and Allocative Efficiencies of Korean Industries," The Journal of Industrial Economics, vol. 35, September, pp. 81-96.

Leibenstein, H., 1960, Economic Theory and Organizational Analysis, New York: Harper & Row.

_____, 1966, "Allocative Efficiency vs. 'X-Efficiency'," American Economic Review, vol. 56, June, pp. 392-415.

_____, 1969, "Organizational or Frictional Equilibria, X-Efficiency and the Rate of Innovation," Quarterly Journal of Economics, vol. 83, Nov., pp. 600-623.

Leibenstein, Harvey, 1976, Beyond Economic Man, Cambridge: Harvard Univ. Press.

_____, 1977, 'X-Efficiency, Technical Efficiency, and Incomplete Information Use: A Comment," Economic Development and Cultural Change, vol. 25, Jan., pp. 311-316.

_____, 1978a, General X-Efficiency Theory and Economic Development, New York: Oxford Univ. Press.

_____, 1978b, "X-inefficiency Xists: A Reply to an Xorcist," American Economic Review, vol. 68, March. pp. 203-211.

_____, 1979a, "A Branch of Economics is Missing: Micro-Micro Theory," Journal of Economic Literature, vol. 17, June, pp. 477-502.

_____, 1979b, "X-Efficiency: From Concept to Theory," Challenge, vol. 22, Sept/Oct., pp. 13-22.

_____, 1982a, "The Prisoner's Dilemma in the Invisible Hand: An Analysis of Intrafirm Productivity," American Economic Review, vol. 72, May, pp. 92-97.

_____, 1982b, "On Bull's-Eye Painting Economics," Journal of Post Keynesian Economics, vol. 4, Spring, pp. 460-465.

_____, 1983, "Property Rights Theory and X-Efficiency Theory: A Comment," American Economic Review, vol. 73, Sept., pp. 831-842.

_____, 1985, "On Relaxing the Maximization Postulate," Journal of Behavioral Economics, vol. 14, Winter, pp. 5-20.

_____, and Maital, S., 1992, "Empirical Estimation and Partitioning of X-Inefficiency: A Data-Envelope Approach," Americal Economic Review Papers and Proceedings, vol 82, May, pp. 428-433.

Lester, R., 1946, Marginal Analysis for Wage-Employment Problems," American Economic Review, vol. 36, March, pp. 63-82.

Levin, H.. 1974. "Measuring Efficiency in Educational Production," Puhlic Finance Quarterly, vol. 2, Nov., pp. 831-842.

Lewis, W. Arthur, 1954, "Economic Development with Unlimited Supplies of Labour," Manchester School, vol. 22, May, pp. 139-191

Lewis, D.. 1969, Conventions: A Philosophical Study, Camhridge: Harvard University Press.

Lin, J, 1992, "Rural Reforms and Agricultural Growth in China," American Economic Review, vol. 82, March, pp. 34-51.

Locke, E., 1976, "The Nature and Causes of Joh Satisfaction," in Handhook of Industrial and Organizational Psychology, edited by M. Dunnette, Chicago: Rand McNally.

Loeb, M., and Magat, W., 1979, "A Decentralized Method for Utility Regulation." Journal of Law and Economics, vol. 22, Oct., pp. 58-73.

McEachern, W., 1978, "Corporate Control and Growth: An Alternative Approach," Journal of Industrial Economics, vol. 26, March, pp. 257-266.

McFetridge, D., 1973, "Market Structure and Price-Cost Margins: An Analysis of the Canadian Manufacturing Sector," Canadian Journal of Economics, vol. 6, August, pp. 244-255.

Maddi, S., and Kobasa, S., 1984, The Hardy Executive: Health Under Stress, Chicago: Dorsey.

Main, J., 1983a, "Anatomy of An Auto Plant Rescue," Fortune, April 4, p. I0X.

_____, 1983b, 'Ford's Drive For Quality," Fortune, April 18, p. 62.

Majumdar, S., 1993, "X-Efficiency in Emerging Competitive Markets: The Case of U.S. Telecommunications," Journal of Economic Behavior and Organization, vol. 266, # 1, pp. 129-144.

Manne, H., 1965, "Mergers and the Market for Corporate Control," Journal of Political Economy, vol. 72, April, pp. 110-120.

Martin, J., 197X, "X-inefficiency, Managerial Effort and Protection," Economica, vol. 45, pp. 273-286.

Marris, Robin, 1963, "A Model of the Managerial Enterprise," Quarterly Journal of Economics, vol. 77, May, pp. 185-209.

_____, 1964, The Economic Theory of Managerial Capitalism, New York: Free Press.

Marshall, A., 1923, Industry and Trade, London: Macmillan.

Maynard, A., 1979, "Pricing Insurance and the National Health Service," Journal of Social Policy, vol. 8(part 2), April, pp. 157-176.

Monsen, R., and Downs, A., 1965, "The Theory of a Large Managerial Firm," Journal of Political Economics, vol. 73, June, pp. 221-236.

Monsen, Chiu, J., and Cooley, D., 1968, "The Effect of Separation of Ownership and Control on the Performance of the Large Firm," Quarterly Journal of Economics, vol. 82, August, pp. 435-451.

McCormick, R., Shughart II, W., and Tollison, R., 1984, "The Dis-Interest in Deregulation," American Economic Review, vol. 75, no. 5, pp. 1075-1079.

Medford, Robert, 1986, "Introducing Management into the Production Function," Review of Economics and Statistics, vol. 68, #1, pp. 96-104.

Mullen, John, and Roth, Byron, 1991, Decision Making. Its Logic and Practice. Savage Maryland, Rowman & Littlefield.

Mundell, R., 1962, "Review of L.H. Janssen, Free Trade, Protection and Customs Union," American Economic Review, vol. 52, June, p. 622.

Muskin, J., and Sorentino, J., 1977, "Externalities in a Regulated Industry: The Aircraft Noise Problem," American Economic Review, vol. 67, March, pp. 347-350.

Newhouse, J., 1973, "The Economics of Group Practice," Journal of Human Resources, vol. 8, Winter, pp. 37-56.

Niitamo, O., 195X, "Development of Productivity in Finnish Industry, 1925- 1952," Productivity Measurement Review. vol. 15. Nov.. pp. 30-41.

Pack, H., 1974, "The Employment-Output Trade-Off in LDC's - A Microeconomic Approach," Oxford Economic Papers (New Series), vol. 26, # 3, pp. 388-404.

_____, 1976, "The Substitution of Labour for Capital in Kenyan Manufactur-ing," The Economic Journal, vol. 86, March, pp. 45-58.

Page, J., 1980, Technical Efficiency and Economic Performance: Some Evidence from Ghana," Oxford Econ. Papers, vol. 32, July, pp. 319-339.

Parish, R., and Ng, Y., 1972, "Monopoly. X-Efficiency, and the Measurement of Welfare Losses," Economica, vol. 39, August, pp. 301-308.

Pasour, Jr., E., 19X2, "Economic Efficiency and Inefficient Economies: Another View," Journal of Post Keynesian Economics, vol. 4, Spring, pp. 454-459.

Peel, D., 1974, "A Note on X-Inefficiency," Quarterly Journal of Economics, vol. 88, Nov., pp. 687-688.

Pittman, Russell, 1990, "Railroads and Competition: The Santa Fe / Southern Pacific Merger Proposal," Journal of Industrial Economics, vol. 39, September, pp. 25-46.

Pratten, C. F., 1976, Labor Productivity Differentials Within International Companies, Cambridge: Cambridge Univ. Press.

Primeaux, W., 1977, "An Assessment of X-Efficiency Gained Through Competition," Review of Economics and Statistics, vol. 59, Feb., pp. 105-113.

_____, 1978, "The Effect of Competition on Capacity Utilization in the Electric Utility Industry," Economic Inquiry, vol. 26, April, pp. 237-248.

_____, 1985, 'Dismantling Competition in a Natural Monopoly," Quarterly Review of Economics and Business, vol. 25, Autumn, pp. 6-21.

_____, 1986, Direct Electric Utility Competition: The Natural Monopoly Myth, New York: Praeger.

Pustay, M., 1978, "Industrial Inefficiency Under Regulatory Surveillance," Journal of Industrial Economics, vol. 27, Sept.. pp. 49-68.

Register, C., 1988, "Wages, Productivity, and Costs in Union and Nonunion Hospitals," Journal of Labor Research, vol. 9, # 4, pp. 325-345.

_____, and Grimes, P., 1991, "Collective Bargaining, Teachers, and Student Achievement," Journal of Labor Research, vol. 12, Spring, pp. 99-107.

Rostas, Laszio, 1964, Comparative Productivity in British and American Industry, Research Paper #13, Cambridge: National Institute of Economic Sociology.

Rozen, M., 1985, "Maximizing Behavior: Reconciling Neoclassical and XEfficiency Approaches," Journal of Economic Issues, vol. 19, Sept., pp. 661-685.

Salter, W., 1960, Productivity and Technical Change, Cambridge: Cambridge Univ. Press.

Schap, D., 1985, "X-inefficiency in a Rent-Seeking Society: A Graphical Analysis," Quarterly Review of Economics and Business, Spring, pp. 19-27.

Scherer, F., Beckenstein, A., Kaufer, E., and Murphy, R., 1975, The Economics of Multi-Plant Operations: An International Comparisons Study, Cambridge: Harvard Univ. Press.

Schiller, B., 1986, The Microeconomy Today (3rd. ed.), New York: Random House.

Schive, C., 1988, "An Intra-Firm Study of X-Efficiencyof Taiwan's Sugar Industry," The Developing Economies, vol. 26, June, pp. 161-171.

Schoemaker, P., 1982, "The Expected Utility Model: Its Variants, Purposes, Evidence and Limitations," Journal of Economic Literature, vol. 20, June, pp. 529-564.

Scitovsky, T., 1943, "A Note of Profit Maximization and Its Implications," Review of Economic Studies, vol. 11, no. 1, pp. 57-60.

_____, 1976. The Joyless Economy, New York: Oxford Univ. Press.

Seiford, M.L., 1990, "A Bibliography of Data Envelope Analysis (1978-1990): Version 5.0," Technical report, Department of Industrial Engineering, University of Massachusetts, Amherst.

_____, and Thrall, M., 1990, "Recent Developments in DEA: The Mathematical Programming Approach to Frontier Analysis, " Journal of Econmometrics, vol. 46, Oct-Nov., pp. 7-38.

Shapiro, K., and Muller, J., 1977, "Sources of Technical Efficiency: The Roles of Modernization and Information," Economic Development andCultural Change. vol. 25, Jan. pp. 293- 310.

Shelton, J., 1967, "Allocative Efficiency versus 'X-Efficiency': Comment," American Economic Review, vol. 57, Dec., pp. 1252-1258.

Shen, T.Y., 1973, "Technology Diffusion, Substitution, and X-Efficiency," Econometrica, vol. 41, March, pp. 263-284.

_____, 1984, "Estimation of X-Inefficiency in Eighteen Countries," Review of Economics and Statistics, vol. 66, Feb., pp. 98-104.

_____, 1986, "Putting X-Efficiency In Its Place at a Pinnacle," Journal of Behavioral Economics, vol. 15, Winter, pp. 29-34.

Shepherd, W., 1972a, "The Elements of Market Structure," Review of Economics and Statistics, vol. 54, Feb., pp. 25-37.

_____, 1972b, "Elements of Market Structure: An Inter-Industry Analysis," Southern Economic Journal, vol. 38, April, pp. 531-537.

Siegfried, J., and Wheeler, E., 1981, "Cost Efficiency and Monopoly Power: A Survey," Quarterly Review of Economics and Business, vol. 21, Spring, pp. 25-46.

Silkman, R., and Young, D., 1982, "X-Efficiency and State Formula Grants," National Tax Journal, vol. 35, Sept., pp. 383-397.

Simon, H., 1957, Models of Man, New York: John Wiley & Sons.

_____, 1959, "Theories of Decision Making in Economics and Behavioral Science," American Economic Review, vol. 49, June, pp. 253-283.

_____, 1965, Administrative Behavior, New York: Free Press.

_____, 1978, 'Rationality as Process and as Product of Thought," American Economic Review, vol. 68, May, pp. 1-16.

Singh, A., 1975, "Takeovers, 'Natural Selection,' and the Theory of the Firm," Economic Journal, vol. 85, Sept., pp. 497-515.

Smiley, R., 1976, "Tender Offers, Transactions Costs and the Theory of the Firm," Review of Economics and Statistics, vol. 58, Feb., pp. 22-32.

Solow, R. M., 1957, "Technical Progress and the Aggregate Production Function," Review of Economics and Statistics, vol. 39, August, pp. 312-320.

_____, 1959, "Investment and Economic Growth," Productivity Measurement Review, vol. 16, Feb., pp. 62-68.

Stevenson, R., 1982, "X-inefficiency and Interfirm Rivalry: Evidence From the Electric Utility Industry," Land Economics, vol. 58, Feb., pp. 52-66.

Stigler, G., 1976, "The X-istence of X-Efficiency," American Economic Review, vol. 66, March, pp. 213-216.

Sudit, E., 1979, "Automatic Rate Adjustment Based on Total Factor Productivity in Public Utility Regulation," in Problems in Public Utility and Economics and Regulation, edited by M. Crew, Lexington, Mass.: Lexington Books.

Tanner, W., and Swets, J., 1954, "A Decision-Making Theory of Visual Detection, Psychological Review, vol. 61, pp. 401-409.

Thaler, Richard, 1980, "Toward a Positive Theory of Consumer Choice," Journal of Economic Behavior and Organization, vol. 1, pp. 39-60.

Thomas, H., and Logan, C., 1982, Mondragon: An Economic Analysis, London: George Allen and Unwin.

Timmer, Peter, 1971, 'Using a Probabilistic Frontier Production Function to Measure Technical Efficiency," Journal of Political Economics, vol. 79, July/August, pp. 776 - 794.

Tullock, G., 1967, "The Welfare Costs of Tariffs, Monopolies, and Theft, " Western Economic Journal, vol. 5, June, pp. 224-232.

_____, 1980. "Efficient Rent Seeking," in Toward a Theory of the Rent-Seeking Society," edited by J. Buchanan, R. Tollison. and G. Tullock, College Station: Texas A & M Univ. Press.

Tversky, Amos, and Kahneman, Daniel, 1974, "Judgement Under Uncertainty: Heuristics and Biases," Science, vol. 185, pp. 1124-1131.

Tyler, W., 1979, "Technical Efficiency in Production in a Developing Country: An Empirical Examination of the Brazilian Plastics and Steel Industries," Oxford Econ. Papers, vol. 31, Nov., pp. 477-495.

Ullmann-Margalit, E., 1977, The Emergence of Norms, New York: Oxford Univ. Press.

Vining, A., and Boardman, A., 1992, "Ownership versus Competition: Efficiency in Public Enterprises," Public Choice, vol. 73, March, pp. 205-239.

Weiss, H., and Ilgen, D., 1985, "Routinized Behavior in Organizations," Journal of Behavioral Economics, vol. 14, Winter, pp. 57-68.

Weiss, L., and Pascoe, G., 1985, 'Concentration, X-Inefficiency and Mr. Peltzman's Superior Firms," Social Systems Research Institute Working Paper No. X501, Madison: University of Wisconsin.

Wells, L., 1973, "Economic Man and Engineering Man: Choice and Technology in a Low-Wage Country," Public Policy, vol. 21, Summer, pp. 319-342.

White, L., 1979, "Appropriate Technology, X-Inefficiency, and a Competitive Environment: Some Evidence From Pakistan," Quarterly Journal of Economics, vol. 90, Nov., pp. 575-589.

Wilder, R., and Stansell, S., 191974, "Determinants of Research and Development Activity by Electric Utilities," Bell Journal of Economics and Business, vol. 5, Autumn, pp. 646-650.

Wilson, G., 1975, "Regulation, Public Policy, and Efficient Provision of Freight Transporation," Transportation Journal, vol. 15, Fall, pp. 5-20.

Williamson, O., 1964, The Economics of Discretionary Behavior: Management Objectives in a Theory of the Firm, Englewood Cliffs, N.J.: Prentice-Hall.

_____, 1970, Corporate Control and Business Behavior, Englewood Cliffs, N. J.: Prentice-Hall.

Williamson, 1975, Markets and Hierarchies, New York: The Free Press.

_____, 1985, The Economic Institutions of Capitalism, New York: The Free Press.

Yerkes, R., and Dodson, J., 1908, "The Relation of Strength of Stimulus to Rapidity of Habit Formation. J. Comp. Neurology, vol. 18, no. 5, pp. 459-482.

INDEX